Books Are Not Life, But Then What Is?

Books Are Not Life, But Then What Is?

Marvin Mudrick

With a new introduction by Jervey Tervalon

A BERKSHIRE CLASSIC published 2018
by Berkshire Publishing Group, by arrangement with the estate of Marvin Mudrick.

Copyright © 1979 by Marvin Mudrick.
Introduction copyright © 2018 by Berkshire Publishing Group.

All rights reserved. No part of this publication may be reproduced or transmitted in any form or by any means electronic or mechanical, including photocopying, recording, or any other information retrieval system, without permission in writing from:

Berkshire Publishing Group LLC
122 Castle Street, Great Barrington,
Massachusetts 01230-1506 USA
www.berkshirepublishing.com
Tel +1 413 528 0206
Fax +1 413 541 0076

Library of Congress Cataloging-in-Publication Data

Names: Mudrick, Marvin, author.
Title: Books are not life but then what is? / by Marvin Mudrick ; with an new introduction by Jervey Tervalon.
Description: Great Barrington, Massachusetts : Berkshire Publishing Group, [2016] | Includes bibliographical references.
Identifiers: LCCN 2016052056 | ISBN 9781614720270 (pbk. : alk. paper) | ISBN 9781614728863 (ebook)
Subjects: LCSH: Literature, Modern—History and criticism.
Classification: LCC PN710 .M757 2016 | DDC 809—dc23 LC record available at https://lccn.loc.gov/2016052056

Cover illustration by Mike Solomon shows Marvin Mudrick reading a student's story. Watercolor and ink on paper, 9 × 12 inches, © Mike Solomon 1977, www.mikesolomon.com.

Table of Contents

In Gratitude: Marvin Mudrick Gave Me All the Life I Could Live
by Jervey Tervalon ix
Preface by the Author. xv

I. People: Just Like You and Me. 1

The Emperor of China 3
Su Cosa Mi Cosa; or, Busy Busy Busy 9
The Offending Member 19
The Entertainer. 27
I Don't Care What Mama Don't Allow 36
Pushkin in English 45
The Ugly Duck 60
Father Knows Best 67
Portnoy's Bachelor Uncle 80
Agèd Eagles and Dirty Old Men 90
Issues and Answers: or, If You've Tried It Don't Knock It 97
The Smell of Mortality 106

II. Scholars: The Soft Recesses of Uneasy Minds 117

The Blind Men and the Elephant. 119
Twenty-Three Stone-Deaf Theologians 129

III. Operators: If They Don't Like It Here Why Don't
They Go Back Where They Came From? 141

Adorable Ideas and Absent Plenitudes 143
Mad Dogs and Anglo Shrinks 152
A Thrust in the Hand Is Worth Two in the Bush 157

IV. Books in Bunches: The Fox and the Grapes 163
Old Pros with News from Nowhere. 165
Fiction and Truth 186

V. Four Ways of Looking: Books Are Not Life But Then What Is? 203
Chamber of Horrors 205
Good and Proper (I) 209
Good and Proper (II) 217
Mrs. Harris and the Hend of All Things 227

The Return of Marvin Mudrick 235
About Marvin Mudrick 239
About Jervey Tervalon 241

"A freewheeling, earthy entertainer." —*Kirkus Reviews*

". . . A literary curmudgeon, a randy iconoclast, and a delight."
 —*Washington Post*

"Masterful is what Marvin Mudrick unmistakably and invigoratingly is."
 —*The Times Literary Supplement*

". . . the Mickey Spillane of Belles Lettres." —*Village Voice*

"Who the hell is Marvin Mudrick and what gives weight to his pronouncements anyway?" —*New York Review of Books*

BERKSHIRE CLASSICS
The Marvin Mudrick Collection

Jane Austen: Irony as Defense and Discovery (1952) by Marvin Mudrick,
with a new introduction by Karen Christensen

On Culture and Literature (1970) by Marvin Mudrick,
with a new introduction by Kia Penso

The Man in the Machine (1977) by Marvin Mudrick,
with a new introduction by William Pritchard

Books Are Not Life, But Then What Is? (1979) by Marvin Mudrick,
with a new introduction by Jervey Tervalon

Nobody Here But Us Chickens (1981) by Marvin Mudrick,
with a new introduction by James Raimes

Mudrick Transcribed: Classes and Talks (1986), edited by Lance Kaplan,
with a new introduction by James Raimes

Find out more about this series and Berkshire Publishing Group's revival of selected authors at http://www.berkshirepublishing.com/classics/

In Gratitude: Marvin Mudrick Gave Me All the Life I Could Live

Jervey Tervalon

I THOUGHT I was pretty flawed: bad at math, horrible at spelling, illegible handwriting, and still sleeping in bed with my mother and wetting the bed until age six. I also got my ass kicked for being the fat, light-skinned New Orleans kid at a mostly black elementary school in South Central Los Angeles. Yet I grew into myself, more or less—got taller, sprouted an Afro. My brother enrolled me in a martial arts school and I figured out how to calm my mind—or maybe reading did that. I started having a life, hanging with buddies who read all the time and weren't fat or pootbutts getting their asses kicked. I went from fat to stout, and I had a bookish, pretty girlfriend. College was drawing near, and I was leaving for the University of California, Santa Barbara, at the right time, avoiding the escalating gang violence in my neighborhood inspired by the rise of rock cocaine. I was worried, though, that without the tremendous pressure of "hood mayhem", I might be like a deep-sea fish that explodes at sea level.

The reality was that I wasn't trapped by circumstances like so many people that I knew: I was an avid reader so I had already left the neighborhood. All my close friends were similar in that reading seemed to propel most of us elsewhere. I read everything: science fiction, comics, cereal boxes, Victorian porn sold, for some reason, at the liquor store up the street. I never felt intellectually deprived—I had Richard Pryor, Chaucer, Bram Stoker—and I thought I was ready for university life and the Wonder Bread world.

I was wrong. The Wonder Bread world ate me alive. I hadn't known many white people other than teachers, and suddenly everyone was white, whiter, whitest! I knew that they weren't intellectually superior, but I also knew that I actually didn't know shit except for the stuff I was interested in, and I knew I wouldn't get graded on science fiction, comics, porn, and martial arts movies.

I didn't take notes—I didn't know how. I just wanted to listen to lectures and not scribble frantically. I had one writing course that I enjoyed taught by Ms. Driscoll, a former nun who thought I had talent as a writer, but I received no credits for that class since it was remedial. I had to drop Chemistry, and I had a major disaster in Introduction to Philosophy: I plagiarized from the *Encyclopedia of Philosophy* because we were supposed to write our term paper using notes; I listened intently as the philosophy professor defined philosophical terms and cursed in class, saying "fuck" regularly, and I was enthralled, but didn't take notes. I think I had a negative GPA, and I had to plead with a panel of sympathetic white people not to be thrown out of the school.

Soon, I discovered the College of Creative Studies, where Marvin Mudrick was provost. For me this was the promised land of higher education. No grades! I hated grades, but I loved the money I was getting from financial aid. I tried to enroll in a poetry workshop taught by Robyn Bell that was already full, but I was so insistent—I needed the credits to keep my financial aid—that Robyn let me into the class. All I needed to do was write poetry and I would get credits! My future at the university was secure! I guess I wasn't bad at poetry either. I ended up winning the Society of American Poets Award and came in third in the Ina Coolbrith Memorial Poetry Prize for University of California undergrads (though I lost the award check, had to ask the university president to send another, and he was snarky about going to the trouble).

At UCSB, I was amazed at the girls tanning in their bikinis all over our beach campus. No one tanned at my African American and Asian high school, and at first I thought the sunbathing girls wanted to be ogled, until I finally realized their looks of disgust meant they probably thought I was a letch with an Afro.

I went home every weekend to hang out with my girlfriend and my buddies. I had a black life at home and a white life at school, but the bifurcation was manageable. Sometimes I'd invite a friend to campus, and one time a buddy shouted at the café that seeing all these hot white women made him want to get some cock. That was awkward, since he meant the opposite of what he said. Oddly enough, some southerners referred to vaginas as cocks. He quickly returned to LA after this incident, ashamed of mistakenly outing himself.

Doris, my high school girlfriend, began at UCSB the following year and it was disaster. Turns out that skinny girls received a lot more attention from white dudes than from black guys. She was so skinny that if she went to basketball practice without eating lunch she'd pass out. At UCSB she had that anorexic look without having to throw up. Suddenly she was popular and I was left by myself as she disappeared into popularity.

I was still broken-hearted when I went to my "Troilus and Criseyde" class with Professor Mudrick. I was fairly lost in the course, since I didn't read Middle English with much facility. Against his advice, I had bought a parallel translation and was trying to survive. That day, the topic turned to the problem of maintaining intimacy in relationships. Having just recently experienced a degree of romantic intimacy, the shock of losing it was too much, and I found the discussion paralyzing. As Mudrick casually explained the difficulties of relationships, all the problems I had been having with Doris revealed themselves with an intensity that made me insane. Paranoia descended on me right there in class. I attributed it to Mudrick having crazy paranormal powers: he knew my relationship with Doris was dead. Yet I didn't want to accept it, and as soon as class was over, I hurried to her dormitory with the hope that I still might lose my virginity to her.

The door to her dorm was open and she was lying on the bed reading as I hurried inside. She didn't seem interested that I was there and barely turned her head to say hello. I tried for a kiss and she jerked away. I was crushed and confused, but I was sure of one thing: Mudrick had been right.

In Gratitude: Marvin Mudrick Gave Me All the Life I Could Live

How did this professor know everything about me? Who was this Mudrick? I didn't care that he was a respected critic who published constantly. I cared that he understood my life better than I did. I continued to attend his class, I did find a girl to lose my virginity to, and I started to listen more carefully to Mudrick (I actually did listen to him more carefully). What my eighteen-year-old self figured out was that Mudrick believed literature had all the information about human life that one needed, and he was right.

His courses were explosions of conversations. He would discuss Chaucer and segue into Anthony Trollope and Jane Austen as though this was more important and exciting than anything we'd ever experience in life. Soon a few brave students would venture an opinion and we'd be off in what seemed like a roller coasters of ideas. I had read almost nothing he brought up but he made me want to read it all. I wanted to be there. I didn't want to miss anything. He never made me feel that I should accept his opinions, though they were compellingly argued. What he wanted us to do was to read, react to it, and talk about it.

Some of what he covered in class, like Chaucer, Pepys, Rochester, Boswell, Austen, Pushkin, Tolstoy, and Kafka, found its way into *Books Are Not Life But Then What Is?* Mudrick would also give us his reviews for the *Hudson Review* when you'd visit his office (if he was there, and he often was, his door open: you were welcome to come in) and those essays he gave to us would often find their way into his books as well. It felt like we were kind of indirectly involved in his writing process. I think he often tried his ideas out on us. For me, reading *Books Are Not Life But Then What Is?* was like being tied to a roller coaster of ideas, as Mudrick whips through Pepys as though all our lives depended on it, and it was extraordinarily entertaining.

This was the opposite of what grad school would feel like: the necessity of assimilating the ideas and language of the literary fashion of the moment, and a kind of compulsory mimicry of the ideas of your betters without ever having to evaluate or challenge those ideas. Years later, when I started my MFA in Fiction at UC Irvine, one of the professors said he wanted to be my literary guru. Immediately suspicious, I never trusted another word he said about my writing.

Taking a workshop with Mudrick involved walking into class and tossing your story onto his desk. The anonymity was a relief for me, and by the time the class started there would be a stack of stories that he would work his way through. Mudrick read everything with the same affect, but he didn't try to hide his reactions. The first story I submitted was a science fiction story that won twenty-five dollars and a gift certificate from Merlin's, the science fiction and fantasy bookstore in Isla Vista. Mudrick began reading it and within a couple of paragraphs said it made him want to vomit—it was too cute, or stupid, or something along those lines.

After this playful, and much-needed, shredding of my story, I stopped trying to write science fiction and I started to write about my own life, the people I knew, and the neighborhood I grew up in. The next story I submitted was about my handsome, and brilliant in his way, friend Earl. Earl was good with the ladies, to say the least. By the time he got to college he said he had slept with forty-two women, while studying to be a chess master, playing basketball, and reading the *Encyclopedia of Philosophy*.

He dated my high school girlfriend's sister, and as a virgin I was astonished at his commitment to getting laid while I just fooled around and didn't get the job done. My girlfriend's sister allowed Earl to hop though her bedroom window at the night, and then he'd hop back out and continue sleeping outside of her window like a faithful golden retriever. I thought it was the most romantic thing I had ever heard.

Mudrick loved the story, and his praise gave me the kind of momentum to keep writing. He'd rip other's stories as he had done mine earlier, and would do again, but eventually I came to understand what he hated and what he wanted: he hated artifice, preciousness, and an emphasis on style. He wanted to be entertained by our lives as directly as possible: He wanted *our* voices and *our* stories. He didn't want self-consciousness—something that tends to happens at competitive MFA programs. Writers think about how a critic will read their work instead of having the arrogance and confidence to think their work and writing intrinsically matter. Sure, that might be a delusional belief, but it's necessary to do the best work. More precisely, stories weren't shredded for being stupid in his workshops; the problem was triviality.

Actually, after writing workshops with Mudrick, the process of conventional writing workshops seemed clumsy and unnecessarily intrusive. When I was at UC Irvine, I wrote against the workshop—I wasn't looking for their approval, just their reaction; criticisms were more useful than praise. I didn't expect that they'd understand what I was doing—writing about black life in all its complexities, but it turned out that Mudrick did. He grew up in Philadelphia, in a Jewish neighborhood bordered by a black neighborhood on one side and an Irish on the other. He said he'd get up beat up walking either way, and I had nodded with the satisfaction of meeting someone who shared some of my own experience. Mudrick supported my work without reservation. He sent my stories about growing up in South Central to an editor friend of his at a major publishing house while I was still at UCSB. I didn't get published, but the editor's words were so supportive that I wrote with even more enthusiasm. Mudrick also hired me to teach without having an advanced degree, so I had the best of all worlds—gainful employment with time to write and chase girls somewhere beautiful, and to not have to deal with grad school.

I continued to take his courses, particularly his narrative prose workshop. I never want to forget something he said to me about novel writing. I was in his office as he talked to another student about how difficult it was to write a novel, how the minefields were almost impossible to avoid. Suddenly, I blurted, "I can do that." He looked at me with astonishment, and I thought he might ridicule me for my hubris—he was very good at saying something that would sting. Instead he smiled, and, as I remember, it was a tender smile. He said, "That's good, Jervey. It's good to have ambition."

I owe my writing life to him, and everything good in my life comes from writing. The books I've written affirm his belief in me and my belief in him. I owe him everything.

Jervey TERVALON
Author of *Understand This* and *Monster's Chef: A Novel*,
College of Creative Studies '80

To Jeanne

Preface

"Books are not life" comes from Lawrence's essay "Why the Novel Matters," "soft recesses of uneasy minds" from Pope's poem "To Mr. Gay." To be exhaustive, I must also credit Stevens's "Thirteen Ways of Looking at a Blackbird," Lear's "it smells of mortality," Eliot's "aged" eagle, Philip Roth's Portnoy, and Andersen's ugly duckling. Otherwise the titles in this book are mostly catch-phrases, folk-poetry, or independent efforts along the same line, and I intend the pieces they designate to have something of the same vernacular quality.

For their permission to reprint parts of this book originally published by them, I am grateful to The New American Library and The Macmillan Company; and especially to *The Hudson Review*, in which all but the last four pieces first appeared.

M. M.
Santa Barbara, California
July 1978

I

People: Just Like You and Me

The Emperor of China

This is the story[1] of an Emperor who set out on his progress in nothing more than his birthday suit but unlike some other Emperors wasn't ever a tailor's dummy and didn't need a bright-eyed little tyke to put him wise:

> My birth was nothing miraculous—nor did anything extraordinary happen when I grew up. I came to the throne at eight, fifty-seven years ago. I've never let people talk on about supernatural influences of the kind that have been recorded in the Histories: lucky stars, auspicious clouds, unicorns and phoenixes, *chih* grass and such like blessings, or burning pearls and jade in front of the palace, or heavenly books sent down to manifest Heaven's will. Those are all empty words, and I don't presume so far. I just go on each day in an ordinary way, and concentrate on ruling properly.

The date is December 23, 1717, five years before his death, and the Emperor is delivering his valedictory edict to an audience made up of all his sons and the senior court officials. He has had a good and useful life, a very long and "more or less" peaceful reign; he has never been afraid of thinking for himself and attending to everything—

> All the Ancients used to say that the emperor should concern himself with general principles, but need not deal with the smaller details. I find that I cannot agree with this. Careless handling of an item might bring harm to the whole world, a moment's carelessness damages all future generations.

But now he is old and ailing ("Now that I am ill I am querulous and forgetful and terrified of muddling right with wrong, and leaving my work in chaos"), and he has other reasons besides for shedding "tears of bitterness" (the audience, in which his sons are assembled, knows that he means to implicate three ungrateful and treacherous sons, and, among the three, in particular the one who will succeed him); "so I have prepared these notes to make my own record, for I still fear that the country may not know the depth of my sorrow":

> Many emperors and rulers in the past made a taboo of the subject of death, and as we look at their valedictory decrees we find that they are not at all written in imperial tones, and do not record what the emperor really

---

[1] Jonathan D. Spence, *Emperor of China: Self-Portrait of K'ang-Hsi* (Knopf, 1974).

wanted to say. It was always when the emperors were weak and dying that they found some scholar-official to write out something as he chose.

With me it is different, I am letting you know what my sincerest feelings are in advance.

(Of course the "final" valedictory edict issued to the country after his death omitted every one of the passages cited here.) At length, having told all, he takes his leave in a serenity of despair:

> I have enjoyed the veneration of my country and the riches of the world; there is no object I do not have, nothing I have not experienced. But now that I have reached old age I cannot rest easy for a moment. Therefore, I regard the whole country as a worn-out sandal, and all riches as mud and sand. If I can die without there being an outbreak of trouble, my desires will be fulfilled. I wish all of you officials to remember that I have been the peace-bearing Son of Heaven for over fifty years, and that what I have said to you over and over again is really sincere. Then that will complete the fitting end to my life.
>
> I've been preparing this edict for ten years. If a "valedictory edict" is issued, let it contain nothing but these same words.
>
> I've revealed my entrails and shown my guts, there's nothing left within me to reveal.
>
> I will say no more.

(Of course the "final" edict omitted K'ang-hsi's peroration, and substituted somebody else's: "My Fourth Son Yin-chen—Prince Yung—has a noble character and profoundly resembles me; it is definite that he has the ability to inherit the empire. Let him succeed me to the throne and become emperor. Obedient to the rituals, don the mourning clothes for twenty-seven days, then doff them. Announce this to the people, make it known to all.")

Emperor of China is a beautiful book, though one would like to know more than the editor-translator seems willing to reveal about his method and his materials. The 1717 edict is K'ang-hsi speaking for himself, and there is also a series of letters he wrote home while on a military campaign. The rest of the book, however, is the result of Professor Spence's risky decision to select and rearrange characteristic bits and pieces ("personal expressions"), picked out and put together from this or that imperial document ("scattered and often fragmentary, dispersed in a mass of formal edicts and utterances . . . couched in stereotyped language"); and one would feel obliged to complain (maybe the publisher believed that explanations and parallel passages would scare off the common reader) if it weren't for the fact that out of these constructions, representing various times and preoccupations of K'ang-hsi's long life, comes the voice which will also be heard at the end of his life sounding out the words of his valediction, the same plain-speaking voice whether old and despairing or in the prime of vigorous authority:

The so-called *Seven Military Classics* are full of nonsense about water and fire, lucky omens and advice on the weather, all at random and contradicting each other. I told my officials once that if you followed these books, you'd never win a battle. Li Kuang-ti said that in that case, at least, you should study classical texts like the *Tso-chuan,* but I told him no, that too is high-flown but empty. All one needs is an inflexible will and careful planning.

This is the brisk military theoretician, but he isn't a desk soldier, he can speak just as plainly about the look and smell of all-out war:

Our troops have chased the Ölöds now for five days. I have seen their abandoned Buddhist scriptures and tents, the women and children and the sick whom they slew themselves, their fish kettles and their brewing apparatus, their hunting nets and their armor, their saddles and bridles and clothes, their food, the wooden spoons still standing in the bowls of soup, their leather skins filled with kumiss—all these poor items of their daily life, all thrown away.

War is waste. K'ang-hsi wants to use things and people (including himself) properly; nothing disturbs him more than waste, lack of use, improper or inadequate use. He disapproves of suicide because it isn't useful! "I refused my retainers' requests that we visit the precipices [of Mount T'ai] where people sometimes killed themselves, hoping that by offering up their own lives they might save those of their dying parents. I refused to condone such acts by visiting the place where they occurred; for even if the suicide was committed in the name of filial piety, by killing himself the victim cut off forever all chances of helping his parents." Almost anybody can be used—for instance a cloistered scholar, with the customary scholarly weakness for superstition and sycophancy, who may in time and upon attentive cultivation be turned into a useful provincial governor:

At first his memorials were too long and in the wrong format, and he passed on a report that magical *chih* fungus had been found on a mountaintop under a fragrant cloud, sure proof of the Emperor's virtue and promise of long life to come; and even though he knew I did not value such auspicious omens, he was duty-bound to send it in to the palace, so I could examine it or use it for medicine. I replied that the *Histories* are full of these strange omens, but they are of no help in governing the country, and that the best omens were good harvests and contented people. Later his memorials were shorter, there was no more *chih* fungus, and he became a sensible governor.

In a world of unexhausted usefulness, compassion itself can be practical: when another governor, appointed because of his incorruptible honesty, is "condemned to death by the Board of Punishments for panicking about pirates and unlawfully killing several innocent people in jail," the Emperor "refused to punish him, but told the

Grand Secretaries: 'He is truly not a man fit to be a governor. Yet he can prevent bribery, and has great integrity. Let him be put in charge of some financial post where there's not too much going on.'" Authority is life and death: "Giving life to people and killing people—those are the powers that the emperor has"; and K'ang-hsi prefers life: "administrative errors in government bureaus can be rectified, but . . . a criminal who has been executed cannot be brought back to life any more than a chopped string can be joined together again."

Not religions so much as their practitioners puzzle and exasperate him. Heaven is hope but earth is labor. "This is what we have to do: apply ourselves to human affairs to the utmost, while remaining responsive to the dictates of Heaven. In agriculture one must work hard in the fields *and* hope for fair weather." With the Jesuit missionaries in Peking he is pleased to study "Western arithmetic and the geometry of Euclid," surveying, astronomy, horology, hydrostatics, mechanics, music ("in the early 1690's I often worked several hours a day with them"), and he learns a great deal and uses it; but when they begin to talk doctrine he turns them back politely ("I asked Verbiest why God had not forgiven his son without making him die, but though he tried to answer I had not understood him. . . . I would gladly witness some of the miracles they talked about, but none was forthcoming"), and when the Roman Curia tries to move in with one of its own roving agents he denies the request brusquely (because at least the resident missionaries have been dedicated enough to choose to live out their lives in China). Among the Chinese themselves, the Taoists are quick to promise believers long life and unfailing health, but K'ang-hsi notes that "I have seen them age like other men." The trouble with religious people is that their experience of religion seems limited to a sort of frivolous sacrilege:

> The meaning of the Great Way is not lightly to be explained. Some of these adepts' words are even harder to believe, they chill the heart and make me shiver—claims to "arrogate to oneself the cosmic creativity and rival the shaping forces," to "bring together the Five Phases and reconcile the Eight Trigrams," or to "never grow old," or "become like Buddha or the Jade Emperor."

What religious people look for is the end of the line, revelation, stasis, "understanding." In a conversation with Stravinsky (as reported in Robert Craft's *Stravinsky*), the poet Henri Michaux extolled the "understanding" he derived from his experience of hallucinogenic drugs, whereupon Stravinsky retorted: "I prefer thinking to understanding, for thinking is active and continuous, like composing, while to understand is to bring to an end." K'ang-hsi prefers thinking too, and doesn't find it incompatible with mysteries. Doubtless there are unencompassable mysteries, mysteries beyond words (and beyond understanding), but we have only words and the human voice—"the primal sound in the whole world"—with which to approach them, now here now there, from this side or that:

> I have never tired of the *Book of Changes* . . . ; the only thing you must not do, I told my court lecturers, is to make this book appear simple, for there

are meanings here that lie beyond words. The written word has its limits and its challenges; for the primal sound in the whole world is that made by the human voice, and the likeness of this human voice must be rendered in dots and strokes. Therefore, I have practiced my Chinese calligraphy regularly, often writing more than a thousand characters a day; I use my own hand to write my edicts, I copy ancient calligraphic styles in my old age (as I used to when I was a boy, studying with my eunuchs in the palace), and I also practice my Manchu writing, to keep it clear and fast. Yet I never forget that the voice, too, is important: when my name appears in the invocations to the gods, I tell my ritual officials: don't mumble or hesitate. Speak it in a loud voice, clearly, and without fear.

K'ang-hsi, second Emperor of the Ch'ing dynasty, was only one generation removed from the Manchu tribes his great-grandfather and grandfather had united into a confederation that would eventually take over all of China. "As a Manchu who had learned the Chinese language in his later boyhood, K'ang-hsi wrote with a simplicity and directness rarely found among those scholars (or emperors) whose deeper knowledge of the language led them to frequent flights of literary hyperbole and allusion." For more than sixty years, during a reign nearly contemporaneous with Louis XIV's, he ruled an immense and populous country (150,000,000 people, at a time when France, the major power of Europe, had one-eighth as many). He shared some of Louis's problems: dominated in his boyhood and youth by a regency that he threw off as soon as he dared; early involved in a civil war which, even after he had won it, darkened the remainder of his reign; living so long that he was plagued by cabals which inevitably formed round the Heir-Apparent and other possible successors: but, though the formally denominated "Son of Heaven," no unique Sun King; an active and prudent administrator, not a despotic chief clerk; a man thinking, not a superb pattern of manners. He was a Manchu warrior, and had little to say about women: "I keep only three hundred women around the palace, and those who have not served me personally I release when they are thirty and send them home to be married." He spent many months of his life on military campaigns: his "reign was a time of territorial expansion and border warfare, and his troops captured the island of Taiwan in 1683, defeated Russian forces and leveled the fortifications at Albazin in 1685, waged protracted campaigns against the Zungars in the far west and northwest during the 1690's"—

> And so it was that, in the far northwest in the bend of the Yellow River in the early summer of 1697, I heard the news that Galdan, abandoned by nearly all his followers, had committed suicide. As I wrote to my eunuch Ku Wen-hsing: "Now Galdan is dead, and his followers have come back to their allegiance. My great task is done. In two years I made three journeys, across deserts combed by wind and bathed with rain, eating every other day, in the barren and uninhabited deserts—one could have called it a hardship but I never called it that; people all shun such things but I didn't shun them. The

constant journeying and hardship has led to this great achievement. I would never have said such a thing had it not been for Galdan.

"Heaven, earth, and ancestors have protected me and brought me this achievement. As for my own life, one can say it is happy. One can say it's fulfilled. One can say I've got what I wanted."

He loved hunting (especially in the bleak north country of his ancestors), and now he remembered another time of rejoicing:

> Five years ago, on one of my hunts, in the autumn of 1692, just as I was finishing dinner, came news that a bear had been cornered among some rocks in a small wood. I rode out immediately, reaching the wood just before sunset. At first neither shouting, nor beating on trees, nor cracking our whips would dislodge that bear, but finally he roared and came out into the open country. My huntsmen rode along beside him, at a distance of fifteen or twenty paces, and steered him to a defile between two hills. There I shot an arrow at him, which hit him in the side and pierced his stomach. He tore at the arrow, breaking it in pieces, ran a few paces and stopped. I dismounted and took a pike in my hands and, with four hunters at my side, carefully approached the bear and speared him, killing him outright. Never, I told my retinue, had I enjoyed a hunt so much.

Could anybody but the Emperor of China have commanded such pleasures, and on such a scale?

This is the story of a man who dreamed he was Emperor of China.

Su Cosa Mi Cosa; or, Busy Busy Busy

On October 20, 1663 Elizabeth Pepys sat in a coach outside a London shop waiting for her husband; and while Pepys

was in Kirtons shop, a fellow came to offer kindness or force to my wife in the coach. But she refusing, he went away, after the coachman had struck him and he the coachman. So I being called, went thither; and the fellow coming out again of a shop, I did give him a good cuff or two on the chops; and seeing him not oppose me, I did give him another; at last, I found him drunk, of which I was glad and so left him and home; and so to my office a while and so home to supper and to bed.[1]

"No other diarist lays himself so bare as Pepys does," declares Professor Matthews in his Introduction, reminding the rest of us how equivocal we are, implicating us against our will but for our own good in the bare facts of the all too human. Isn't Pepys our patsy and double (hypocrite readers!), doesn't his "passion for microscopic observation of himself as he actually was" end by exposing us all as we actually are? Sometimes we aren't much. The masher's way with a lady (that was no lady, that was my wife), the way of a man with a maid (chamber-, bar-, upstairs-, downstairs-), is "kindness or force"—if kindness doesn't work the alternative is naturally force—which are the two sides of a man's mettle (brass), because according to Pepys *nulla puella negat* though occasionally for appearance' sake she balks a little (sooner or later she can't say no: e.g. the lady in the coach doesn't rage or swoon, merely "refuses" and summons her handy husband; maybe next time . . .). Chivalry is dead and the Pepysian *coup de grâce* is that gratuitous cuff on the chops, which he delivers when he's sure the masher won't strike back: who else would not only let it fly at the moment but indite it with unembarrassed deliberateness hours or days later, and note besides how invigorating it is to discover that one's adversary is drunk (and therefore *can't* strike back)? Whatever the moral questions that keep popping up, editors understand all and forgive all because the Pepys of their dreams is Everyman except "incredibly honest":

> Much of the matter that is printed for the first time in the present edition might be labelled pornographic and [Pepys is often troubled with wind, one onset of which he describes at considerable length in pungent detail]

---

[1] *The Diary of Samuel Pepys.* A new and complete transcription edited by Robert Latham and William Matthews. (University of California Press, 1970-1976), Vols. I-IX. These volumes include the full text of the Diary. There will be two more volumes: X (A Companion) and XI (Index).

scatological. Since most of it is written in Pepys's own *lingua franca* and hedged with shorthand and dog-Latin devices, it may be judged to deal with behaviour that Pepys himself thought shameful. Yet his presentation of this record of his moral deviations is clinical rather than moral or erotic; much of it reads like material for a scientific report on sexual behavior in the human male. That Pepys included it, although ashamed, is the most evident testimony to the full objective reporting, the scientific outlook, the Baconian-ism that went into the diary and the manner in which it was reported.

But Pepys won't be caught so easily. Why not infer that not just the *lingua franca* but the whole diary—private, secret, written in shorthand, locked away from prying eyes—"deal[s] with behaviour that Pepys himself thought shameful"? Or who knows, perhaps the lingo is just a device for indicating something rich and strange, i.e. the sexy parts, so that when Pepys wants a quick charge he can look them up by skimming for word-clusters characteristic of the lingo, and shame has nothing to do with it: after all, when his sexual relations with his wife take a turn for the better, he uses it to record even those ("Waked betimes, and lay long hazendo doz vezes con mi moher con grande pleasure to me and ella"); and, for anyone who bothered to crack the simple shorthand, this mostly "Spanish" pidgin is so elementary and so peppered with—intentionally eye-catching?—giveaways ("I only did hazer her para tocar my prick con her hand, which did hazer me hazer"[2]) that either Pepys is ashamed past the need for concealment (he *needs* to be found out and humiliated!) or he isn't as ashamed as he ought to be for perpetrating such a witless exercise. Anyhow Pepys doesn't begin to use it till far along in the diary, years after his "moral deviations" have become so inextricable from the pattern of his daily life—like the man in Mark Twain's story who falls into a carpet-making machine and gets woven into the carpet—that dalliances and curds and cream and a shilling tip to Nell who lets him rub her thing with his thing and a salmon-pie in the nick of time for sending on to his wife in the country can all be looped together continuously in the crazy carpet:

> thence I back to the King's playhouse and there saw *The Virgin Martyr*—and heard the music that I like so well; and entended to have seen Knipp, but I let her alone; and having there done, went to Mrs. Pierce's back again where she was, and there I found her asleep on a pallet in the dark, where yo did poner mi manos under her jupe and tocar su cosa and waked her; that is, Knipp. And so to talk, and by and by did eat some Curds and cream and thence away home; and it being night, I did walk in the dusk up and down, round through our garden, over Tower Hill, and so

---

[2] As the two parenthetical passages suggest, the operative word of Pepys's pidgin is "hazer," which means "make" or "do" and is used for a range of compulsive, brutal, insulting, merely ejaculatory sexual activity. The second passage proceeds to the payoff: "and so to a milliner at the corner shop going into Bishopsgate and Leadenhall-street, and there did give her eight pair of gloves, and so dismissed her.

through Crutched Friars, three or four times; and once did meet Mercer and another pretty lady, but being surprized, I could say little to them, though I had an opportunity of pleasing myself with them [?]; but left them, and then I did see our Nell, Payne's daughter, and her yo did desear venga after migo, and so ella did seque me to Tower-hill to our back entry there that comes upon the degres entrant into nostra garden; and there, ponendo the key in the door, yo tocar sus mamelles con mi mano and su cosa with mi cosa et yo did dar-la a shilling; and so parted, and yo home to put up things against tomorrow's carrier for my wife; and among others, a very fine salmon-pie sent me by Mr. Steventon, W. Hewer's uncle; and so to bed.

This is as idyllic as the gallivanting ever gets, very likely because the women here aren't the low types with whom he dares to push his luck. It's the latter, of course, who provoke the Pepysian unbuttoning that obliges editors to clear their throats and emphasize the "clinical" and "Baconian" qualities of the sexy parts; but mere laymen might be inclined to substitute such epithets as "humorless," "mechanical," probably "anesthetic," possibly "sadistic," and to notice how readily the tone modulates into something like megalomania. Once Pepys discards his Puritan hang-ups and stops invoking God whenever he masturbates in church during a Sunday sermon or "spends" with one or another of his faceless, bodiless, mindless, unimaginable women ("I find myself, both head and breast, in great pain. . . . It is a cold, which God Almighty in justice did give me while I sat lewdly sporting with Mrs. Lane the other day with the broken window in my neck"), once he has the habit, there's no limit to his self-assurance and his sense of impunity. Thus, as a pretext for visiting the man's wife, he befriends a carpenter at one of the naval shipyards (Pepys is a Principal Officer of the Navy Board): "After dinner I found occasion of sending him abroad; and there alone avec elle je tentoy à faire ce que je voudrais, et contre sa force je le faisoy, bien que pas à mon contentment" (i.e. against her physical resistance I did what I would, though not to my satisfaction). Another time with Mrs. Bagwell "I had sa compagnie, though with a great deal of difficulty; néan-moins, enfin je avais ma volonté d'elle"; but the next day he complains of a "mighty pain in my forefinger of my left hand, from a strain that it received last night in struggling avec la femme que je mentioned yesterday." Or, in a coach with another woman and her husband, "did prender su mano with some little violence" and forces her to masturbate him (under a lap-robe? with her husband sitting on the other side of her? Pepys never brings up such trifles) "all the way home," where once they arrive he is surprised to detect that she seems out of sorts:

> there she did seem a little ill, but I did take several opportunities afterward para besar la [to kiss her], and so goodnight. They gone, I to my chamber, and with my brother and wife did Number all my books in my closet and took a list of their names; which pleases me mightily, and is a jobb I wanted much to have done. Then to supper and to bed.

Or plays the role of rough trade with his barmaid and shopgirl regulars:

> So to Westminster, where to the Swan; and there I did fling down the fille there upon the chair and did tocar her thigh with my hand; at which she begin to cry out, so I left off and drank, and away to the Hall and thence to Mrs. Martin's to bespeak some linen, and there yo did hazer algo with ella and drank and away. . . . . So by coach home, and there find our pretty girl, Willet, come, brought by Mr. Batelier; and she is very pretty, and so grave as I never saw little thing in my life.

That unaccustomed touch of character and interest is really there in Pepys's first sight of Deb Willet, and commentators have always been grateful for the opportunity to carry on about the intensity and pathos of Pepys's involvement with her; but in fact the first sight of her remains the most moving, Pepys's appetite grinds everything down to its usual quick inventory, and his emotional repertoire never expands:

> going down Holburn-hill by the Conduit, I did see Deb on foot going up the hill; I saw her, and she me, but she made no stop, but seemed unwilling to speak to me; so I away on, but then stopped and light and after her, and overtook her at the end of Hosier-lane in Smithfield; and without standing in the street, desired her to follow me, and I led her into a little blind ale-house within the walls; and there she and I alone fell to talk and besar la and tocar su mamelles; but she mighty coy ["quiet," "unresponsive"], and I hope modest ["virtuous"]; but however, though with great force, did hazer ella con su hand para tocar mi thing, but ella was in great pain para be brought para it. I did give her in a paper *20s*, and we did agree para meet again in the Hall at Westminster on Monday next; and so, giving me great hopes by her carriage that she continues modest and honest, we did there part. . . .

Pepys is sentimental about those of his women who not only have a virtuous look but, before he lays them out, put up a desperate fight; he tends, understandably enough, to worry about the risks to other people's virtue while in the very act of assaulting it "with some little violence" or "with great force." Vice is what happens to other people: what he himself seeks is "pleasure" (he often reproaches himself for "my love of pleasure") while others are the subjects or the objects of "vice": "how rude some of the young gallants of the town are become, to go into people's arbors where there are not men, and almost force the women—which troubled me, to see the confidence of the vice of the age"; but, on a typical "Lords day," Pepys

> turned into St. Dunstan's church, where I hear an able sermon of the Minister of the place. And stood by a pretty, modest maid, whom I did labour to take by the hand and the body; but she would not, but got further and further from me, and at last I could perceive her to take pins out of her pocket to prick me if I should touch her again; which seeing, I did forbear,

> and was glad I did espy her design. And then I fell to gaze upon another pretty maid in a pew close to me . . . .

and so on. Vice, however, is something else and mustn't be left unmoralized: Mrs. Martin, his Westminster Hall regular, having married the wrong man, i.e. not the one Pepys urged on her for some special conveniences to Pepys in the arrangement,

> begins a sad story how her husband, as I feared, proves not worth a farding, and that she is with child and undone if I do not get him a place. I had my pleasure here of her; and she, like an impudent jade, depends upon my kindness to her husband; but I will have no more to do with her, let her brew as she hath baked—seeing she would not take my counsel about Hawly.

True, in this instance Pepys's love of pleasure wins out over his moral indignation, and soon and often he returns to the Hall and takes his position again at the old stand, sometimes "backward" for "convenience," sometimes "devante" for variety. Impudent jade or modest maid; su cosa mi cosa. Pepys thinks of himself as a connoisseur of women, by playing the field he is faithful to them all; he piques himself—and editors drop like flies with delight at the vividness of the phrasing—on the "strange slavery that I stand in to beauty": i.e. to any moher's cosa against which, having contended con mucho pièce de résistance, yo did rub mi cosa para hazer in mi hand. Women, on the other hand, are unreliable and fickle even when not yet vicious: *la donna è mobile*, as Pepys might have reflected: "no passion in a woman can be lasting long," as he does reflect, having joked with a woman and made her laugh after she enters the office solemn-faced to ask his help about housing for her family; and, "the best instance of a woman's falseness in the world," Mrs. Martin's sister is shameless enough to

> come home all blubbering and swearing against one Captain Vandena, a Dutchman of the Rhenish wine-house, that pulled her into a stable by the Dog tavern and there did tumble her and toss her; calling him all the rogues and toads in the world, when she knows that ella hath suffered me to do anything with her a hundred times.

The logic here, though murky, seems to go as follows: If a woman gives way to any one man, doesn't put up a desperate fight against him, indeed "suffers" him to do and do with her at his will and pleasure, then she is by such evidence bursting (and in some sense *obligated*) to be done to and done to by all the men in the world.

Other people, not just women, keep disappointing him, "vexing" him, they seldom fail to hurt Pepys more than he hurts them: "I having from my wife and the maids complaints made of the boy, I called him up and with my whip did whip him till I was not able to stir"; "I took a broom and basted her till she cried extremely, which made me vexed"; "Up betimes; and with my salt Eele went down in the parler, and there got my boy and did beat him till I was fain to take breath two or three times"; "became angry and boxed my boy when he came, that I do hurt my Thumb so much, that I was not able to stir all the day after and in great pain." Or consider such a milestone of injured delicacy as this:

> coming homeward again, saw my door and hatch open, left so by Luce our cookmaid; which so vexed me, that I did give her a kick in our entry and offered a blow at her, and was seen doing so by Sir W. Penn's footboy, which did vex me to the heart because I know he will be telling their family of it, though I did put on presently a very pleasant face to the boy and spoke kindly to him as one without passion, so as it may be he might not think I was angry; but yet I was troubled at it.

Small wonder that when in a fit of temper he pulls his wife's nose or blacks her eye, he can't bear to think that people will *know* (he's a very private man), and is "vexed at my heart to think what I had done, for she was forced to lay a poultice or something to her eye all day, and is black—and the people of the house observed it."

Although if worse comes to worst he can usually beat her up, Pepys is well matched with his wife, above all after she catches him *in flagrante* at home under her very nose: "my wife, coming up suddenly, did find me imbracing the girl con my hand sub su coats; and endeed, I was with my main [i.e. Fr. "hand"] in her cunny." What follows is the most interesting episode in the diary. Pepys is the little boy caught playing doctor with the girl next door; Elizabeth is Big Mama, a volcano of latent and sometimes actual hysteria (one night she advances toward him with red-hot tongs), she is enigmatic and implacable, she is demanding (especially in bed: "I have lain with my moher"—what a difference a "t" makes—"as a husband more times since this falling-out," he writes three weeks later, "then in I believe twelve months before—and with more pleasure to her then I think in all the time of our marriage before"), she is Argus-eyed (insists he have a full-time keeper! herself or his young assistant, either or both of whom must accompany him whenever he leaves the house, e.g. for appointments at Whitehall where he discusses Navy business with the Duke of York or the King), levitating at last to an ecstasy of omniscience from which she denounces him for having evil *dreams* and passes the night (if Pepys's tangled way of putting it doesn't allow some doubt) keeping a judicial hand ready to check on his unconscious erections: "My wife mighty peevish in the morning about my lying unquietly a-nights, and she will have it that it is a late practice, from my evil thoughts in my dreams; and I do often find that in my dreams she doth lay her hand upon my cockerel to observe what she can."

Professor Matthews has the presumptuousness to rate Pepys with Shakespeare and more particularly with Chaucer, "of all English writers, perhaps the only one who is his equal in gusto. . . . Who else among English writers has Pepys's enthusiasm for everyday people, everyday life, or his habit of judging everything he liked the best that ever there was?" Pepys does frequently express enthusiasm for one thing and another, for a good dinner he prides himself on giving to friends and eminent acquaintances (especially once he is prosperous enough to be able to show off a handsome house and excellent plate), for music, for dancing; and he can even make a few qualifications and wax philosophical:

> we to dancing and then to a supper of some French dishes (which yet did not please me) and then to dance and sing; and mighty merry we were till about 11 or 12 at night, with mighty great content in all my company; and I did, as I love to do, enjoy myself in my pleasure, as being the heighth of what we take pains for and can hope for in this world—and therefore to be enjoyed while we are young and capable of these joys.

But which dishes he objected to, or who did what at the party, or how the guests responded to one another, or almost whether anybody but Pepys was there—such matters scarcely ever intrude into the text: Pepys's "pleasure"—as when he is with his women—radiates an aura of self-satisfaction blinding enough to fade out everything in the neighborhood. Pepys is enthusiastic about plays too, goes to them as often as by surrealistic chains of reasoning[3] he can neutralize his Puritan sense of guilt about going, considers himself a connoisseur of plays (on one occasion sits by an acquaintance "who understands and loves a play as well as I, and I love him for it"), but his capsule comments don't inspire a corresponding enthusiasm in the reader: *Romeo and Juliet* is "the worst [play] that ever I heard in my life"; *Sir Martin Mar-all* is "the most entire piece of Mirth . . . that certainly was ever writ"; *The Siege of Rhodes* is "certainly the best poem ever wrote"; *The Adventures of Five Hours* is "the best play I ever saw" (in comparison with which *Othello*, "which I have heretofore esteemed a mighty good play, . . . seems a mean thing"); *Twelfth Night* is "but a silly play and not relating at all to the name or day"; *A Midsummer Night's Dream* is "the most insipid ridiculous play that ever I saw in my life." One might as well be reading the movie reviews in the New York *Times*.

Pepys isn't like Chaucer, rather he's like those of Chaucer's characters who are authorized and camouflaged by a vocation: the Pardoner, the Friar, the Summoner, the Merchant, the Man of Law—

> *Nowher so bisy a man as he ther nas,*
> *And yet he semed bisier than he was.*

Chaucer's Man of Law could be Samuel Pepys, Clerk of the Acts of the Navy Board, member of the Fishery Corporation, Treasurer of the Tangier Committee, ubiquitous civil servant trusted and consulted by the Duke of York and the King, confidant to

---

[3] For example: "after dinner by coach to White-hall, thinking to have met at a Comittee of Tanger; but nobody being there but my Lord Rutherford, he would needs carry me and another scotch lord to a play; and so we saw, coming late, part of *The Generall*. . . . And here I must confess breach of a vow [not to go to theaters more often than once a month] in appearance, but I not desiring it but against my will, and my oath being to go neither at my own charge nor another's, as I had done by becoming liable to give them another, as I am to Sir W. Penn and Mr. Creed. But here I neither know which of them paid for me; nor, if I did, am I obliged ever to return the like, or did it buy desire or with any willingness. So that with a safe conscience, I do think my oath is not broke, and judge God Almighty will not think it otherwise."

the Earl of Sandwich and Sir William Coventry and Sir George Carteret and Lord Crew, Fellow of the newly established Royal Society, in the prime of his young manhood (he is twenty-six at the beginning of the decade covered by the diary) busy busy busy doing his jobs and maintaining his "interest" with all the right people and accumulating "profits" (bribes) on the side and enjoying convivial dinners and outings almost nightly, yet not so busy that he doesn't have time for a secret life that behind the perfect competence of his rôle grins like an idiot, chasing after housemaids and barmaids and subordinates' wives and petitioners' daughters up and down stairs and all over the shadier sections of town, gorging on awful plays, planning the definitive treatise on the theory of music though he still hasn't got round to asking somebody the difference between concords and discords, trying without luck to follow the lectures and comprehend the experiments at the Royal Society, thrilled by scientific books he can't make sense of (like Boyle's *Hydrostatics*) as he indulges his intermittent determination to become an up-to-date know-it-all (what his age called a "virtuoso"), skeptical about Court gossip but (like Chaucer's old carpenter in *The Miller's Tale* who falls for a cock-and-bull story about the Flood) delighted to get the real dope on the Ark from a book by a Dr. Wilkins, "wherein he doth give a very good account thereof, showing how few the number of the several species of beasts and fowls were that were to be in the arke, and that there was room enough for them and their food and dung; which doth please me mightily—and is much beyond whatever I heard of that subject. And so to bed." The world is his cosa, and with some little violence all the animals fit inside.

Chaucer is the touchstone all right, not because he and Pepys are soul-brothers but because Chaucer is the only writer whose subject is the split between "gusto" and consciousness, the fact that vitality and consciousness ordinarily exist at cross-purposes, that each ordinarily functions at the expense of the other, that vitality is the fundamental good and yet can be incompatible with goodness—Chaucer's "moral vertu," which is the summit of consciousness. Chaucer knows exactly how marvelously vital such characters as the Pardoner and the Wife of Bath are, how full of shrewdness and truth, how interesting and indispensable and generous when their interest isn't at stake (as when Pepys spins out his marvelously detailed account of the Great Fire of London: "a piece of glass of Mercer's chapel in the street, where much more was, so melted and buckled with the heat of the fire, like parchment"), how exhilaratingly sure of themselves, and yet what horrors they would be to confront in the flesh or live with, what freaks and monsters, what liars and moral idiots, how gigantic and invulnerable, how abstract and human. Here is Pepys's Vitality head to head with the Prick of Conscience, on a field of Consciousness Dormant: At his bookseller's he looks into a dirty book which seems to him "the most bawdy, lewd book that ever I saw . . . so that I was ashamed of reading in it"; three weeks later, "to my bookseller's, and there stayed an hour and bought that idle, roguish book, *L'escholle des Filles;* which I have bought in plain binding . . . because I resolve, as soon as I have read it, to burn it"; the next day (Sunday of course), "I to my chamber, where I did read through *L'escholle des Filles;* a lewd book, but what doth me no wrong to read for information sake (but it did hazer my prick para stand all the while, and una vez to decharger); and after I had done it, I burned it, that it might not be among my books to my shame." How cute and *all-zu-menschlich!* chortle the professors, striking a conscious blow for gusto.

There's nobody here but us monsters. For Pepys the Puritan and churchy jerk-off and mad secret fucker and ambitious bureaucrat and lunatic playgoer, Charles II is the ultimate monster—A King and No King—and a wit besides. By his indolence and quite unsecret profligacy Charles has managed to disillusion the populace (and Pepys) in record time and make them yearn for the good old Cromwellian repressions. In March 1668, for instance, there is serious and prolonged rioting in the London streets by mobs of apprentices, who indicate their temper by "pulling down of bawdy-houses, which is one of the great grievances of the nation. To which the King made a very poor, cold, insipid answer: 'Why, why do they go to them, then?' and that was all, and had no mind to go on with the discourse." Pepys, who fancies himself a connoisseur of sermons, no doubt intends the parallel with truth and Pilate; but the King is speaking for Pepys, and neither speaks for Chaucer. Gusto isn't the last word.

Pepys stands up for public order and lies low for private expedience, and many nights before he goes beddy-bye he makes lists of unfinished business that don't distinguish between the two: "so to supper and to bed—vexed at two or three things—*viz.* that my wife's watch [her new timepiece, not her surveillance over him] proves so bad as it doth—the ill state of the office and Kingdom's business—at the charge which my mother's death for mourning will bring me when all paid [his mother had died the week before]." Pepys didn't much care for his mother, he had wept for his brother's death, surely he will weep for his wife's and father's deaths later. Still, Death the Leveler reduces the number of items (categories don't matter) to be ordered and expedited, as when the Lord Treasurer is about to give up the ghost:

> Sir Ph. Warwick doth please himself like a good man, to tell some of the good ejaculations of my Lord Treasurer concerning the little worth of this world, to buy it with so much pain, and other things fit for a dying man. So finding no business likely to be done here for Tanger, I having a warrant for tallies to be signed, I away to the New Exchange and there stayed a little and then to a looking-glass shop to consult about covering the wall in my closet over my chimney, which is darkish, with looking-glasses....

and then and then and then and then "and then to bed, resolving to rise betimes tomorrow to write fair the report."

There is a single exception in the diary: William Coventry, Secretary to the Lord High Admiral, the only person whom Pepys loves, admires, is undeviatingly loyal to, and indeed may be said to reverence from beginning to end. Moreover, on the evidence Pepys gives, it's clear that Coventry deserves Pepys's near-idolatry and it's equally clear that he not only trusts but likes and esteems Pepys:

> and then at noon rise [from a Navy Board meeting] and I with Mr. Coventry down to the waterside, talking; wherein I see so much goodness and

endeavours of doing the King service that I do more and more admire him. It being the greatest trouble to man, he says, in the world, to see not only in the Navy, but in the greatest matters of State, where he can lay his finger upon the soare (meaning this man's faults, and this man's office the fault lies in), and yet dare or can not remedy matters.

Pepys's most courageous public act is recorded near the end of the diary—visiting Coventry in the Tower, where he has been committed by the King after being goaded by the Duke of Buckingham into a challenge. Coventry is too conspicuously strong and good to survive in such a government—he seems to have been the only effective, hard-working, brave, far-sighted, and incorruptible official in the inner circle of government policy (Burnet's *History* sums him up as "a man of the finest and the best temper that belonged to the court")—whereas Pepys survives wars and revolutions because he is useful to everybody and not least to himself. Pepys must have been a charmer as well as a useful functionary; at any rate Coventry was charmed and convinced. But Coventry didn't read the diary.

The Offending Member

Rochester died a Christian, and thereby hangs a tale. (Dr. Johnson was almost alone in being unimpressed: "he lived worthless and useless, and blazed out his youth and health in lavish voluptuousness, till . . . he had exhausted the fund of life, and reduced himself to a state of weakness and decay.") If only Rochester had died a few years earlier in his usual condition, drunk, disgusting, and impenitent among "the merry gang"—say, in 1676 during the brawl at Epsom, where he managed to behave brutally and stupidly enough to get his companion Downes killed while he and Etherege ("Easy Etherege") saved their necks by running away. Then Burnet might never have become a bishop (it couldn't have hurt his chances for the appointment that he was renowned for converts in the *beau monde*) and would certainly never have written his little book on Rochester. It's a sober, thoughtful, sensible book about sin as the motor of salvation; not a memoir but an exemplum and saint's life, a manual of conversion, by a clergyman who couldn't refrain from telling the world that he had just helped to accomplish the holy dying of the most outrageous libertine of Charles II's wicked Court: "Some/Passages/of the/Life and Death/ of the Right Honourable/John/Earl of Rochester,/who died 26th of July, 1680./Written by his own Direction on his Death-Bed,/By Gilbert Burnet, D.D."

Burnet's hot-from-the-presses apologia set the pattern for later and less hasty Christian lives of Rochester: the Great Sinner justified and redeemed. For instance, Professor Pinto's *Enthusiast in Wit* (1962) reveals its intentions well in advance of page 1, opening with the Miltonic epigraph that approximately evokes Byron, Prince Hamlet, and either notorious Rochester (the second Earl or Charlotte Brontë's)—

> *his form had not yet lost*
> *All her Original brightness, nor appear'd*
> *Less than Arch Angel ruin'd, and th'excess*
> *Of Glory obscur'd . . .*

—an image that, especially out of context, suggests to romantic readers all sorts of paradoxes: Big is beautiful, Bad is thrilling, Black is off-white; and Pinto uses up most of the rest of his book explaining to us that Archangels don't really *like* to be naughty—

> It was still possible to escape from the nightmare of boredom and despair by plunging into dissipation. He would call for louder music and for stronger wine. It was possible, but it was becoming more and more difficult.

> The lights were blinding his tired eyes and the music was stunning his dizzy brain. The Utopia of Gallantry was turning into a kind of weird *danse macabre*, a ballet of figures that were becoming ghostly and incredible. . . .

Greene the Catholic novelist is sleeker, less evangelical, less exhilarated by Archangels, but equally susceptible to paradoxes: "The spirit was always at war with the flesh; . . . [Rochester's] unbelief was quite as religious as . . . [Donne's] faith. He hated the thing he loved with something of the same dark concentration, the confusion of love and lust and death and hate."[1] So Greene's Lord Rochester not only derives from Burnet but comfortably associates himself with Greene's own fictional heroes, oxymoronic, sepulchral, crypto-metaphysical; unbelieving and therefore devout, loathing and therefore loving, empty and therefore stuffed with substance, random (randy) and therefore aimed like an arrow, damned and therefore saved. Thank God neither Pinto nor Greene makes a fuss about Rochester's dying at thirty-three (Jesus's terminal age, according to legend; Joe Christmas's, according to Faulkner); but there isn't much otherwise to be thankful for among the Christians. "Why should the *Devil* have all the good tunes?" asked a psalm-singing divine once, and wouldn't stay for an answer, which anyhow was perfectly obvious: "Because, old cock, the Devil's got something to sing about"—

> *Naked she lay, clasped in my longing arms,*
> *I filled with love, and she all over charms;*
> *Both equally inspired with eager fire,*
> *Melting through kindness, flaming in desire.*
> *With arms, legs, lips close clinging to embrace,*
> *She clips me to her breast, and sucks me to her face.*
> *Her nimble tongue, Love's lesser lightning, played*
> *Within my mouth, and to my thoughts conveyed*
> *Swift orders that I should prepare to throw*
> *The all-dissolving thunderbolt below.*
> *My fluttering soul, sprung with the pointed kiss,*
> *Hangs hovering o'er her balmy brinks of bliss.*
> *But whilst her busy hand would guide that part*
> *Which should convey my soul up to her heart,*
> *In liquid raptures I dissolve all o'er,*
> *Melt into sperm, and spend at every pore.*
> *A touch from any part of her had done't:*
> *Her hand, her foot, her very look's a cunt.* . . .

---

[1] Graham Greene, *Lord Rochester's Monkey* (Viking, 1974). Greene wrote it more than forty years ago but his publisher rejected it at the time, presumably because Rochester's verses were still under lock and key in the basement alcove behind the men's room in the university library. Greene's title refers to a portrait of Rochester with a pet monkey, and doubtless has symbolic significance.

The quadruple climax (orgasm, obscenity, both high point and ending of the passage) doesn't have the effect of complication or ingenuity or shock, it doesn't express the Greene-sickness of a man who "hated the thing[! what the Wife of Bath calls her *belle chose*] he loved," it isn't a pun or conceit on the subject of passion ("O my America! my new-found-land") but rather an account of the plain facts for which Rochester has found all the words including the last one. "The Imperfect Enjoyment" goes on to describe, with the same unfailing energy, exactness, and candor, the lady's loving reproach to her failed lover—

> *Smiling, she chides in a kind murmuring noise,*
> *And from her body wipes the clammy joys,*
> *When, with a thousand kisses wandering o'er*
> *My panting bosom, "Is there then no more?"*
> *She cries. "All this to love and rapture's due;*
> *Must we not pay a debt to pleasure too?"*

—the lover's helpless self-contempt—

> *Trembling, confused, despairing, limber, dry,*
> *A wishing, weak, unmoving lump I lie.*

—and (again quite unlike Greene's construction) the lover's all-too-effective awareness of the *difference* between love and lust:

> *What oyster-cinder-beggar-common whore*
> *Didst thou e'er fail in all thy life before?*
> *When vice, disease, and scandal lead the way,*
> *With what officious haste dost thou obey!*
> *Like a rude, roaring hector in the streets*
> *Who scuffles, cuffs, and justles all he meets,*
> *But if his King or country claim his aid,*
> *The rakehell villain shrinks and hides his head;*
> *Ev'n so thy brutal valor is displayed,*
> *Breaks every stew, does each small whore invade,*
> *But when great Love the onset does command,*
> *Base recreant to thy prince, thou dar'st not stand.*
> *Worst part of me, and henceforth hated most,*
> *Through all the town a common fucking post,*
> *On whom each whore relieves her tingling cunt*
> *As hogs on gates do rub themselves and grunt,*
> *Mayst thou to ravenous chancres be a prey,*
> *Or in consuming weepings waste away;*
> *May strangury and stone thy days attend;*
> *May'st thou ne'er piss, who didst refuse to spend*

> *When all my joys did on false thee depend.*
> *And may ten thousand abler pricks agree*
> *To do the wronged Corinna right for thee.*

This vindictive peroration is funny and wild and, in the rage of the moment, justifiable—not at all a burst of Swiftian revulsion—but, so the details attest, it's no joke either. As if lust with the oyster-cinder-beggar-common whores weren't bad enough, it's followed by a train of familiar diseases and disabilities (not to speak of the treatments at Mrs. Fourcard's "Baths" in Leather Lane). The curse that the lover calls down on the head of his offending member is mainly an acknowledgment of the inevitable.

How does a critic place and tame such impudence? Deliver it over to Freud, and Rochester becomes a psychically impotent Don Juan with a mother-fixation: "'The Imperfect Enjoyment,' on an unconscious level," says Dustin H. Griffin, "may in fact represent a hatred not of the penis but of the woman. If she, like other women in the poems, is thought of as an omnivorous mouth, then he denies her the demanded meal." Pinto, who dotes on Rochester, tries to salvage him as "the great poet of unbelief." Professor Leavis, who doesn't, snaps back that "Rochester is not a great poet of any kind." According to Leavis, the great lyric poems of the seventeenth century are emanations of "the old fine order . . . the 'Court culture,'" from which Charles's "mob of gentlemen" were debarred by the interval of the Commonwealth, a decade or more of exile, and their consequent readiness to be satisfied with writing "cheaper things" (i.e. filth): the Restoration poet's affinity wasn't with "the country house" (Penshurst and such) but with "the coffee-house" and (actresses!) "the Green Room." In the meantime, while Griffin, Pinto, Leavis, and Greene debate the criteria for mental health and sexual happiness in man and society, the Restoration poet can't find anything better to do than commiserate with Nell Gwyn as she busily ministers to the aging, complaining King:

> *This you'd believe, had I but time to tell ye*
> *The pains it costs to poor, laborious Nelly,*
> *Whilst she employs hands, fingers, mouth, and thighs,*
> *Ere she can raise the member she enjoys.*

Under Charles's auspices, life for anybody who gave it a thought reduced itself sooner or later to such scenes as this: no wonder Rochester was a disappointed man. He had entered upon his career at Court with every prospect: the first Earl, who had been one of Charles's most faithful supporters in exile, had died shortly before the Restoration and left his son with the title and the King's good will and patronage; after a year and a half at Oxford and three years on the obligatory grand tour of France and Italy, Rochester made his debut at Court in 1664. He was seventeen, and a contemporary describes him as he appeared then:

> His person was graceful, tho' tall and slender, his mien and shape having something extremely engaging; and for his mind, it discover'd charms not

to be withstood. His wit was strong, subtle, sublime, and sprightly; he was perfectly well-bred, and adorned with a natural modesty which extremely became him. He was master both of the ancient and modern authors, as well as of all those in the modern French and Italian, to say nothing of the English, which were worthy of the perusal of a man of fine sense. From all which he drew a conversation so engaging, that none could enjoy without admiration and delight, and few without love.

By the summer of 1666 (he was nineteen) he had served with spectacular and officially commended bravery in two major sea-battles against the Dutch.[2] As for the Court wits who were to become his drinking, whoring, and brawling companions ("the merry gang"; "the Ballers"), they had already begun to practice their customary amusements as early as 1662, when "a tanner named Hoppy [was robbed and murdered] by Lord Buckhurst, his brother Edward Sackville, Sir Henry Belasyse and others," and "the next year at Oxford Kate's tavern in Covent Garden, when Sir Charles Sedley and Lord Buckhurst appeared naked upon the balcony and preached to the crowd which gathered below." The King knew all and forgave all; and many years after the little book on Rochester, Bishop Burnet wrote an immense *History of My Own Times* in which the most memorable passage is his summation of the character of the King who found such courtiers congenial and amusing:

> He had great vices, but scarcely any virtues to correct them: he had in him some vices that were less hurtful, which corrected his more hurtful ones. He was, during the active part of life, given up to sloth and lewdness to such a degree, that he hated business, and could not bear the engaging in any thing that gave him much trouble, or put him under any constraint: and though he desired to become absolute, and to overturn both our religion and our laws, yet he would neither run the risk, nor give himself the trouble, which so great a design required. He had an appearance of gentleness in his outward deportment, but he seemed to have no bowels nor tenderness in his nature; and in the end of his life he became cruel. . . . He had the art of making all people grow fond of him at first, by a softness in his whole way of conversation, as he was certainly the best bred man of the age. But when it appeared how little could be built on his promise, they were cured of the fondness that he was apt to raise in them. When he saw young men of quality, who had something more than ordinary in them, he drew them about him, and set himself to corrupt them both in religion and morality; in which he proved so unhappily successful, that he left England much changed at his death from what he had found it at his restoration. . . .

---

[2] Years afterward, his enemies at Court accused him of cowardice (on the basis of stories and inferences that now seem at least questionable), and of course the Epsom incident was regarded as confirmation. "For all men would be cowards if they durst," Rochester wrote in his "Satyr Against Mankind": maybe cowardice was another dare he couldn't resist taking.

Books Are Not Life, But Then What Is?

(Was Burnet, especially in that last count of the indictment, thinking back across the years to the dying Rochester, who at the time might well have made the bitter case against Charles which Burnet recapitulated a generation later?)

Burnet was a Scottish parson writing about a profligate King who had died a secret Catholic and passed the British throne on to his Catholic brother; and the parson wasn't inclined to celebrate the handsome, cultivated, intelligent, amiable, witty man Charles seemed to others and must have seemed to Rochester at the outset. Rochester was—how could Charles fail to take note of him?—a young man of quality with something more than ordinary in him, therefore worth corrupting or at any rate worth indulging, and the King

> allowed him remarkable freedoms. At an entertainment given to the Dutch ambassador on the night of 16 February 1668/9, there was heavy drinking after dinner and we are told that the company was "pretty merry." The next day Pepys heard that among those present were "that worthy fellow my lord of Rochester," and Tom Killigrew, the dramatist, manager of the King's company of players, self-appointed King's jester and father of Rochester's friend Harry Killigrew. According to Pepys, Tom's "mirth and raillery" offended Rochester so much that he gave him "a box on the ear in the King's presence." This was a serious offence in the seventeenth century, and, if blood had been drawn, Rochester would have been liable to the medieval penalty of losing his hand. The incident, Pepys heard, gave "much offence to people . . . at Court, to see how cheap the King makes himself, and the more, for that the King hath not only passed by the thing, and pardoned it to Rochester already." Pepys was shocked to see with his own eyes on the morning of 17 February how, "The King did publickly walk up and down, and Rochester I saw with him as free as ever, to the King's everlasting shame, to have so idle a rogue as his companion."[3]

A month later, visiting at the French Court with a letter of introduction from the King, Rochester was refused an audience by Louis XIV, who had heard of the incident. The English King, however, less finicky than Louis (or Pepys), continued to encourage him to go as far as he liked, and he did, seeing how far he could go before he drew blood instead of ichor ("His scepter and his prick are of a length;/And she may sway the one who plays with th' other,/And make him little wiser than his brother"):

> *God bless our good and gracious King,*
>   *Whose promise none relies on;*
> *Who never said a foolish thing,*
>   *Nor ever did a wise one.*

But Charles is reported to have gone the epigrammatist one better by "interpreting" the epigram into a compliment: "My words are my own, but my acts are my

---

[3] *Enthusiast in Wit*, p. 71.

ministers'.". Rochester, for all his brilliance and waywardness, had no master suit with which to trump this King of hearts.

Rochester is praised (even by Leavis) for his formal satires—the "Satyr Against Reason and Mankind," "An Allusion to Horace," "Timon," "Tunbridge Wells," "A Letter from Artemisia in the Town to Chloe in the Country," "Upon Nothing"—all impressive performances, sardonic and shrewd (though not so carefully thought out as they try to appear), more vivacious and less full-dress than Dryden, a bit too unkempt to be taken for Augustan, peppered with the details of common life; set-pieces to fill out period anthologies that have the room for something of Rochester's besides his little love-lyrics with their vein of gloomy pathos. Then there is the Rochester who went like a shot off a shovel through the membrane of decorum (which never felt a thing), raging back to a Bedlam of particulars:

> *Had she picked out, to rub her arse on,*
> *Some stiff-pricked clown or well-hung parson,*
> *Each job of whose spermatic sluice*
> *Had filled her cunt with wholesome juice,*
> *I the proceeding should have praised*
> *In hope sh' had quenched a fire I raised.*
> *Such natural freedoms are but just:*
> *There's something generous in mere lust.*
> *But to turn damned abandoned jade*
> *When neither head nor tail persuade;*
> *To be a whore in understanding,*
> *A passive pot for fools to spend in! . . .*

This is from "A Ramble in St. James's Park," the most ferocious of Rochester's outlaw poems. Sometimes the particulars have a more genial air, as in "The Disabled Debauchee" or the almost never wholly unfriendly animadversions on the King's sexual appetite:

> *'Tis sure the sauciest prick that e'er did swive,*
> *The proudest, peremptoriest prick alive.*
> *Though safety, law, religion, life lay on't,*
> *'Twould break through all to make its way to cunt.*
> *Restless he rolls about from whore to whore,*
> *A merry monarch, scandalous and poor.*

And just once, in "The Imperfect Enjoyment," Rochester's rage for particulars is free and comprehensive enough to be called Chaucerian.

Rochester's first notable escapade at Court was the abduction of a young heiress, for which he was confined a month in the Tower till he begged the King's forgiveness. A year later, at nineteen, he married her. She bore him four children; there are characteristically straightforward letters—domestic, loving, occasionally angry and even agitated—from husband to wife (of course she stayed at home in the country, mostly patient and putting up with his despotic mother, while mostly he carried on at Court); when she "sent a servant on purpose desiring to hear from him, being very uneasy at his long silence," he took the opportunity to reply—not altogether ironically and with a more affectionate sort of sensuality than he revealed in his public poems—"To My More Than Meritorious Wife":

> *I am, by fate, slave to your will*
> *And shall be most obedient still.*
> *To show my love, I will compose ye,*
> *For your fair finger's ring, a posy,*
> *In which shall be expressed my duty,*
> *And how I'll be forever true t' ye.*
> *With low-made legs and sugared speeches,*
> *Yielding to your fair bum the breeches,*
> *I'll show myself in all I can,*
> *Your faithful, humble servant,*
>
> John.

One pair of breeches he didn't begrudge her was control of the estate she had brought to the marriage. In an age when a woman's property became the property of the man she married, Rochester acted as her honest steward, reserving her estate entirely (as he wrote her) "to the use of yourself and those who depend on you," though living and carousing on his own limited income he was himself continually in debt and short of money. He had no pretensions; he talked straight; he kept nothing back; he was not a mean, vain, greedy, unkind, or self-righteous man.

Toward the end, ill, dispirited, "a man whom it is the mode to hate" at Court, out of fashion as his fellow Ballers grew older and dwindled into politics, Rochester nevertheless didn't yield to Burnet's Christian testimony without a fight. He didn't, for instance, admire the Christian insistence on faith: he thought nobody should be compelled to accept mysteries,

> since it is not in a man's power to believe that which he cannot comprehend and of which he can have no notion. The believing mysteries, he said, made way for all the jugglings of priests, for they getting the people under them in that point, set out to them what they pleased, and giving it a hard name, and calling it a mystery, the people were tamed and easily believed it. The restraining a man from the use of women, except one in the way of marriage, and denying the remedy of divorce, he thought unreasonable impositions on the freedom of mankind.

Burnet answered that such impositions need not be considered unreasonable in view of what was promised: "all that propose high rewards have thereby a right to exact difficult performances." But Rochester must have heard the argument before under less exalted circumstances, and he was ready for it with his last piece of impudence: "We are sure the terms are difficult, but we are not so sure of the rewards." He was bracing himself for another disappointment.

The Entertainer

BOSWELL never ran out of questions, but Johnson occasionally ran out of patience: "I will not be put to the *question*. Don't you consider, Sir, that these are not the manners of a gentleman? I will not be baited with *what*, and *why;* what is this? what is that? why is a cow's tail long? why is a fox's tail bushy?"[1] Boswell was no gentleman, he had questions which hardly anybody except a child would think of asking or even think of, questions which, if Johnson sulked, only God Almighty would be competent to answer. (Johnson, if he could be got to answer, was for all practical purposes God: "I must really," Boswell mused in his journal after a depressing session with a clergyman on the question of original sin, "get Mr. Johnson to put me down a short, clear system of religion." Or: "Mr. Wood raved ignorantly about the uncertainty of the soul's being immortal or immaterial. But I had not arguments ready to silence him. I must get a *summary* from Mr. Johnson.") When Boswell visited his brother who had gone mad, what shocked him most about the change was its unbounded and self-evident questionableness: "I could not conceive *how* he did not talk as usual." (God will not be baited with how and what and why.) Worse, Boswell had a child's helpless apprehension that the answers whenever they came and wherever they came from wouldn't necessarily be reassuring:

> At night after we were in bed, [his six-year-old daughter] Veronica spoke out from her little bed and said, "I do not believe there is a GOD." "Preserve me," said I, "my dear, what do you mean?" She answered, "I have *thinket* it many a time, but did not like to speak of it." I was confounded and uneasy, and tried her with the simple Argument that without GOD there would not be all the things we see. It is He who makes the sun shine. Said She: "It shines only on good days." Said I: "GOD made you." Said she: "My Mother bore me." It was a strange and alarming thing to her Mother and me to hear our little Angel talk thus. . . . [The next day] By talking calmly with Veronica, I discovered what had made her think there was not a GOD. She told me, "She did not like to die." I suppose as She had been told that GOD takes us to himself when we die, she had fancied that if there were no GOD, there would be no death. . . . I impressed upon her that we must die at any rate; and how terrible it would be if we had not a Father in Heaven to take care of us. . . .

---

[1] After one such occasion, Boswell recorded in his journal that "Langton told me . . .[Johnson] said when they were in the coach, 'When Boswell gets wine, his conversation consists all of questions.'"

Out of the mouths of babes, and months afterward the implacable voice was still carrying on—"The children said divine lessons in the evening. But some bad fit had seised Veronica, for she said to me in a kind of plaintive, upbraiding tone, 'I am not to go up to Heaven. I am just to rot.'"

Ask a childish question, get a childish answer. As a boy, Boswell was "subject to fits of depression, and in his seventeenth year suffered a protracted illness that sounds like a nervous collapse."[2] At nineteen, imagining that the Church Universal was the answer, he ran away from Presbyterian Scotland (away from his unsympathetic father and—as he would cry out in exasperation years later—"the narrowness of this damned country") to London, where he made his submission to Roman Catholicism and considered entering a monastery in France. But his father appealed in the nick of time to an Ayrshire neighbor, a Scottish lord then living in London, who rescued Boswell for posterity by initiating him into the metropolitan pleasures and opportunities that during the rest of his life would have the power to divert him intermittently from "the gloomy *ground*"[3] of his mind. But at any time in his life he could be knocked flat in a moment:

> My affliction was a kind of *faintness of mind,* a total indifference as to all objects of whatever kind, united with a melancholy dejection. I saw death so staringly waiting for all the human race, and had such a cloudy and dark prospect beyond it, that I was miserable as far as I had animation. Either this morning or yesterday I awaked in terrible melancholy. I found however immediate relief by instantaneously praying to GOD with earnestness; and I felt the comfort of piety. I absolutely was reduced to so wretched a state by my mental disease that I had right and wrong and every distinction confounded in my view. I loved my wife with extraordinary affection, but I had distinctly before me the time which *must* come when we shall be separated by death. I was fond of my children. But I unhappily saw beyond them; saw the time when they too shall be dead, and seeing that, I could not value them properly at present.

Boswell was a very limited man: how can we not be sure since he so often tells us? He talked about his shortcomings freely, not only in his journals but in letters to friends, who concluded that doubtless anybody who volunteered thoughtful and exact accounts of his own shortcomings must be a fool. "I always remember Sir John Pringle's saying to me some years ago in London, 'You know nothing.' And now the remark is as just as then. There is an imperfection, a superficialness, in all my notions. I understand nothing clearly, nothing to the bottom." "My misery is that . . . I am

---

[2] Frederick A. Pottle, "Introduction" to Boswell's London Journal (McGraw-Hill, 1950), p. 3.

[3] "Such is the gloomy *ground* of my mind, that any agreeable perceptions have an uncommon though but a momentary brightness." Letter to William Johnson Temple: 28, 30 November 1789. Marshall Waingrow (ed.), *The Correspondence and Other Papers of James Boswell Relating to the Making of the Life of Johnson* (McGraw-Hill, 1969).

convinced by the last book which I have read. I have a horror at myself for doubting thus." "I am too concave a being. My thoughts go inwards too much instead of being carried out to external objects. I wish I had a more convex mind. And yet the happiness of a rational being is reflection. But I am too minute." Sometimes the self-deprecation had a pathetic little plume of vanity stuck into the end of it: "I am not a great man, but I have an enthusiastic love of great men, and I derive a kind of glory from it"; "I find myself an amiable, pretty man of moderate abilities, but a soul truly noble." He could never resist self-revelation ("I have a kind of strange feeling as if I wished nothing to be secret that concerns myself. This is a weakness to be corrected"), though Johnson "cautioned me against too much openness. 'A man,' said he, 'should never tell tales of himself. People may appear to laugh and be entertained, but they treasure them up, and bring them out against him.'" The result is that Boswell has persuaded just about everybody that he didn't have the brains or gumption or moral awareness to put together the *Life of Johnson* except as the all-time fluke of luck and circumstance.

So a stuffed prune of a biographer as late as 1932 could summarize Boswell in terms appropriate to a character sketch of Frank Harris by Queen Victoria:

> he is not to be regarded as a great man or as a figure of profound significance. . . . If Johnson had not taken a liking to him, it is doubtful if we should have remembered Boswell at all. . . . The sordid particulars which are revealed by his private journals can only be of legitimate interest if they are studied as data of a purely relative importance. Whether the ample and elaborate presentation of such data can be justified, or whether they ought not to have been preserved in the decent obscurity of private archives, if it was desirable to preserve them at all, are matters for doubt; but we are grateful to Colonel Isham for presenting them in a form that places them for ever beyond the reach of a wide, curious and undiscriminating public.[4]

No doubt about it, among the journals' thousands of pages of brilliant evocation and unfailingly fresh and personal reflection over a range of encounters with hundreds of the most interesting people in England and Scotland and various nations of the Continent, Boswell doesn't spare the sordid particulars of what he accurately called his "rage" for whoring and drinking and all-night card-playing—

> About one in the morning I sent a note to my wife by Joseph, who had found me out, told her I was sober, and hoped she would go to bed; and then I indulged my love of gaming, and insensibly resolved to make a night of it.

---

[4]C. E. Vulliamy, *James Boswell* (Geoffrey Bles, 1932), pp. 210-11. "For ever" is quite a while though, and the journals (which were first published between 1928 and 1934 in a collectors' edition "for ever beyond the reach" of human beings) have been coming out in a popular edition since 1950, when the first volume—the *London Journal*—was issued with best-seller success.

> About seven in the morning my clerk, Mr. Lawrie, came and found us sitting like wizards. He told me that my wife had been up all night and was quite miserable. This shocked me. I thought, however, that it was in vain to go home now, but that I would play on till within a little of nine, when I was obliged to be in the Parliament House, having fifteen causes in the rolls, as Mr. Lawrie mentioned with much earnestness. He had the dismal look of a faithful servant who saw his master doing what was quite wrong. . . .If the Court had not been sitting, I believe we should have played on all day, for I was not at all saturated with gaming. . . .

(But who else would have noticed from the outside himself as well as the others, cards in hand, in their tranced hieratic pose around the table after a sleepless night among the knaves and deuces "sitting like wizards"?)

> I madly drank a bottle of claret by myself, none of them drinking with me, and this, meeting what I had taken at dinner, made me brutally feverish. So I sallied to the Park again, and again dallied. But, what was worse, as I was coming home to General Paoli's, I was picked up by a strumpet at the head of St. James's Street, who went with me to the entry to the passage from Hay Hill by Lord Shelburne's, and in my drunken venturousness, I lay with her. Oh, what a sad apprehension then seized me! I got home between three and four, or a little earlier.
>
> **SATURDAY 30 MARCH.** Awaked very ill with sickness and headache; wished to conceal my illness, or rather the cause of it. Got up at ten. The General discovered it, and genteelly reproved my drunkenness as a vice which hurts the character, and gives envious people an advantage over a man of parts. . . .

(But what other drunkard was so beloved of two great men as Boswell, about whose drinking Paoli, the hero of Corsica, conferred anxiously with Johnson? One evening Boswell turned up "sadly in liquor" at the Club and not only went out of his way to insult Johnson but "harangued" Charles James Fox, who "did not like my vinous compliments, and went to another part of the table from that where I sat"; next day, meeting Johnson, Boswell expected thunder and lightning but received only a mild rebuke; when later Johnson was asked what Boswell had said to make amends, he replied, "Sir, he said all that a man should say. He said he was sorry.")

Because Boswell had a talent for persuading even his friends that—good-hearted and well-meaning as he was—he was obviously too shallow, irresponsible, indolent, injudicious, self-doubting, vain, and silly ever to accomplish anything valuable, they awaited the publication of the *Life of Johnson* with skepticism and something like embarrassment (yet his *Journal of a Tour to the Hebrides* had appeared years earlier, and ought to have demonstrated to everybody his mastery of the method and the subject). Lord Hailes, a family friend and lifelong confidant of Boswell's, wrote when the *Life* was already in press to warn him against including Johnsonian trivia and—so easy was it to feel free to treat him like an idiot child—against featuring himself as the hero!

> Your work will, I doubt not, be very entertaining, but I am afraid that your admiration of your friend may lead you to be too minute and to record *dicta* of little moment. I hope that you have observed an advice which I once gave, namely to remember that Dr. J. is the principal figure in the piece. . . .

William Johnson Temple, Boswell's closest friend from boyhood, merely gaped in disbelief: "Have you the vanity to think your Biography preferable to Mason's [*Life of Gray*]?" (Boswell's answer must have seemed quite lunatic to Temple: "I am absolutely certain that *my* mode of Biography which gives not only a *History* of Johnson's *visible* progress through the World and of his Publications, but a *View* of his mind, in his Letters, and Conversations is the most perfect that can be conceived, and will be *more* of a *Life* than any Work that has ever yet appeared.") Once the *Life* was published, fellow members of the Club like Burke and Bishop Percy were confirmed in their opinion that, though it was of course "entertaining" (the correct word that many who wished to disregard the book's originality and magnitude used as a sneer; but Boswell himself had written exultantly to Langton just before publication, "It will be the most entertaining Book that ever appeared"), though he might manage to amuse them, for gentlemen the decisive fact about Boswell was that he was no gentleman and couldn't be trusted in the same room with gentlemen. Burke was one of many who took offense at Boswell's "practice of recording and publishing private conversation"[5]: questioned by Boswell about his reaction to the *Life,* he replied in an ignoble letter that damned with faint praise and ended by asseverating that "many particulars there related might as well have been omitted." Boswell's particulars, sordid or not, have a tendency to wrinkle the noses of stuffed prunes.

"As to the conversation I had the honour of having with the King at his Levee with regard to your Work and to Johnson," sniffed Burke in the same letter, "I gave you the account of it with as much exactness at the time, as I am able ever to relate any thing; not being much in the habit of precision with regard to particular expressions." Gentlemen take their stand by ideas and convictions and meanings, of which words are only more or less temporary receptacles. But Boswell has the habit of precision, he demands the words themselves, the very body of the temporary and unpredictable and irresponsible:

> I talked of Sheridan's saying and persisting to say that Dr. Johnson had a black heart because Dr. Johnson had said, "If they have given him a pension, it is time for me to give up mine." He said Macpherson had told this

---

[5] Letter from Sir William Scott: 2 August 1791 (Note 1). Charles N. Fifer (ed.), *The Correspondence of James Boswell with Certain Members of the Club* (McGraw-Hill, 1976).

to Sheridan, for there were none present but he and Mr. and Mrs. Strahan, at whose house it was said. But that the half of what passed only was told, for he added, "I am glad he has got a pension, for he is a very good man." And he said now to me, "I'll tell Sheridan so when I see him. But supposing I had not added this, how absurd is it in a man to load the saying with a black heart. It accused him of nothing. It was what everybody will at a time say of everybody in a fit of frowardness or bad humour."

Johnson is comfortable with Boswell because Johnson isn't a gentleman either, he is always answering for his life in the full tide of his feelings, what he says at the moment is not only what he feels but what he is, even his apologies are affirmations. Boswell's Johnson is the word made flesh (too too solid and maybe sullied for the likes of Burke and Percy), an extemporaneous man talking himself into the thick of every occasion (in a world of occasions if nothing else) and therefore no monument at all but all that can be saved of a man alive in the pages of a book.

A few months after Johnson's death Boswell had an exchange of his own with the King at his Levee, who said, "I believe you knew him more intimately than any Man"; and Boswell replied, "He was very good to me, Sir. And I was very forward with him." The only life ever written is Boswell's *Life of Johnson,* because only Johnson lived so fully in unpremeditated words and only Boswell, besides being so forward in provoking so many of them, had the genius, the love, the attentiveness, the perseverance, and the opportunity to gather so very many of them in. Boswell must have been pleased that at least one member of the Club and an old friend of Johnson's, Dr. Burney, understood immediately and prophetically what he had done:

> it is impossible to open either of your two Volumes without finding some sentiment of our venerable Sage worth remembering. His wit and his wisdom are equally original and impressive; and I have no doubt but that both will become proverbial to Englishmen, and long continue to direct their taste as well as morals. For my own part, I think myself infinitely obliged to you for embalming so many of his genuine sentiments which are not to be found in his works. Indeed if all his writings which had been previously printed were lost, or had never appeared, your book would have conveyed to posterity as advantageous an Idea of his Character, genius, and worth as Xenophon has done of those of Socrates. . . .

(In fact Johnson's conversation was the whole man, livelier and more characteristic than his writing, as only Boswell at the time could dare to think. In the journals Boswell notes that he asked Johnson's opinion on a legal case he was engaged in, about which Johnson first talked freely and then dictated a statement: Boswell concludes with the comment, "I could perceive that what he threw out upon the subject in conversation was stronger and had more fire than what he dictated." But even Boswell couldn't make public such heresy, and his comment is omitted from the account as it appears in the *Life*.⁶) And Boswell was delighted (his letter in response to Elford has survived) by a really champion fan letter from a man he didn't know, William Elford, Fellow of the Royal Society, devout admirer of Johnson:

> This kind of Biography appears to me perfectly new, and of all others the most excellent—it constitutes a fund of the highest intellectual entertainment, by giving the portrait of the mind of perhaps the greatest man the world has produc'd—enlivened with anecdotes, and conversations of most of the great literary characters of his time—and as these works of Yours [he includes, quite rightly, the *Tour of the Hebrides*] are, I believe the first of their kind, so it will be long before Your example will be follow'd, for Your plan requir'd not only great Ability, and Capacity of selection, but a degree of labour and attention which very few persons will be found willing to submit to. In short instead of describing Your characters, You exhibit them to the Reader. He finds himself in their Company, and becomes an Auditor of Conversations, which have all the dignity of the best moral writings, soften'd by the ease, the wit and the familiarity of Colloquial manners.

So when Burke frowned and turned aside or Sir William Scott invited him to a party with the admonition, "no Letter Press upon the Occasion!" Boswell, fortified by such appreciations as Burney's and Elford's, could confidently elucidate the difference between a scandal sheet and the greatest biography ever written:

> If others, as well as myself, sometimes appear as shades to the Great Intellectual Light, I beg to be fairly understood, and that you [Scott] and my other friends will inculcate upon persons of timidity and reserve, that my recording the conversations of so extraordinary a man as Johnson with its concomitant circumstances, was a *peculiar* undertaking, attended with

---

⁶In the anecdote about Sheridan, quoted above as it appears in the journals, Boswell omitted from its transcription into the *Life* Johnson's entire last statement, beginning "I'll tell Sheridan so. . . ."—much the best part, indeed the *point*, of the anecdote—and there are other regrettable and often inexplicable omissions as Boswell mines the journals for Johnsoniana to be used in the *Life*. One nerve-racking anecdote that the journals preserve but that it isn't hard to make out why Boswell decided against including in the *Life*—he disliked calling attention to Johnson's convulsive mannerisms—takes place at Beauclerk's:

> after dinner Mr. Johnson rose and walked to the end of the room in a fit of meditation and threw himself into some of those attitudes which he does when deep in thought. [Captain] Brodie, who knew nothing of his character but was just a jolly sea-officer, a blunt tar who wished to put the bottle about and did not like to see a man who did not drink as the rest of the company did, turned to Mr. Johnson and said, "Sir, if you be for dancing a minuet, had not you better go to the ladies?" Brodie had no bad intention. But it may be well conceived what a shocking speech this was to the majestic Rambler. A dreadful explosion was to be expected. Mr. Johnson took no notice whatever of the speech for a good while. At last he came and sat down, and all at once turning to Mr. Beauclerk, said, "Don't you think this Brodie a very coarse fellow?" [Presumably Brodie was at the moment out of earshot, because Boswell mentions nothing further.]

much anxiety and labour, and that the conversations of people in general are by no means of that nature as to bear being registered and that the task of doing it would be exceedingly irksome to me. . . .

Boswell had a special license to strike back at his touchy friends—so fearful of being reduced to shades and contexts—because the sole important figure in the *Life* who may be said to be misrepresented is Boswell himself. Certainly, having only the *Life* to go by (the journals had another century to wait before being turned up at Malahide Castle), early critics like Croker and Macaulay could find Boswell pushy and light-minded, the indefatigable interlocutor and snoop, too ready to appear as shade to the Great Intellectual Light, less fond of the man Johnson than of the perfect target for an upstart's literary ambition; and it may be that the warnings of his editorial associate, Edmond Malone, and of friends like Lord Hailes, against admitting evidences of his personal vanity into the *Life* had the effect of persuading him to delete more of himself and of his intimacy with Johnson than the plan of the work required.

In any case the journals make clear Boswell's uninterrupted and virtually religious devotion to Johnson from the day they met until his own death thirty-two years later. "I am never with this great man without feeling myself bettered and rendered happier," he noted a few weeks after their first meeting. Away from Johnson for two and a half years during his studies and travels on the Continent, subjected and susceptible to every kind of distraction, in his own grandiose phrase a man "of wavering faith and strong passions" (by the last two words Boswell meant his hair-trigger horniness[7]), at a most impressionable age (when he left England he was twenty-two and had known Johnson less than three months), a vain and gregarious young man living among cultivated Europeans who had never heard of his idol and so could hardly make sense of his devotion, he continued notwithstanding to regard Johnson as the pole star of his existence, the greatest and best of men, the sovereign palliative if not cure for his melancholy, the beloved and steadfast comforter and counselor.

Yet what, after Boswell's heroic omissions of evidence in the *Life*, shows up most brightly and most surprisingly in the journals is Johnson's love of Boswell. When Boswell returned from the Continent and came to see Johnson, "he hugged me to him like a sack, and grumbled, 'I hope we shall pass many years of regard.'" (In the

---

[7]Which was a question he seems never to have been able to bring up frankly with Johnson. Still, he was eager to hear Johnson's opinion on an occasion when Johnson cautiously mentioned "the mechanical reason" for marriage: said Boswell, "'But imagination makes it much more important than it is in reality. It is . . . a delusion in us as well as in women.' 'Yes, Sir,' said he, 'and a delusion that is always beginning again.' This was admirably observed. I said I imagined there was more evil than good produced by that appetite. He said, 'I don't think so.' I must hear him more fully upon this." When Boswell transcribed this exchange from the journals to the *Life*, he did some tidying (changed his own first sentence from declarative to interrogative, changed "and" before Johnson's "a delusion" to "but," dropped his own approving comment, tacked a "Sir" on at the end of Johnson's last statement); censored "appetite" into "passion"; and deleted the altogether personal last sentence. Johnson's startlingly unconventional and generous "I don't think so" comes very near absolving Boswell, for the moment, of his sense of guilt. But Boswell never did hear Johnson more fully on the question.

Life: "He received me with much kindness.") On a visit to London two years later, he found Johnson gone to Oxford and traveled there to meet him: "He took me all in his arms and kissed me on both sides of the head, and was as cordial as ever I saw him. . . .I told him I was settled as a lawyer and how I had made two hundred pounds by the law this year. He grumbled and laughed and was wonderfully pleased. 'What, Bozzy? Two hundred pounds! A great deal.'" (Not a word or gesture of this greeting survives in the *Life*.) On a later visit: "He seemed happier to see me than ever. He said, 'I do love thee. I do love thee'; and when I left him he said, 'Good-night, dear Sir. I am glad to see you again, very glad to see you again.'" (In the *Life*: "I am glad you are come. . . .") Writing to Lord Kames a year after his introduction to Johnson, Boswell called it "the happiest incident of my life"; but the mutuality was explicit when, a decade later, Boswell recalled that Johnson "said to me at Edinburgh, before Dr. Blair and some more, that he reckoned the day on which he and I became acquainted one of the happiest days in his life." And, after fifteen years of intimacy, they were able to acknowledge to each other in all the complacency of love how well they went together:

> Dr. Johnson said, "You make yourself agreeable wherever you go. Whoever has seen you once wishes to see you again." BOSWELL: "That is a very pleasing circumstance, Sir." JOHNSON: "Yes, Sir, very pleasing indeed." BOSWELL: "You and I do quite well to travel together. The composition just fits. I love to be under some restraint, some awe, and you're as easy with me as with anybody."

These characteristic facts and instances appear in the journals, and none of them is transcribed into the *Tour of the Hebrides* or the *Life*. Boswell must have been drawn or driven to the conclusion that omitting them was necessary because nothing is less entertaining and more ungentlemanly than love.

I Don't Care What Mama Don't Allow

KLEIST goes too far (does he always know he goes too far?), for instance in "The Marquise of O—" when Mama rejoices to witness through a keyhole the not quite uninhibited reconciliation of father and daughter:

> as she was able to see through the keyhole, her daughter was sitting on the Commandant's lap, something he had never in his life allowed her to do. Finally she opened the door and peered in—and her heart leaped for joy: her daughter lay motionless in her father's arms, her head thrown back and her eyes closed, while he sat in the armchair, with tear-choked, glistening eyes, and pressed long, warm and avid kisses on her mouth: just as if he were her lover! Her daughter did not speak, her husband did not speak; he hung over her as if she were his first love and held her mouth and kissed it. The mother's delight was indescribable; standing unobserved behind the chair, she hesitated to disturb the joy of reconciliation that had come to her home. At last she moved nearer and, peering around one side of the chair, she saw her husband again take his daughter's face between his hands and with unspeakable delight bend down and press his lips against her mouth. On catching sight of her, the Commandant looked away with a frown and was about to say something; but calling out, "Oh, what a face!" she kissed him in her turn so that his frown went away, and with a joke dispelled the intense emotion filling the hushed room. She invited them both to supper, and they followed her to the table like a pair of newlyweds; the Commandant, to be sure, seemed quite cheerful during the meal, but he ate and spoke little, from time to time a sob escaped him, and he stared down at his plate and played with his daughter's hand.[1]

There's no place like home, be it ever so humid. Here in the to go no further very bosom of the family (archetypal *ménage à trois*), Denys Dyer coughs nervously and notices something: "There is a strong hint of an unconscious incest motif."[2] Besides:

---

[1] From Martin Greenberg's translation of the stories: Heinrich von Kleist, "*The Marquise of O—*" *and Other Stories* (Criterion Books, 1960).

[2] Denis Dyer, *The Stories of Kleist* (Holmes and Meier, 1977). In a footnote Dyer also notices that the scene was "strongly influenced by the erotic scene between father and daughter in Rousseau's *Nouvelle Héloïse*, Letter 63." He doesn't quote from Letter 63 or otherwise try to support his assertion, though it's just as well he doesn't, because the similarities are only schematic, and Rousseau's scene is all deliberate

I Don't Care What Mama Don't Allow

"He fires a revolver at his daughter—a sexual act, one might say . . . ."; at least Dyer might say so, doing his best here to make sense out of a writer who isn't content to settle for brilliance, power, and mastery.

What Dyer deals with when he's being helpful is Kleist's mastery of complex, lucid, and endlessly explicable short fiction. He pays tribute to Kleist's thunderclap opening sentences; carefully summarizes the intricate and economical plots; describes Kleist's reliance on lengthy and astonishingly vivid passages of indirect discourse; describes his commitment to paradox and chance, contrast and contradiction, misunderstanding and error; discusses the large and serious philosophical issues raised by the stories; solemnly demonstrates the expressiveness of the punctuation: "This book on Kleist's stories is intended to help those who study his works at universities and to interest readers with little knowledge of German literature in stories that are commonly regarded as masterpieces of prose fiction." But Dyer is helpless to deal with the outreaches and outrages, the moments like that family free-for-all in "The Marquise of O—" from which he rashly gleans a strong hint of unconscious hoo-hah (of which there may well be a strong hint in Dyer himself as he invents his own version of another such moment in the same story: "Kleist tells how, immediately after the rape, the count helped put out a fire . . . running around with a dripping fire hose in his hand"; but Kleist's text reads as follows: "The Russian officer . . . was scrambling among the burning gables, hose in hand, aiming the stream of water at the flames." Why does Kleist's stream dwindle into Dyer's drip? Maybe Dyer "unconsciously" rejected Kleist's image because he found it too energetic to be decent "immediately after the rape"; and he would probably refuse to believe that the outrageous symbolism works because this isn't Kleist trying to impress the reader, it's the inexhaustible count—great balls of fire!—obliged by still another wartime emergency to reconsider and reënact his nature). At any rate, Kleist is the inexhaustible extremist who, by scattering them everywhere, insists on the importance of such moments.

It remains a temptation to see them as mere highlights of Kleist's elegantly machined plots, which can have the look of bearing the full weight and meaning—and gloom or joy—that the stories have to offer:

> Of all the stories Kleist wrote *Der Findling* [*The Foundling*] may reasonably be held to be the most sombre and depressing. . . . Out of the goodness of his heart a worthy middle-class tradesman, happily married with wife and child, adopts a foundling child whom he finds by the side of the road. By the end of the story the man's son is dead, his wife is dead, the foundling

---

masturbatory hallucination told from the point of view of the daughter: the father, angered by the daughter's choice of suitor, strikes her; later, remorseful and ashamed, with a "sort of involuntary gesture" he seats her on his lap (the mother present and approving), whereupon "in this embarrassing attitude" she kisses him and "felt his arms pressing my breast with a rather poorly smothered sigh" (the dangling prepositional sigh in this literal, accurate translation is the father's). "I told him [she tells her no doubt fascinated confidante], and I mean it, that I would be happy to be beaten every day for the same reward, and that there isn't any treatment however harsh which a single one of his caresses wouldn't efface to the bottom of my heart." Kleist read and admired Rousseau, but "The Marquise of O—" inhabits a different planet.

has been murdered by him, he is strung up in a deserted Piazza del Popolo for this crime, and he goes eagerly to hell, hoping there to find his victim and carry out further revenge on him. All the good [sic] human virtues are questioned and perverted, and human institutions, such as law and religion, seem to aid and abet the satanic foundling. It is a bleak and chilling view of life that Kleist presents in this story, which is compressed into some sixteen pages of print.

Dyer has the plot right, drear as can be, and he notices its extraordinary compactness, but what he manages to ignore is the sunburst of personal energy that irradiates it at the very end:

> In short. . . wickedness triumphed and the government, upon the priest's intervention, issued a decree confirming Nicolo in his possession [of Piachi's house] and commanding Piachi to cease from troubling him about it.
>
> Just the day before, Piachi had buried the unfortunate Elvira, who had died from the effects of a high fever brought on by the episode. Maddened by this double grief, he put the decree in his pocket, went to the house, and, with the strength that rage lent him, threw Nicolo, who was the naturally weaker one, to the floor and dashed his brains out against the wall. The deed was done before the people in the house knew he was there; when they found him, he was holding Nicolo between his knees and stuffing the decree down his throat. After which he got up and surrendered all his arms; he was put in jail, tried, and condemned to be hanged by the neck until dead.

Piachi goes on to stuff the decree down the throat of the government also because though "in the Papal States there is a law forbidding a criminal to be executed without his first receiving absolution," Piachi "obstinately refused absolution":

> he was led out to the gallows. On one side stood a priest who, with the voice of the last trumpet, depicted all the terrors of that hell whither his soul was about to depart; on the other side another, with the Body of Christ, the holy means of atonement, in his hand, extolled to him the abode of eternal peace.
> "Do you wish to share in the blessings of redemption?" both demanded. "Do you wish to receive the Holy Communion?"
> "No," Piachi answered.
> "Why not?"
> "I don't want to be saved. I want to go down to the lowest pit of hell. I want to find Nicolo again, who won't be in heaven, and take up my revenge again, which I could only partly satisfy here!"

So for three successive days they go through the same rigmarole on the gallows and can't get him to coöperate in a proper hanging:

When, on the third day, he again had to come down the ladder without having been hanged, he raised his hands up in a fierce gesture and cursed the inhuman law that kept him from going to hell. He summoned all the host of devils to come and fetch him, swore his only wish was to be executed and damned, and promised he would take the first priest that came along by the throat just so he could lay his hands on Nicolo again in hell!

When this was reported to the Pope, he gave orders for him to be executed without absolution; unaccompanied by any priest, he was hanged, very quietly, in the Piazza del Popolo.

"The tragedy is absolute and unresolved," says Dyer, but he's taken in by his own summary; the story isn't tragic, nothing here has the effect of irresolution or waste or loss: indeed Piachi fulfills himself, overcomes all his enemies, dies triumphant—"unrepentant" would give a false impression—and glowing with anticipation; rather, this extravagance of energy is comic or farcical or even transcendent, comparable to the effect of *Oedipus at Colonus*, whose hero is also a furious old man who embraces his death in a sublimity of self-approbation.

Kleist is less concerned with the momentousness of issues or events than with the momentum of feeling. The gallant officer, having materialized in the nick of time to save the Marquis of O—from a marauding gang of his own soldiers, is so carried away by the excitement of the rescue and the defenseless beauty of the unconscious Marquise that he rapes her and precipitates the comedy of a rapist turned suitor who is unknown as the former and unsuitable as the latter to his bewildered lady and victim:

> In M—, a large town in northern Italy, the widowed Marquise of O—, a lady of unblemished reputation and the mother of several well-bred children, published the following notice in the newspapers: that, without her knowing how, she was in the family way; that she would like the father of the child she was going to bear to report himself; and that her mind was made up, out of consideration for her people, to marry him.

Kleist's characteristically abrupt and crammed opening sentence introduces with appropriate sly sympathy the innocent (and well-bred) spring of all the wild oscillations of the story. Everybody else—her parents as well as her gallant rapist—is driven or thwarted by desire for the beautiful and beleaguered Marquise, who in the course of the story while just standing around waiting for a streetcar is first raped and afterward courted by her lover, thrown out of her father's house and later reclaimed by him with uncontrollable sobs and "warm and avid kisses on her mouth," scornfully rejected by her mother and later worshiped as "saintly" and "purer than the angels":

> "From now on . . . I will wait upon you hand and foot, my darling child. You shall have your confinement in my house; if the circumstances were different and I were expecting you to present me with a young prince, I

> shouldn't take care of you with greater tenderness and consideration. I'll not budge from your side again the rest of my days. I defy the whole world; from now on your shame is the only glory I wish, if only you will think well of me again and forget the cruel way in which I repudiated you." The Marquise tried to comfort her with endless caresses and reassurances, but the evening came, and then midnight, before she succeeded. The following day, when the old lady's excitement, which gave her a fever during the night, had somewhat abated, mother, daughter, and grandchildren drove back to M——. The journey was like a triumph. . . .

In the vicinity of the fated and unavoidable young widow, feelings are likely to get out of hand. Aphrodite begins as an innocent bystander. (Aphrodite, not Galatea, because Kleist skips all the preliminary stages of creation. Goethe, who ought to have seen himself in his own work as Pygmalion trying to pray some life into a gallery of plaster busts, found Kleist's work unbalanced and morbid, perhaps because—in the fiction at any rate—even so "passive" a figure as the Marquise is instantly breathing and dangerous, a provocation and a source, a fuse if not a bomb.)

The title character of "Michael Kohlhaas" begins as an innocent bystander too, but the world—in the persons of brutal lackeys, mean-spirited knights, and graceless princes—makes the mistake of passing him off as a nobody to whom the inadvertent and impersonal injustices of the world will be as sourly acceptable as they are to the rest of us. For the first twenty-five pages of this tremendous story Kleist slowly and patiently puts together the scores of circumstances that one by one deprive the respectable and God-fearing horse-dealer of all his reasons for trusting in God and going through channels; and then—

> With this handful of men, at nightfall of the third day, he attacked the castle, riding down the tollkeeper and gateman as they stood in conversation in the gateway, and while Herse [Kohlhaas's groom, the earliest victim of the train of injustices], amid the sudden bursting into flames of all the barracks in the castle yard, raced up the winding stairs of the castle keep and with thrusts and blows fell upon the castellan and the steward, who were sitting half undressed over a game, Kohlhaas dashed into the castle in search of the Junker Wenzel. In such fashion does the angel of judgment descend from heaven. The Junker, who was in the middle of reading aloud the decree sent him by the horse-dealer, amid uproarious laughter, to a crowd of young friends staying with him, had no sooner heard the latter's voice in the castle yard than he turned pale as a corpse, cried out, "Brothers, save yourselves!" and vanished. Kohlhaas, entering the hall, grabbed hold of a Junker Hans von Tronka as the latter came at him and flung him into a corner of the room with such force that his brains splattered over the stone floor, and asked, as the other knights, who had drawn their swords, were being routed and overpowered by his men: where was the Junker Wenzel von Tronka? But, seeing that the stunned men knew nothing, he kicked open the doors

of the two rooms leading into the castle wings, searched up and down the rambling structure and, finding no one, went down, cursing, into the castle yard to post guards at the exits. In the meantime, dense clouds of smoke were billowing skywards from the castle and its wings, which had caught fire from the barracks, and, while Sternbald and three other men were busy heaping up everything that was not nailed down tight and heaving it out among the horses for plunder, the corpses of the castellan and the steward, with those of their wives and children, came hurtling out of the open windows of the castle keep accompanied by Herse's exultant shouts. . . .

Within days and weeks "the dragon" has spread confusion and terror throughout the land: issues the "'Kohlhaas Manifesto,' in which he called upon the country to give no aid or comfort to the Junker Wenzel von Tronka, against whom he was waging righteous war, . . . on pain of death and the certain destruction by fire of everything they called their own"; keeps recruiting followers for his guerrilla band; routs a sheriff's force and sets fire to the outskirts of Wittenberg; routs an armed troop under the Prince of Meissen; advances to Leipzig and sets fire to the city; issues a new manifesto according to which he is "a viceroy of the Archangel Michael, come to punish with fire and sword, for the wickedness into which the whole world was sunk, all those who should take the side of the Junker in this quarrel," and which concludes, "Done at the Seat of Our Provisional World Government, the Chief Castle at Lützen"; routs a cavalry troop from Leipzig; panics "all Saxony," so that the Elector, whose weakness and indifference in Kohlhaas's case have precipitated the catastrophe, "announced he was assembling a force of two thousand men . . . to capture Kohlhaas"; eventually draws the attention of Martin Luther himself, who in a public notice denounces Kohlhaas and demands his submission to the laws of God and man. Much is yet to come: an interview between the two intractable rebels; a time of negotiation during which the dragon seems tamed or in chains; a mysterious gypsy woman and a locket; a triumphant execution (like Piachi's), during which Kohlhaas opens the locket that holds the secret of the Elector of Saxony's line, reads the paper through, then "looking steadily" at the Elector standing below him sticks the paper into his mouth and swallows it, and submits his neck to the axe while the Elector lies before him in a fit unconscious on the ground. It's a very long story, a comedy of self-interest and circumstance that couldn't have been expected to open out more or less accidentally toward such possibilities; but Kohlhaas is a man in touch with the quick of his uncharted nature, and, as the Elector discovers, there are dragons out there.

Kleist (by the evidence of a friend's letter) saw himself as a dramatist and regretted the time he had to spend on his stories, which he considered pot-boilers and occasional pieces; and it's a fact that the critics and outline-histories classify him as a dramatist who also wrote some impressive and idiosyncratic fiction. But in this respect Kleist resembles Chekhov: each is less an instrument through which powerful stories tell themselves than an authoritative voice which tells them; each, in his plays, having lost his voice delegates authority to the protagonist—in Chekhov, the yearning middle-class woman of the Russian boondocks (Emma Bovary minus gonads); in

Kleist, the headlong and undependable sensibility which resembles his own without being answerable to the authoritative voice which nerved him to put up with his sensibility for thirty-four years before he had to put an end to it.

Prince Frederick of Homburg is said to be Kleist's masterpiece, but prodigies of interpretive gymnastics don't dissipate the aura of neurotic self-dramatization: Kleist, despised and rejected by his monocled family of Prussian generals past and future, writes a fairytale about a young commander susceptible to daydreaming, inattention, fainting-fits, disobedience, and fear of death who redeems himself by accepting—actually, *over*-accepting—the ideal of self-sacrifice for one's country; and after a mechanical reprise of the opening scene (the hero as dreamer) the play concludes quite unironically with the following lines:

Officers	To horse! Away!
Truchss	Into battle!
Dörfling	To victory! To victory!
All	Death to all the enemies of Brandenburg!

—which aren't notably more literary than "Heil Hitler!" or "Kill the gooks!" or "Death to the German invader!" Kleist's "tragedy," *Penthesilea,* seems to be about the awful violence of passionate love (it does come up with one interesting character, Achilles, presented as a shrewd and amiable ladies' man), has Greek pretensions, and concludes with a peripeteia in which—offstage of course—the heroine not only kills her lover Achilles, she bites chunks out of him too; but when Kleist's voice isn't there reporting matter-of-factly on the palpable brains that Piachi or Kohlhaas splatters over nearby floors and walls, the characters speaking for themselves have such an attack of stage fright they can't do better than make like the woe-is-me or oy-vay school of drama:

Meroe	She is terrible!
Penthesilea	I kissed him dead?
First Priestess	O Heavens!
Penthesilea	Surely I kissed him? Or did I tear him? Speak!
High Priestess	Woe! Woe upon thee! Hide thyself! Eternal darkness cover thee from sight!
Penthesilea	So—it was a mistake. Kissing—biting—Where is the difference? When we truly love It's easy to do one when we mean the other.
Meroe	Help her, ye gods!

Kleist's only play in which the medium doesn't hopelessly cramp his style is *Amphitryon,* a rather grim adaptation of Molière's witty and uncommitted comedy of appearances. In Kleist Alkmene becomes the protagonist, and the relation between Alkmene and Jupiter is a more abstract and much talkier (*less* dramatic!) version of the relation between the Marquise of O—and her Russian officer: woman "purer than the angels" besieged by circumstances and the male principle that doesn't take no for an answer—

> *Jupiter* What would you do if he were to appear now?
> *Alkmene* If he would now appear to me—you're torturing me.
> How can Amphitryon appear now
> When I have dear Amphitryon here—in my arms?
> *Jupiter* And yet, it easily could be the god in your embrace,
> Because you thought he was Amphitryon.
> Why should your feeling then surprise you?
> Suppose that I, the god, held you in my embrace
> And thereupon Amphitryon, your husband, showed himself.
> What would your heart say then, do you suppose?
> *Alkmene* If you, the god, held me in your embrace,
> And thereupon Amphitryon, my husband, showed himself,
> Then I should be most sad indeed, and wish
> That he would be the god and you
> Would stay Amphitryon for me, just as you are.

It isn't (though Thomas Mann says so) "the wittiest, most charming, most intellectual, profoundest, and loveliest theater piece in the world"; nor Molière with a Prussian accent; it's an interesting if coarse-grained personal adjustment of one of the theater's great plots to a characteristic theme of Kleist's. Maybe adaptation was more congenial to Kleist than invention when he was writing drama: anyhow, in this instance he had the luck to be working with characters none of whom—divine or human—had the kind of sensibility he couldn't as a playwright resist identifying with and losing himself in. But none of them sounds at all like Kleist either, and we miss him.

Writing fiction Kleist has no problems, he can be himself without being at the mercy of himself: it may have helped that writing fiction seemed to him a waste of his time which he ought to have spent writing those heroic dramas suffused with Shakespearean pathos which represented his notion of masterpieces. He couldn't have imagined that every one of his eight stories—from the shivery vignette "The Beggarwoman of Locarno" to the epic novella "Michael Kohlhaas"—is a masterpiece and unlike anything written by anybody else before or after. Who but Kleist could have written a story that emerges from the opening sentence of "The Earthquake in Chile" and doesn't turn into a Beerbohm parody?

> In Santiago, the capital of the kingdom of Chile, at the very moment of the great earthquake of 1647 in which many thousands of lives were lost, a young Spaniard by the name of Jeronimo Rugera, who had been locked up on a criminal charge, was standing against a prison pillar, about to hang himself.

Anything is possible, and it all happens at once. (Kafka, who esteemed Kleist—he did a public reading from "Michael Kohlhaas"—and was influenced by him, redid him inside out: Nothing is possible, and it never happens together.) In Kleist's fiction, which is heroic as his plays never are, the personal is always besieged by social proscriptions or social or natural or even supernatural catastrophes and always a match for them. Life can be, it had better be, beautiful. "The Duel" is an inexorable and catastrophic story about the death of chivalry, in consequence of which the irreproachable knight and his virtuous lady live happily ever after. Kleist specialized in happy endings: during the last hours before he blew out his brains (splattering them over the shore of the Wannsee), he said goodbye to his friends and family in the liveliest and most joyous letters he ever wrote; and Piachi and Kohlhaas on the scaffold are shamelessly jubilant as they wait for the trap to be sprung or the axe to fall.

Pushkin in English

ENGLISH-SPEAKING readers have long heard rumors about a Russian poet who wrote Byronic poems with hollow-eyed Byronic heroes stalking through them, also lived recklessly and died young like Byron, and whom the Russians expect us to take as a dramatic and lyric poet on the level of Shakespeare! a century or more after we have stopped taking Byron himself very seriously. So, hoping to solve the puzzle quickly, we look up some of Pushkin's shorter poems in the available translations:

Alas! where'er my gaze I cast
—everywhere whips, everywhere irons;
the perilous disgrace of laws,
the helpless tears of servitude.
Unrighteous Power everywhere
in condensed fog of prejudices
has been enthroned—the awesome Genius
of slavery, and fame's fatal passion.

This is a representative stanza from Vladimir Nabokov's translation of "Liberty: An Ode"—done according to Nabokov's literalist prescription, "with the iambic tetrameter preserved, but with the rhymes sacrificed to literal sense." The poem is reminiscent, at any rate in Nabokov's English, of "Sonnet on Chillon," in which Byron addresses the "Eternal Spirit of the chainless mind . . . Liberty": "And when thy sons to fetters are consigned—/To fetters, and the damp vault's dayless gloom . . . ."[1] (the abolitionist rhetoric must have been in the air of the time, because the two poems were written within a year of each other—"Chillon" in 1816, "Liberty" in 1817—and Pushkin hadn't yet read any Byron at all). Nabokov says that the Liberty ode is Pushkin's "first great work," and what a blessing he lets us know, since how would we ever guess from the banal images and mechanical syntax of its "literal sense"? The stanza is equally representative of Nabokov's other translations of the shorter poems, all glumly poetic, many of which he quotes, in his brilliant and painstakingly informative monograph on Pushkin,[2] to unmask the criminal incompetence of ev-

---

[1] There is an alternative reading of the second line in a manuscript doubtfully attributed to Byron, in the British Museum: "To tar and fetters, and the damp vault's gloom."

[2] Disguised as a multi-volumed commentary on his translation of *Eugene Onegin*: Pushkin, *Eugene Onegin*, Translated from the Russian, with a Commentary, by Vladimir Nabokov (Pantheon, 1964). In Four Volumes.

erybody else's Englishings of Pushkin; but his own aren't notably better at dispelling the condensed fog wherein this awesome Genius of the steppes, imperiled by (alas!) unrighteous Power, solicits and enthrones fame's fatal passion. Nor is the English language unique in its lack of hospitality to Pushkin: Flaubert, having scratched his head over a French version, remarked to Turgenev, "Il est plat, votre poète"—which means, "He certainly isn't the whole wide world's plate of *zakuski*, this parochial delusion of yours."

One might begin to hypothesize that, after all, translations—of poetry anyhow—are unreliable, unbearable, and unusable; but of course Pushkin used them with prodigal indiscriminateness as sources and inspirations, and gratefully dubbed translators "the post horses of enlightenment": what they brought him was the mind of Europe—they brought for example Byron, Napoleonic conqueror of nineteenth-century Continental poetry, whom (having no English) Pushkin was obliged to make out through the only medium available to him, a hack translation into French prose,[3] and if this hasty trot hadn't turned up in the nick of time at his remote posting station, he would have become a very different poet from the one the Russians are mad about. On the other hand, Pushkin's availability in English has electrified no writers whatever and very few readers.

And no critics either: even the most intelligent of them, bilingual and authoritative, lapse into prettiness and phrase-making when they try to describe what the translator has the task of carrying over from Pushkin's Russian. Nabokov, for instance, rhapsodizes on the theme of "Pushkin's genius for extracting meaningful and noble music out of the most trivial words; in fact, it is exactly the contrast between their humdrum, subservient nature and the sonorities they develop within the acoustical paradise of Pushkin's tetrameter that produces the impression [if not the reality?] of noble sense." Prince Mirsky, straining just as hard to extract noble music out of the most trivial words, is just as anticlimactic:

> there is in Pushkin . . . an element . . . which I do not know what other name to give than perfection. . . . Pushkin's perfection is classical, for it is composed of precision and harmony. His diction is always precise and entirely exempt from all looseness and vagueness. If, for instance, he gives a woman's kisses the epithet of "incisive," he means to say that she bites when she kisses; if he makes a Circassian sleep under a "wet cloak" he is prepared to explain that, though wet, it is quite comfortable to sleep in, because being waterproof it is wet only on the outside. It is doubtful if poetry ever

---

[3]Nabokov: "in Pushkin's day Russian writers knew the literatures of England, Germany, and Italy, as well as the works of the ancients, not from original texts but from the stupendous exertions of French paraphrasts. . . . By 1820, eager Russian readers had already at their disposal the first four volumes of Pichot's and de Salle's first edition (1819) of Byron's works in French, and it is in these prose versions, pale and distorted shadows of the original, that Pushkin read for the first time . . . *Le Corsaire, Manfred,* and the first two cantos of *Le Pèlerinage de Childe-Harold.* . . . Pichot not only made no attempt to be accurate, but methodically transposed the text into the most hackneyed, and thus most 'readable,' French of the previous age." Ibid., II, pp. 158-59.

approached to precision of verse more than in the work of Pushkin. But precision alone does not constitute Pushkin's perfection. Its most essential element is *harmony*, by which I mean firstly a sound-pattern in which the poet answers for every single vowel and consonant, pause and intonation, each of them playing its indispensable part in the effect of the whole; and secondly a harmony of sense—a complete adequacy and consistency of the overtones and associations of all the sense elements of a given phrase, passage or poem. . . .[4]

"Il est plat, votre poète." The best that Nabokov and Mirsky can come up with is a list of qualities—noble music, harmony, perfection, the impression of noble sense—which generate the impression of infracritical hot air, and which prove to be the very qualities unrepresented in the available translations. Pushkin's verse is a challenge or a mirage for translators, it must be so unreasonably difficult for them that they can't resist laboring away at it to the limit of our patience and without useful results. ("Difficult!" exclaimed Dr. Johnson, when he was told that the musical performance he had just suffered through was very difficult for the performer; "I wish it were impossible!")

Pushkin's verse doesn't travel well. His prose, though, is something else again, and the translators are evidently incapable of getting in its way. It's the most beautiful prose in the world. There is in it (as Mirsky might have said) an element which I do not know what other name to give than perfection. It's accommodating, alert, lithe, precise, incisive, classical, harmonious, nobly musical, the marriage of wit and passion, not merely the impression but the substance of noble sense,[5] a perpetual fountain of high spirits, and withal so perfectly free and unpretentious that to the blurred eye of custom it might look narrow and bare.

The narrator of *The Captain's Daughter* is a young officer named Grinyov, serving in a remote fortress during the time of the rebellion by the Cossack pretender to the throne, Pugachov. The routine of the fortress is so domestic and unmilitary (the first five chapters are devoted to establishing our sense of it) that, when Pugachov mounts a siege, the fatherly old Captain exhorts his garrison as if they were children in a game; but he knows perfectly well what the end will be, having had his brisk and loving farewell with his wife and daughter moments before he marches out to confront the rebels:

> "Well, lads," the Commandant said, "now open the gates, beat the drum. Forward, lads; come out, follow me!"

---

[4] Prince Mirsky, "Introduction" to *Russian Poems*, translated with Notes by C. Fillingham Coxwell (C. W. Daniel, 1929), p. 19.

[5] "Precision and brevity are the most important qualities of prose. It demands ideas—and then more ideas; without them glittering phrases serve no purpose. Poetry is another matter (although it wouldn't hurt our poets to have a sum of ideas rather more significant than is usually the case with them. Our literature will not move far ahead on reminiscences of past youth)." Carl R. Proffer (ed.). *The Critical Prose of Alexander Pushkin* (Indiana University Press, 1969), p. 19.

> The Commandant, Ivan Ignatyich, and I were instantly beyond the rampart; but the garrison lost their nerve and did not move.
> "Why do you stand still, children?" Ivan Kuzmich shouted. "If we must die, we must—it's all in the day's work!"
> At that moment the rebels rushed upon us and burst into the fortress. The drum stopped; the soldiers threw down their rifles; I was knocked down, but got up again and entered the fortress together with the rebels. The Commandant, wounded in the head, was surrounded by the villains, who demanded the keys; I rushed to his assistance; several burly Cossacks seized me and bound me with their belts, saying: "You'll see what'll happen to you, you enemies of the Czar!"

It doesn't sound like Homer or Shakespeare, this threat to an empire in the image of a scuffle at a tiny outpost. Because it's a family matter: Grinyov since his arrival has been treated like a son by the good-hearted old Commandant; he is in love with the Commandant's daughter; here in the square, as he watches, the Commandant refuses to acknowledge "the Czar" ("you are a thief and an impostor, let me tell you!") and is "dragged to the gallows. The old Bashkir, whom we had questioned the night before, was sitting astride the cross-beam. He was holding a rope and a minute later I saw poor Ivan Kuzmich swing in the air." The Commandant's wife, Vasilisa Yegorovna, is an energetic, bossy, sensible, affectionate woman, never at a loss for words and advice, reassuringly in control of her husband and her household, the inviolate old mother; now, suddenly and unthinkably,

> a woman's cry was heard. Several brigands had dragged Vasilisa Yegorovna, naked and disheveled, onto the steps. One of them had already donned her coat. Others were carrying featherbeds, boxes, crockery, linen, and all sorts of household goods.
> "My dears, let me go!" the poor old woman cried. "Have mercy, let me go to Ivan Kuzmich!"
> Suddenly she saw the gallows and recognized her husband.
> "Villains!" she cried in a frenzy. "What have you done to him! Ivan Kuzmich, light of my eyes, soldier brave and bold! You came to no harm from Prussian swords, or from Turkish guns; you laid down your life not in a fair combat, but perished from a runaway thief!"
> "Silence the old witch!" said Pugachov.
> A young Cossack hit her on the head with his saber and she fell dead on the steps. Pugachov rode away; the people rushed after him.

Grinyov never stops to express his feelings about their deaths, events move too rapidly, he is too busy trying to rescue his beloved and dealing with the savage, sly, and magnetic rebel leader; but hours later, summoned by Pugachov, he passes the death scene: "The gallows, with its victims, loomed menacingly in the dark. Poor Vasilisa Yegorovna's body was still lying at the bottom of the steps, where two Cossacks were mounting a guard." The next morning, waiting in the square for Pugachov to appear, he has a final look at "the gallows, where the victims of the day before were still hanging. . . . I searched with my eyes for Vasilisa Yegorovna's body. It had been moved a little to one side and covered with a piece of matting. At last Pugachov appeared in the doorway. . . ." Grinyov's eyes seek out the bodies as the tongue seeks out spaces left by pulled teeth: they were there, and now where are they? The mystery of death and transience dominates the square, into which new life keeps pouring nevertheless.

The translation is, mostly, by Natalie Duddington.[6] I have replaced Duddington's vulgarism "poor old lady" with Gillon R. Aitken's[7] "poor old woman" (no doubt correctly rendered from the original); Duddington's solecism "astride on the crossbeam" with Aitken's "astride the cross-beam"; Duddington's nonsensical "ran up to us and rushed into the fortress" with Aitken's "rushed upon us and burst into the fortress"; Duddington's "walked into" with Aitken's "entered"; Duddington's mincing British "You will catch it presently" (spoken by the Cossack rebels) with Aitken's likelier "You'll see what'll happen to you." Otherwise Aitken's English tends to be fussier and less idiomatic: "in a twinkling" for "instantly," "hurled to the ground" for "knocked down," "Quieten the old witch!" for "Silence the old witch!"; but it's the same village square in the same clear and present light of terrible violations, nothing in Duddington or Aitken can throw it out of focus. The diction, considered from the standpoint of either imperfect translation, seems basic and exact enough to bypass altogether the problems of translation. The action down to its elements is unmistakable, and even mistakes don't seem to matter: "in a twinkling" is so jarringly wrong for *The Captain's Daughter* that it can't weaken the briefest passage, it reads like a misprint; whereas it is just the sort of phrase we are led to expect in every third tetrameter of "the first complete English translation of the first Russian masterpiece in the narrative genre," *Ruslan and Liudmila*:

> *But reader! What about our maiden?*
> *Let's leave the horsemen for the nonce;*
> *We'll soon be back there, but before,*
> *It's more than time now to be turning*
> *To the fair prisoner and learning*
> *Her fate with dreaded Chernomor.*[8]

Ruslan and Liudmila is the poem that prompted Vasily Zhukovsky, the most celebrated Russian poet of the time, to proclaim young Pushkin's poetic supremacy. According to Mirsky, *Ruslan* "is pure play, like the classical ballet." In Walter Arndt's translation, however, it is sprightly rather than high-spirited, jocose rather than witty, often coy: a protracted skit that is neither romance nor folktale nor—like Chaucer's *Tale of Sir Thopas*—an amusing takeoff on both. It won't make any English or American converts.

---

[6] Pushkin, *The Captain's Daughter and Other Stories* (Modern Library, 1936).
[7] *The Complete Prose Tales of Alexandr Sergeyevitch Pushkin* (Norton, 1966).
[8] Alexander Pushkin, *Ruslan and Lindmila*, tr. Walter Arndt (Ardis, 1974).

It was completed shortly before Pushkin read Byron (in Pichot's French prose) for the first time. Of the narrative poems that followed, *The Gypsies* is (says Mirsky) "Pushkin's first attempt at tragedy, and one of his greatest. . . .It is too easy to philosophize about *The Gypsies*—the most temptingly universal imaginative work in the Russian language." Perhaps. Aleko, the hero, is a disillusioned young cosmopolite who returns to nature among the simple and unspoiled Gypsies, takes up with a Gypsy girl, accepts the job of keeper of the dancing bear, and lives in idyllic happiness till the girl sings a Gypsy love-song and takes up with one of the locals. Aleko has the customary unexplicit and unspeakable past of the Byronic hero: "Why does the young man's heart shudder in his bosom? what secret weariness torments him?"[9] Pushkin never tells us what's bothering Aleko, as Byron never tells us what's (somewhat incoherently) bothering the Corsair:

> *Mark—how that lone and blighted bosom sears*
> *The scathing thought of execrated years!*
> *Behold—but who hath seen, or e'er shall see,*
> *Man as himself—the secret spirit free?*

On March 5, 1814 Jane Austen, unscathed and execrably provincial, wrote to her sister: "Do not be angry with me for beginning another Letter to you. I have read the Corsair, mended my petticoat, & have nothing else to do." Despite such skeptics, it was the Age of the Blighted Bosom. *The Corsair* had been published on February 1, 1814 and 10,000 copies were sold—maybe one of them to Jane Austen!—on the first day of publication. Many a secret heart must have shuddered in unison with the Byronic hero's best-selling acid indigestion, which, as soon as he discovered it in Pichot, Pushkin fell for enthusiastically.

Aleko is a derivative of the Corsair and Childe Harold and Manfred—the Byronic nocturnal avatar exuding its own circumambience—accessible to Pushkin as early as 1820. By 1823, having read Pichot's first five cantos of *Don Juan* ("What a marvel!" he wrote to a friend, and called it Byron's masterpiece), Pushkin conceived the promising idea of crossing the two Byronic strains in a single work: How, that is, would Childe Harold stand up to the brittle brightness of *Don Juan?* and *Eugene Onegin* is intended as the answer. In the first two chapters of *Onegin*, though, Pushkin seems uncertain and a bit amateurish, he has trouble sustaining without fatuity the *Don Juan* manner of worldly-wise chitchat, and still more trouble trying to establish Eugene's importance by means of unsupported assertion—his "somber epigrams," his "unexpected epigrams," his "genius" in the art of love—when in fact all that Pushkin has him think or do (he finds almost nothing for him to *say* till Chapter 3) causes him to appear a dull and ill-tempered fop.

---

[9] The only translation I have found of *The Gypsies* is Prosper Mérimée's into French prose, from which I translate Pushkin's Byronic mystagogy back into the language of the poet from whom Pushkin borrowed it by way of the medium of Pichot's French prose. (Later my attention was called to Walter Arndt's translation into English verse: "What sets the youthful heart to pining,/What private torment, what dismay?" I still say it's spinach and I still say the hell with it.)

At the beginning of *Onegin* Pushkin isn't quite Byron but he isn't Pushkin yet either: his aim is to have the use of more of himself, to put together a characteristic and effective persona out of the materials of his personality; and *Onegin* is the work, his first work of large ambition, in which he gives himself the room for his grand and deliberate attempt. By Chapter 3 he is learning to assimilate the *Don Juan* manner to his own livelier and more sympathetic worldliness, which, a quality of his prose as far back as his earliest letters, now for the first time makes itself at home in his verse. Besides he is learning to exercise his talent for fiction, not just his knack for stock romantic figures and conjunctions: the story itself rather than the theme it proposes or the way of telling it or the hero it glorifies comes to dominate, un-Byronically, this long poem ("A Novel in Verse" is Pushkin's subtitle), so that (1) Eugene's masquerade-ball gloom and boredom soon become less important than his involvements with others, and (2) the English-speaking reader, reading the poem, can ignore the verse, which in the available translations isn't anything like an acoustical paradise or a model of semantic economy but at least subordinates itself to the absorbing skills and satisfactions of the plot. Finally, at the moment when Tatyana appears on the scene, the reader in any language whatever begins to understand that he is about to be carried along on the tide of a great and original work of fiction.

Creating Tatyana, Pushkin must have been thinking of Byron's Haidée, as uncontaminated by books as Tatyana is bookish. Are books a drag if not worse? Byron, having filed away his latest royalty statement, enjoins his armies of readers to discover in Haidée's (and Don Juan's) illiteracy the virtuous charm against the vice of reading:

> *What was it made them thus exempt from care?*
> *Young innate feelings all have felt below,*
>   *Which perish in the rest, but in them were*
> *Inherent; what we mortals call romantic,*
> *And always envy, though we deem it frantic.*
>
> *This is in others a factitious state,*
>   *An opium dream of too much youth and reading,*
> *But was in them their nature or their fate:*
>   *No novels e'er had set their young hearts bleeding,*
> *For Haidée's knowledge was by no means great,*
>   *And Juan was a boy of saintly breeding;*
> *So that there was no reason for their loves*
> *More than for those of nightingales or doves.*

(the writing is as slapdash as it usually is even at Byron's best: the general chaos of the "argument"; "what we mortals call romantic"—what do the *im*mortals call it?—and the silly rhyme "romantic"/"frantic"; "hearts bleeding" for a rhyme; the howler of an unintended *double-entendre*, "below," in a context in which the poet needs most of all to avoid localizing the lovers' dovelike love): if you'd like to blight a bosom, says Byron, books will do it every time; whereas Pushkin, unintimidated by books, lovingly describes Tatyana's passionate and dangerous innocence in its relations with all the romantic novels a girl of her time and temperament and social place would have been reading since puberty:

> *With what attention does she now*
> *read some delicious novel,*
> *with what vivid enchantment*
> *imbibe the ravishing illusion!*
> *Creations by the happy power*
> *of dreaming animated,*
> *the lover of Julie Wolmar,*
> *Malek-Adhel, and de Linar,*
> *and Werther, restless martyr,*
> *and the inimitable Grandison,*
> *who brings upon us somnolence—*
> *all for the tender, dreamy girl*
> *have been invested with a single image,*
> *have in Onegin merged alone.*[10]

The characters learn who they are from books. Tatyana learns from her ladies'-library of novels the straightforwardness of passion. Lensky learns from Schiller the exaltation of self-sacrifice. Eugene learns from Byron to distrust straightforwardness and exaltation, and so to precipitate first a tragedy of love and then a tragedy of friendship and, in the astonishing conclusion, a reprise and reversal of the same tragedy of love. Nothing—including the fatal duel—would happen if it weren't for the rules prescribed by books; and everything (once Pushkin hits his stride) is pristine, spontaneous, wilful, explosive: the plot is as symmetrical as a bomb. Even the rather too chummy auctorial voice, which Pushkin borrows from *Don Juan*, can modulate into a dreamlike personal poignance halfway between art and life, as for example directly after Eugene has killed Lensky in the duel (and even Nabokov's—and Pushkin's?—diction purges itself of ash and redundancy):

> *In due time I shall give you an account*
> *in detail about everything.*
> *But not now. Though with all my heart*

---

[10] I am using Nabokov's translation because so far as I have checked nobody who reviewed it, favorably or unfavorably, denied Nabokov's contention that it is the closest of any to a dependable word-for-word crib. Edmund Wilson's review (*The New York Review of Books*, IV:12, July 15, 1965, pp. 3-6) provoked Nabokov's imperially irritated rejoinder, first printed in *The New York Review of Books*, V:2, August 26, 1965, pp. 25-26, and later, amplified, as "Reply to My Critics," in *Nabokov's Congeries* (Viking, 1968), pp. 300-24. Wilson is right about the numerous and disfiguring perversities of diction and syntax in Nabokov's translation, and all the ingenious perversities of Nabokov's rejoinder won't conjure them away. Nonetheless, losing the battle, Nabokov sinks quite a few barbs into his pontifical and surprisingly incautious opponent; and his unfailing impoliteness gets to be very funny.

> *I love my hero;*
> *though I'll return to him, of course;*
> *but now I am not in the mood for him.*

Pushkin, who has already spent six years on the poem (he will spend two more before completing it), pauses, at the instant of Lensky's death, to memorialize the end of his own youth:

> *Can it be true that really and indeed,*
> *without elegiac conceits,*
> *the springtime of my days is fled*
> *(as I in jest kept saying hitherto),*
> *and has it truly no return?*
> *Can it be true that I'll be thirty soon?*
>
> *So! My noontime is come, and this*
> *I must, I see, admit.*
> *But, anyway, as friends let's part,*
> *O my light youth!...*

His mentor Byron could never have spoken with so pure and literary a pang.

Pushkin's great burst of poetic productivity occurred during and just following his eight-year preoccupation with *Onegin,* and it would be a pleasure to state that his other verse of this period is as attractive and nonpareil in English as *Onegin* but no such luck. *Boris Godunov* (which however Musorgsky turned into a serviceable libretto for his opera) is one of those obligatory oversized blank-verse historical neo-Shakespearean dramas, turkeys all, that the Romantic poets—e.g. Wordsworth, Coleridge, and Shelley in England—hatched out one per poet in token of their succession from the Bard. The folktales in verse are something of a reversion to *Ruslan:* the reader keeps hoping they will turn out extravagant and shrewd and hilarious (like one of the comic *Canterbury Tales,* say *The Miller's* or *The Friar's Tale*), but they seem slick and complacent instead. The *Little Tragedies* are obvious and—despite their brevity—tedious thesis plays: *The Covetous Knight* warns against avarice (in the opening scene of *Volpone* Jonson shows how such a thesis might be made to come alive); *Mozart and Salieri* contrasts lavish, heedless genius and laborious, vindictive talent; *The Stone Guest* is a lethargic reduction of the Don Juan legend, having neither the wit and energy of da Ponte's version nor the intractable iconoclasm of Molière's; *A Feast in Time of Plague* is death's-head Gothic melodrama (anticipating Poe, and not in the same league with Chaucer's tremendous parable of the Plague, *The Pardoner's Tale*). *The Bronze Horseman* has an impressive allegorical idea and fine descriptions of Peter the Great and St. Petersburg; but the much-admired image of the really and truly galloping equestrian statue isn't hallucinatory enough to frighten anybody except the deranged young man who imagines he's being hunted down, and the young man's pettybourgeois pathos is the sort of thing that will soon be done better in prose fiction, and from the inside, by Pushkin's protégé, Gogol.

Pushkin's own prose fiction came late in his short life; but it was immediately absolute and inimitable, nothing like Gogol's after or anybody else's before. *The Captain's Daughter* is the last, longest (though still only of novella length), and crowning work, full of the delights of being young, masculine, susceptible to wine, women, and gambling, sentimental, impulsive, and thoughtlessly brave; full of incidents and—like the dream Grinyov has of the bearded peasant with the ax—marvels; written in the clear-water prose that Pushkin turned out as naturally and unstintingly as if it were impossible to tell a lie. *The Queen of Spades* is almost equally wonderful, more limited in its intentions and more compact, a genuine horror story (unlike the theatrics of *A Feast in Time of Plague*):

> The clock struck one, then two; and he heard the distant rumbling of carriage wheels. In spite of himself, excitement seized him. The carriage drew near and stopped. He heard the sound of the carriage step being let down. All was bustle within the house. The servants were running hither and thither, voices were heard, and the house was lit up. Three antiquated chambermaids entered the bedroom, and they were shortly afterwards followed by the Countess who, more dead than alive, sank into an armchair. Hermann peeped through a chink. Lizaveta Ivanovna passed close by him, and he heard her hurried steps as she hastened up her staircase. For a moment his heart was assailed by something like remorse, but the emotion was only transitory. He stood petrified.
>
> The Countess began to undress before her looking glass. Her cap, decorated with roses, was unpinned, and then her powdered wig was removed from off her white and closely cropped head. Hairpins fell in showers around her. Her yellow satin dress, embroidered with silver, fell down at her swollen feet.
>
> Hermann witnessed the repulsive mysteries of her toilette; at last the Countess was in her nightcap and nightgown, and in this costume, more suitable to her age, she appeared less hideous and terrifying.
>
> Like all old people in general, the Countess suffered from sleeplessness. Having undressed, she seated herself at the window in an armchair and dismissed her maids. The candles were taken away, and once more the room was lit only by the sanctuary lamp. The Countess sat there looking quite yellow, moving her flaccid lips and swaying from side to side. Her dull eyes expressed complete vacancy of mind, and, looking at her, one would have thought that the rocking of her body was not voluntary, but was produced by the action of some concealed galvanic mechanism.
>
> Suddenly the deathlike face changed incredibly. The lips ceased to move, the eyes became animated: before the Countess stood a stranger.
>
> "Do not be alarmed, for Heaven's sake, do not be alarmed!" said he in a low but distinct voice. "I have no intention of doing you any harm, I have only come to ask a favor of you."

The Tales of Belkin, Pushkin's first attempts at prose fiction (he was thirty-one), are five of the best stories ever written, shapely, lucid, inquiring, generous, straightforwardly and continuously entertaining while the author does inconspicuous virtuoso tricks with narration, suspense, perspective, and point of view: a story about the circumstances of a duel half of which is postponed for many years; about a wedding that Pushkin must have intended to appear predestined, since the coincidences he invents to make it happen have to be called miraculous; about a drunken undertaker who has an appropriate nightmare; about the way of a man with a maid who wins a young gentleman by playing the maid; about a postmaster's daughter who goes to the bad and ends up all the better for it, but starts modestly enough—

> Dunya returned with the samovar. The little coquette saw at the second glance the impression she had produced upon me; she lowered her large blue eyes; I began to talk to her; she answered me without the least timidity, like a girl who has seen the world. I offered her father a glass of punch, to Dunya herself I gave a cup of tea, and then the three of us began to converse together, as if we were old acquaintances.
>
> The horses had long been ready, but I felt reluctant to take leave of the postmaster and his daughter. At last I bade them good-bye, the father wished me a pleasant journey, the daughter accompanied me to the coach. In the entry I stopped and asked her permission to kiss her; Dunya consented. . . . I can reckon up a great many kisses
>
> *Since first I chose this occupation,*
>
> but not one which has left behind such a long, such a pleasant recollection.

That ellipsis following "Dunya consented" is the narrator's, as he savors with undimmed appreciation the memory of the kiss. Pushkin was always grateful to women, and was always after them to have a reason for being grateful, as when, on his journey to the Russo-Turkish battlefront in 1829, he paid a tourist's visit to a Kalmyk tent:

> A young Kalmyk girl, quite pretty, was sewing, and smoking tobacco. I sat down beside her. "What's your name?"—***—"How old are you?"—"Ten and eight."—"What are you sewing?"—"Trouser."—"For whom?"—"For self." She handed me her pipe and began to eat. Tea was boiling in the cauldron with mutton fat and salt. She offered me her ladle. I could not refuse and swallowed a mouthful, trying not to take a breath. I do not think that the cuisine of any other people could produce anything more repulsive. I asked for something with which to get rid of the taste. They gave me a small piece of dried mare's meat; I was happy even for that. [After this exploit, I thought I deserved a reward, but my haughty beauty gave me a whack on

the head with her balalaika.] Kalmyk coquetry frightened me; I hurried out of the tent—and rode off from the Circe of the Steppes.[11]

Sometimes he was luckier—as when, a friend's letter having brought up the name of a woman Pushkin has been pursuing for years, Pushkin's reply exuberantly tells all;

> Scatterbrain!
> You don't write me anything about the 2100 rubles I owe you, but you write me about Mme. Kern, whom, with God's help, a few days ago I fucked. Here's what I want to know: if you want to receive that sum from *The Moscow Messenger,* find out whether they are in a position to pay me 2100 for the present year, and give me the answer—if not, you will get it from Smirdin in installments. . . .

Pushkin *needed* God's help—God knows he did his best over the years to come to terms with Anna Kern on his own—and he is thankful, but there are other things in the world too: money, professional obligations and arrangements, friendship. In Pushkin's prose there are no barriers and anything can happen, it's a field of force that incites lightninglike strokes from the most unexpected directions; eventually it takes account of all claims, tragic and comic, divine and worldly, not necessarily to the discredit of any, for the world never stops and new events keep breaking in—as in the fictitious square where the old Captain dangles on a rope and Vasilisa Yegorovna lies naked in the dust, so too on Pushkin's journey home from the battlefront, in the actual Caucasus of 1829, where nobody but Pushkin would encounter such a prodigy as Durov:

> He was being treated for some exotic disease like catalepsy and he played cards from morning till night. Finally he lost everything, and I took him to Moscow in my carriage. Durov had a monomania: he absolutely had to have one hundred thousand rubles. He had thought up and rethought all possible ways of getting it. Sometimes on the road at night he would wake me up with the question, "Alexander Sergeevich! Alexander Sergeevich! How do you think I could get one hundred thousand?" Once I told him that if I were in his place and the one hundred thousand was essential for my tranquillity and well-being, I would steal it. "I've thought of that," Durov answered me—"Well, what then?"—"Simple—you can't find one hundred thousand in every man's pocket, and I don't want to knife or rob a man for a trifle—I have a conscience."—"Well, steal a regimental payroll."—"I've thought of that."—"What?"—"It could be done in the summer when the regiment is in

---

[11] Alexander Pushkin, *A Journey to Arzrum,* tr. Birgitta Ingemanson (Ardis, 1974). This is the first English translation. The sentence in square brackets was deleted by Pushkin before publication—maybe he thought it undignified—and doesn't appear in this translation. It is quoted from Henri Troyat, *Pushkin,* tr. Nancy Amphoux (Doubleday, 1970), p. 360.

camp and the wagon with the payroll stands by the regimental commander's quarters. You could throw a long rope over the wagon tongue and hitch a horse to it from a distance and then gallop off on it; seeing the wagon galloping without horses the sentry would probably be afraid and not know what to do; two or three versts away you could break open the wagon and escape with the payroll. But there are a lot of obstacles in this too. Don't you know any other way?"—"Ask the sovereign for money."—"I've thought of that."—"Well?"—"I even asked."—"What? Without any right?"—"That's what I began with: your majesty! I have no right to ask you for what would make the happiness of my life; but, your majesty, there is no model for charity, and so forth."—"What did he answer?"—"That's surprising. You should turn to Rothschild."—"I've thought of that."—"Well, how did that plan go?"—"Well, do you see, one way of enticing Rothschild to give one hundred thousand was to write him such a weird and amusing request that afterward he would be happy to tell an anecdote which cost one hundred thousand. But so many difficulties! . . ."[12]

Pushkin's life would have been a martyrdom if he hadn't had such a good time of it. He was one of the rare lighthearted geniuses, like Chaucer, like Mozart as W. J. Turner sums him up:

> The old Biblical utterance that the truly virtuous shall be light of heart, if applied to Mozart, would make him out to be one of the most virtuous of men, for his natural buoyancy and gaiety of heart were quite extraordinary. It was this sheer lightheartedness and vivacity which made him do rash things and involve himself in difficulties and responsibilities which his more cautious father would have avoided. After all, a man is not a man of genius for nothing. Men of such genius as Mozart's must be conscious of it. It must be an exhilarating element in their lives to a degree of which we can hardly conceive. It may amount, indeed, to what we might call an intoxication of the spirit to which lesser men can only aspire through being in love or in drink.[13]

But Turner can't mean that this grace is characteristic of all geniuses, for many of whom the power is as burdensome as it was exhilarating for Mozart or for Pushkin—"the only one of those nineteenth-century Russians who wasn't a turd," observed an admirer of his whom I had told I was doing a piece on Pushkin, and who doesn't take to the nagging and bullying, the dissatisfactions, the *gracelessness* of the pandemic apocalypticism culminating in Dostoevsky and Tolstoy.

Pushkin had no complaints, he had a zest for both the idiosyncratic and the ordinary, he wanted what life is ready to offer: friends, women, books, conviviality,

---

[12] Proffer, op. cit., pp. 242-43.
[13] W. J. Turner, *Mozart* (Methuen, 1965), p. 15.

gossip, jokes, travel, fame, money, and when the time was ripe a wife and children and the comforts of respectability. But the same Mozartian high spirits that gave him the world impelled him out of sheer excess of sensibility to do rash and impractical things, to involve himself in avoidable difficulties and responsibilities, to risk his career and his freedom and often his life. The smallest suspicion of a personal slight was intolerable to him, he formally called out dozens of putative offenders and fought at least three duels before the one in which he was killed at the age of thirty-seven. As early as his 'teens he was friendly with political dissidents many of whom would later take part in the Decembrist uprising and be executed or transported to Siberia; he wrote poems that served as manifestoes for the cause: yet his own sentiments were closer to Edmund Burke than to Robespierre, not revolutionary but anti-autocratic, his aim was—what could be better if only it were practical?—to convert Tsar Alexander, co-founder of the Holy Alliance, to political liberalism. For his pains he spent a half-dozen years banished from the capitals (if he hadn't had very influential friends, he would have ended in Siberia); and even when, upon the accession of Nicholas, he was officially restored to favor, he remained for the rest of his life under the surveillance of the secret police and the still more constraining supervision of the Tsar. In the last six years of his life, he was slowly driven to the wall by obligations he had accepted with confidence and now gallantly attempted to manage: a literary and financial dependence on the Tsar, who personally censored his work and treated him as if he were a Court flunky or a political prisoner; an expensive, childish, shallow, imprudent society belle of a wife whom he couldn't afford, or enjoy, or win over, or—at the innumerable Court balls to which she insisted he accompany her—keep from flirting scandalously with the man he called out for his last duel as well as with the Tsar himself.

Meanwhile he continued to write (e.g. *The Captain's Daughter*; but during those last years he had just about given up verse), his mountain of debts grew steadily, he was hemmed in by the stupid and brutal government (which never permitted him to leave the country), and he had no recourse but to hope to make money out of a journal he was putting together, with his usual ebullient energy, in the face of the stupid and brutal censorship:

> You [Pletnev, Pushkin's literary agent] have received the *Journey* [*to Arzrum*] from the censorship, but what did the committee decide with regard to my most humble petition? The little ass Nikitenko won't kick and the bull Dunduk butt me to death, will they? They won't get rid of me so easily, though. My thanks, my great thanks to Gogol for his "Calash"; the almanac can travel a long way in it. However, my opinion is this: don't accept "The Calash" for nothing, but set a price for it; Gogol needs money. You ask a name for the almanac: let's call it Arion or Orion. I love names which don't make any sense; there's nothing for jokes to stick to. Have Langer also sketch a vignette without any sense. There should be some little flowers, and lyres, and chalices, and ivy, as in Alexander Ivanovich's apartment in Gogol's comedy [*Vladimir, Third Class*]. That will seem very natural. I would be glad

to come to you in November; all the more that I've never had such a fruitless autumn in my life. I'm writing, but bungling the job. For inspiration one must have spiritual tranquillity, and I'm not tranquil at all. You're doing badly in becoming indecisive. I have always found that everything which you have devised has succeeded for me. Let's begin the almanac with the *Journey*. Send the proofs along to me, and I'll send you some poems. Who will be our censor?. . .

The strain was becoming too much even for Pushkin, and it broke through in a letter to his wife: "my . . . heart drops into my boots when I recall that I'm a journalist. Though still a decent person, I have received police reprimands, and I have been told, *Vous avez trompé* [You have been deceitful], and such like. What will happen to me now? Mordvinov will look on me as he does on Faddey Bulgarin and Nikolay Polevoy—as a spy. The devil prompted my being born in Russia with a soul and with talent! . . ."

He is one of the great writers of the world, one of the heroes of literature, one of the great spirits of history. The Anglo-Saxons are benighted for not knowing him.

The Ugly Duck

As a boy Hans Christian Andersen was mad about the theater, he yearned and struggled to be an actor, a singer, a dancer, nothing made him happier than to find himself on a stage in front of an audience, but nobody took him seriously. A half-century later, in the uncharacteristically relaxed and amusing story "Auntie," he paid his tribute to those on the other side of the footlights who were as "theater-crazy" as he himself had been:

> "I go to school in the theater," Auntie would declare. "It is the well from which I draw my learning, it has even helped me to recollect what I learned in Sunday school. *Moses* and *Joseph and His Brothers* are both operas, and I have heard them. All that I know about history, geography, and human nature I have learned in the theater. From the French plays I know what life is like in Paris—it is obscene but interesting. Oh, how I cried when I saw *The Family Rigquebourg*. It is all about a poor man who has to drink himself to death so that his wife can marry her young lover. . . ."[1]

Just once Auntie the model spectator becomes, in a sort of apotheosis, Auntie the immodest spectacle:

> It had been a winter day, one of those days when daylight consists of two hours of gray twilight. It was cold and had been snowing, but they were performing *Herman von Unna,* a one-act opera, plus a grand ballet, with both a prologue and an epilogue. It would last until the small hours of the morning. Auntie just had to go! From the lodger who had rented her spare room she borrowed a pair of sled boots with sheepskin lining, though they were too big for her and reached all the way up to her knees.
>
> But she managed to make her way to the Royal Theater and to her box: second circle on the left. It is the better side; and here, too, the royal family have their box. The scenery is arranged so that it looks more beautiful seen from there.
>
> All at once someone screamed: "Fire!" And smoke poured out of the loft. Panic broke out! Auntie had kept the sled boots on during the performance because they were so nice and warm. And that they were, but they were not meant for running. Auntie was on her way to the door of the box when the

---

[1] Hans Christian Andersen, *The Complete Fairy Tales and Stories* (Doubleday, 1974).

terrified person in front of her slammed the door so hard that it locked. She couldn't get out of the door of her own box, nor could she climb into any of the neighboring boxes, for the partitions were too high.

She screamed, but no one heard her. She looked down at the circle of boxes below her; it didn't seem far. In her fear, Auntie felt all the agility of youth returning to her: she would jump down! She got one leg over the balustrade but could not manage to get the other one over. There she sat as if she were riding a horse, with her skirt tucked up under her and her long leg with the sled boot on it hanging in the air. It was a sight! And it was seen and Auntie was saved from her death in flames—which was not so strange, for the theater wasn't burning at all.

It was the most memorable evening in her life, she often remarked; and it was a good thing that she could not have seen herself sitting on the balustrade, for if she had been able to she would have died of shame.

Eventually Auntie dies not of shame but of old age, having supped full with horrors and obscene but interesting information, and her exit line is the theater-lover's all-important unanswered question:

> Auntie deserved to live as long as the Royal Theater stood, but few people get what they deserve. She didn't die in her box either, but decently, at home, in her bed. Her last words are worth quoting: "What are they playing tomorrow?" she asked.

If only the palace of illusions had treated young Andersen as well as it treated Auntie! His application to the Royal Theater in Copenhagen was turned down with the comment that he "lack[ed] both the talent and the appearance necessary for the stage." But of course they were right, weren't they? and the ugly duckling just hadn't found his proper pond yet. Nevertheless he wangled an audition from an actor named Lindgreen, who "told him he had some talent for comic parts, but unfortunately Andersen wanted to play tragic or sentimental parts":

> Lindgreen was adamant, however: "Good gracious, my dear child, your appearance is against you. People would only laugh at such a lanky hero!" All the same he allowed him to learn Correggio's monologue from Oehlenschläger's tragedy. When he played it to Lindgreen, Andersen was so moved by his own performance that he burst into tears. Lindgreen pressed his hand and said, "You have a heart, and by God you also have a head, but you mustn't go on wasting your time here. You ought to study! You're no good as an actor, but there are other wonderful things as well as acting."[2]

Whereupon, at the urging of his friends, Andersen reluctantly went off to grammar school! this naïve and ungainly youth of seventeen looming among the

---

[2] Elias Bredsdorff, *Hans Christian Andersen* (Scribner's, 1975).

eleven-year-olds, for five years of belated formal education; returned to Copenhagen not a scholar but a poet; soon was adapting and inventing the fairy tales with their blend of fantasy, comedy, and pathos that established his world fame; at length achieved the skill and detachment that enabled him to transmute the miseries of his early years into the mellow realism of stories like "Auntie." Or so Bredsdorff's biography, a painstaking and unenamored account of a very peculiar life, pretty much says.

This very peculiar person, so the account goes, gradually settled into his proper place as one of the great storytellers of the world. But the evidence won't bear examination: perhaps the best stories—for example "Auntie" (whose sustained and unforced geniality doesn't appear anywhere else in Andersen)—are the work of a great storyteller; but many of the others seem to have been written or at least skewed by the unprepossessing and moony young reject nursing his grievance, by the suppliant in the wings, the tender ham who was "so moved by his own performance that he burst into tears," the out-sized and over-aged schoolboy with a turn for high-minded moist-eyed verses. The fact is that most ugly ducklings grow up to be ugly ducks, and fairy tales don't do their job by tampering with the truth.

Andersen is less interested in truth than in high-mindedness and justice. "The Swineherd" is one of his better tales—an adaptation, and his adaptations are usually simpler and livelier than his inventions—it's about a prince wooing a beautiful (what else?) and spoiled (who cares?) princess; so far so good, until Andersen reverses the original happy ending and sees to it that the prince casts her off because the princess quite forgivably prefers a couple of charming gadgets to God's precious little creatures (a rose and a nightingale): "'I have come to despise you,' said the prince"; vindictively abandons her in a pouring rain out in the middle of nowhere; "entered his own kingdom and locked the door behind him." Andersen seems to think he does justice to the beauty of women by pretending that what gives so much pleasure has no special privileges. But Perrault, one of Andersen's predecessors, knows just what sort of acknowledgment a true prince owes to a beautiful princess (in "Ricky of the Tuft"): "Beauty is so great an advantage that everything else can be disregarded; and I do not see that the possessor of it can have anything much to grieve about." Moreover the Grimm brothers, doting on the beautiful and spoiled princess of "The Frog-King," don't let some silly promises she has made to the frog get in the way of her amphibicidal revulsion when he demands that she take him to bed with her:

> 'I'm tired, I want to sleep as much as you do: pick me up, or I'll tell your father." Then she really got angry, picked him up, and threw him against the wall with all her might: "Now you can go to sleep if you like, you nasty frog!"
> But when he fell he wasn't a frog but a prince . . .

and of course they live happily ever after. In the world's wish-books virtue is its own reward but beauty takes the cake. Who—certainly not Chaucer!—would ever think of punishing zesty and beautiful Alisoun of *The Miller's Tale* for cuckolding her old husband, humiliating one of her suitors, having a wonderful time herself, and generally making the world a wilder place for anybody who lays his eyes or hands on her?

Andersen persuades himself that fairy tales aren't fiction (articulate fears and wishes, reasonable dreams) but lessons, as for instance: nature is better than art (for towering oaks from teeny acorns grow), feeling is better than thinking, ignorance is better than learning, children are better than grownups ("I can't give her any more power than she already has! Don't you understand how great it is? . . . it is in her heart, for she is a sweet and innocent child"), funerals are better than weddings, mothers are better than people—

> The poor mother kissed the dead child and then kissed the rose, before she placed it on the young girl's breast, as if she hoped that the freshness of a rose and a mother's kiss could make the girl's heart beat again.
>
> The petals of the rose shook with happiness. It was as if the whole rose swelled and grew. "I have become more than a rose, for, like a child, I have received a mother's kiss. I have been blessed and will travel into the unknown realm, dreaming on the dead girl's breast. Truly, I am the happiest of us all."

—(when there are no swelling roses available, Andersen rhymes his pubescent girls with tumescent pearls: "The girl said, '. . . I feel within my closed hand the glow of the jewel. I can feel it pulse and swell . . .'"), as a matter of fact though God is good ("To Him alone belongs all honor") people aren't ("the trash, the cheap tinsel that mankind considered beautiful"), ugly is gorgeous, poor is rich, ad infinitum and caveat emptor. Whoever has read only the few most often reprinted stories (chiefly adaptations) of Andersen's wouldn't guess that most of his hundred and fifty-six are non-denominational tracts, homilies, exempla, with the mixture of mush ("who can distinguish between raindrops and tears of happiness?"), bluff, archness, and spite characteristic of such productions, though usually Andersen's make a not necessarily laudable effort to disguise themselves as fairy tales.

Some of the best-known tales—e.g. "The Little Mermaid," "The Snow Queen," "The Ice-Maiden"—don't even observe the blessed folk convention of brevity; they have their moments (especially "The Ice-Maiden," in which the fine realistic account of a courtship doesn't deserve to be juxtaposed and confused with the claptrap supernaturalism) but they tend to trail off into mazes of fancy, sentiment, Victorian trash and tinsel: Andersen and Dickens were mutual admirers, and much of Andersen reads like the worst of Dickens: "The Little Match Girl," "Grief," "The Dead Child," "She Was No Good." When Andersen is doing an adaptation of a highly vertebrate folk tale that resists invention and pathos and coy asides—as for example "The Emperor's New Clothes," "The Tinderbox," "The Princess and the Pea," "Little Claus and Big Claus," "What Father Does Is Always Right"—he can be economical and entertaining, and give evidence of the great storyteller's conscience and sense of pace and rhythm. On his own, though, he has too many options, his detail is often distracting and irresponsible, the sort that passes itself off in the abominable deserts of children's literature as "imaginative": "He did not ride away on a horse: no, he mounted an ostrich, for that could run faster. But as soon as he saw the wild swans he picked out the strongest among them and rode on that instead, for he liked a change" ("The Philosopher's Stone").

The best of the world's fairy tales have a symmetry and a cutting edge that are quite beyond even the best Andersen. Puss of Perrault's "Puss in Boots" advances through his series of challenges so cleverly and so gracefully that we readers would bet Puss's boots that he won't miss a trick coming up with the most elegant and most profitable means of disposal for the very ogre of ogres:

> Finally Master Puss reached a splendid castle, which belonged to an ogre. He was the richest ogre that had ever been known, for all the lands through which the king had passed were part of the castle domain. . . .
>
> The ogre received him as civilly as an ogre can, and bade him sit down.
>
> "I have been told," said Puss, "that you have the power to change yourself into any kind of animal—for example, that you can transform yourself into a lion or an elephant."
>
> "That is perfectly true," said the ogre, curtly, "and just to prove it you shall see me turn into a lion."
>
> Puss was so frightened on seeing a lion before him that he sprang onto the roof—not without difficulty and danger, for his boots were not meant for walking on the tiles.
>
> Perceiving presently that the ogre had abandoned his transformation, Puss descended, and owned to having been thoroughly frightened.
>
> "I have also been told," he added, "but I can scarcely believe it, that you have the further power to take the shape of the smallest animals—for example, that you can change yourself into a rat or a mouse. I confess that to me it seems quite impossible."
>
> "Impossible,?" cried the ogre; "you shall see!" And in the same moment he changed himself into a mouse, which began to run around the floor. No sooner did Puss see it than he pounced on it and ate it.

That's all for the ogre, whose domain (presumably devolving on Puss by right of transubstantiation) faithful Puss delivers to his master. Andersen, trying to work the same magic (in "How To Cook Soup upon a Sausage Pin"), turns Perrault's witty cat into a mouse who's as stupid as an ogre and stupidly tells us how he expects to become wise: "The queen ant . . . stood up on her two hind legs, you couldn't mistake any of the lesser ants for her, and I ate her. 'Go to the ant and become wise.' Now I have swallowed the queen." But then Andersen doesn't know mice whereas Perrault, an expert on cats and ogres, goes so far in "Little Tom Thumb" as to put on exhibition a whole ogre family:

> Now the ogre had seven daughters who as yet were only children. These little ogresses all had the most lovely complexions, for, like their father, they

ate fresh meat. But they had little round gray eyes, crooked noses, and very large mouths, and long and exceedingly sharp teeth, set far apart. They were not so very wicked at present, but they showed great promise, for already they were in the habit of killing little children to suck their blood.

They had gone to bed early, and were all seven in a great bed, each with a crown of gold upon her head.

Those golden crowns are the crowning touch, surely just the thing for a philoprogenitive ogre bent on pampering his little darlings.

Andersen, on the other hand, has a thing about virtue, he doesn't find enough innocence and piety in the world to suit him, he often stamps his foot with vexation and sinks into lugubriousness, though never quite so uninhibitedly as the Grimms' dwarf Rumpelstiltskin when the Queen outsmarts him and saves her child:

"The Devil told you! the Devil told you!" screamed the dwarf and in his anger drove his right foot so deep into the ground that he went down to his waist. Then in his rage he seized his left foot with both hands and tore himself right in two.

Perrault and the Grimms aren't evangelists, they don't apoplectically insist on their own way or on what the world ought to be, they are satisfied to find it full of passion, mother-wit, daring, competitiveness, ambition, the natural affections. Life is a mixed bag, and stories aren't lessons. When the Grimms tell the story of "The Fisherman and His Wife," they don't deplore or moralize the wife's ambition as from humble beginnings (she lives with her husband "in a pisspot by the sea" but how "miserable to live forever in a pisspot; it stinks and is so shitty") she rockets to level beyond level of glory:

"Oh, wife, how nice that you're king. Now let's not wish for anything more." "Well, husband," said the woman and got quite restless, "time's hanging heavy on my hands and I can't stand it any longer. Go to the flounder! I'm king, and now I must become emperor as well." "Oh, wife," said the man, "why do you want to be emperor?" "Husband," she said, "go to the flounder! I want to be emperor." . . . .

Meanwhile he got to the sea, and the sea was all black and soupy and began to boil up and bubble, and such a gale passed over that the surface frothed and foamed, and the man was frightened. But he stepped up and said,

"Manntje, manntje, timpe te,
Flounder, flounder in the sea!
My wife Ilsebill
Doesn't want what I really want."

"Well, what does she want?" said the flounder. "Alas, flounder," he said, "my wife wants to be emperor." "Just go back," said the flounder, "she's emperor already."

Now emperor, that's something! Surely even a woman will settle for *that*!

> Then the man went back, and when he got there, the whole mansion was of polished marble with alabaster figures and golden ornaments. Soldiers were marching before the door, blowing trumpets and beating drums and kettledrums, and within barons and counts and dukes were walking about as servants and opened the doors for him, and these were of solid gold. And when he went in, there was his wife sitting on a throne wrought of a single piece of gold and two miles high, and she had on a golden crown three yards high and set with brilliants and carbuncles. In one hand she held the scepter and in the other the imperial apple. On both sides she was flanked by satellites standing in two rows, each person shorter than the next, ranging in size from the tallest giant, who was two miles tall, to the tiniest dwarf only as big as my little finger. And before her were standing many princes and dukes. Then the man stepped up and said, "wife, are you now emperor?" "Yes," she said, "I'm emperor." "Husband," she said, "why are you standing there? Now that I'm emperor, I want to be pope, too. Go to the flounder!" . . . .

Faint-hearted husband notwithstanding, pope is all right too; and the flounder balks at last only when the wife demands the one office that never has a vacancy:

> She thought, "Aha! couldn't I, too, make the sun and moon rise?" "Husband," she said and nudged him in the ribs with her elbow, "wake up and go to the flounder. I want to be like God." . . . "Oh, wife," said the husband, falling on his knees before her, "the flounder can't do that. It can make an emperor and a pope. I pray you, think it over and remain pope." Then she got angry, her hair flew wildly about her head, she tore her bodice, and gave him a kick, screaming, "I simply won't stand it any longer. Will you go!" Then he put on his trousers and ran off like mad.
>
> Outside a storm was raging so that he could scarcely stay on his feet. Houses and trees were falling, the mountains shaking, and great boulders rolling down into the sea. The sky was absolutely pitch-black, there was thunder and lightning, and the sea was throwing up black waves as high as church steeples and mountains, and all with crests of white foam. Then he shouted but couldn't hear his own voice,
>
> > "Manntje, manntje, timpe te,
> > Flounder, flounder in the sea!
> > My wife Ilsebill
> > Doesn't want what I want at all."
>
> "Well, what does she want?" said the flounder. "Oh," he said, "she wants to be like God." "Just go home, she's back in the pisspot again."
>
> To this day they're still sitting there.

The moral of this story is: It doesn't hurt to try.

Father Knows Best

SURELY, having been told that Tolstoy wrote the following paragraph, readers would place it at once among the earlier pronouncements by the stuffed shirt Karenin as he tries to bring to her senses his erring wife:

> You have committed one of the most serious and at the same time odious crimes that a wife and mother can commit, and having committed this crime you are not doing what is natural to any, I don't say Christian, but perfectly ordinary woman who has not lost all conscience—you are not shocked at your sin, you don't repent of it, you don't acknowledge your fall and humiliation, you don't try to save yourself from the possibility of repeating your sin, but on the contrary you wish by some deceitful means (divorce) to make it possible for the sin to continue, to make that sin cease to be a sin and become something permitted.

Actually it's in a letter from Tolstoy himself,[1] thirty years after *Anna Karenina*, trying to bring to her senses a married woman who has been carrying on with his son Andrey (whom a few years earlier he enjoins to "give up drinking, smoking, gipsies, horses, dogs"—i.e. all the pleasures that at Andrey's age Tolstoy found just as irresistible). As it happened, Tolstoy had no better luck than Karenin. In fact Yekaterina's divorce came through and she and Andrey were married: this was the way out that Anna and Vronsky might have taken too but somehow missed, perhaps because authors can do anything they please—can turn doors into walls—whereas heavy fathers may well get trampled by the rush for the exit.

Tolstoy isn't a reasonable man, early or late; or his very reasonableness is partial and deceptive—as when in *Anna Karenina* he points out that the sentimental and pietistic Countess Lydia Ivanovna isn't the best judge of Anna: "'I can understand immorality,' she went on, not quite truthfully, because she never could understand what it was that led women to immorality . . . "; and Aha! goes the reader, struck by Tolstoy's tactful sophistication which so plainly implies that passion isn't characteristic of silly women and can overwhelm even the most respectable woman, that Anna (unlike Yekaterina thirty years later) isn't to be merely condemned, that pleasures (unlike Andrey's thirty years later) aren't to be dismissed as alarming and unclean; yet here is Anna in total collapse a moment after "her bewitching dream of happiness . . . [has] come to pass":

---

[1] R. F. Christian, (ed.), *Tolstoy's Letters* (Scribners, 1978). 2 vols.

> Looking at him, she felt her humiliation physically, and could say nothing more. He felt what a murderer must feel when looking at the body he has deprived of life. The body he had deprived of life was their love, the first period of their love. There was something frightful and revolting in the recollection of what had been paid for with this terrible price of shame. The shame she felt at her spiritual nakedness communicated itself to him. But in spite of the murderer's horror of the body of his victim, that body must be cut in pieces and hidden away, and he must make use of what he has obtained by the murder.

Strong stuff, this moment of truth ("'What bliss?' she said with disgust and horror"), which, coming to it in so celebrated a novel, we don't dare question because we're afraid to seem coarse and ignorant: certainly the authoritative voice wouldn't say it if it weren't true (and how do we check it, do we take a poll of murderers' row or the girls at the office?). Only it isn't God talking, it's Tolstoy, who unreasonably needs to assert that this particular married woman (unlike Yekaterina?), voluntarily clasped for the first time in the arms of her lover, will of course find the sex act frightful and revolting (if she can't manage to close her eyes and think of England), will experience it as the "spiritual" equivalent of rape and murder, will see "her bewitching dream of happiness" crumble instantly. Tolstoy is at odds here not only with common sense but with his own creature. Anna gives evidence by everything else she thinks and says and does that she is physically and passionately in love with Vronsky; she was before and will continue to be after; she never regrets her love for him except when she suspects he doesn't return it; nothing in her nature or circumstances suggests that this time as well as innumerable times afterward she wouldn't enjoy the act; and whatever her apprehensions it isn't likely, the bewitching dream having come to pass, that she would react to Vronsky's first completed pass as old Tolstoy hopes that after his letter Yekaterina will react to future scrimmages with Andrey. Tolstoy the novelist has created a woman alive to pleasures which Tolstoy the bluenose implausibly denies her.

Tolstoy is the tensest and most irascible of great novelists, he dislikes fine moral distinctions (as between agreeable love-making and disagreeable), he is suspicious of the range of feelings and works at segregating right feelings from wrong, the sheep from the goats, he is so intent on keeping the gulf between good and bad that, if the story he's telling threatens to narrow it, he intervenes with misrepresentations and omissions and the loud bullying that silences readers who might otherwise venture a doubt. In *War and Peace,* for instance, he plans to show Natasha, imprudently left alone with her impulses for a trial year by Prince Andrey, falling in love with—no, because *love* is what she feels only for Prince Andrey; rather, becoming *infatuated* with Anatole Kuragin. But Natasha is a good girl and would never do such a thing all by herself, there must be witches. So Tolstoy prepares us for Natasha's misstep by bringing her to the opera, a bad place (just look at the ladies in the boxes flaunting their "naked shoulders"!), a place of illusion that gives him his pretext for shouting down the very idea of illusion:

> In the center of the stage sat some girls in red bodices and white skirts. One very fat girl in a white silk dress sat apart on a low bench, to the back of which a piece of green cardboard was glued. They all sang something. When they had finished their song the girl in white went up to the prompter's box, and a man with tight silk trousers over his stout legs, and holding a plume and a dagger, went up to her and began singing, waving his arms about. . . .

Next he brings Natasha to a reading by a fat actress who is, besides, French and immoral: "Mademoiselle Georges, with her bare, fat, dimpled arms, and a red shawl draped over one shoulder, came into the space left vacant for her, and assumed an unnatural pose . . . [,] looked sternly and gloomily at the audience, and began reciting some French verses describing her guilty love for her son. . . ." (It's a relief to learn that in such juvenile travesties Tolstoy, according to the Russian Formalist critics, is using a literary technique, which they call "estrangement.") Poor Natasha, wholesome little home-baked *pirozhok* fresh out of the backwoods, "looked at the fat actress" and, quite disoriented by these scandalous public hoaxes (the arts) to which she has been subjected in the wicked city, "felt herself again completely borne away into this strange senseless world—so remote from her old world—a world in which it was impossible to know what was good or bad": thus Tolstoy has proved beyond a reasonable doubt how "senseless," "unnatural," "bad," unworthy of herself, attributable to external evil forces, and light-years distant from love Natasha's crush on the quite sufficiently insipid Anatole will turn out to be. Anyhow, clearing a space around the nearly faultless Natasha is easier than having to think about women at large, the community of women, all those uncontrollables out there infatuated or in love or on a stage dancing and singing (but thank God actresses are always fat and stupid) or at a ball or the opera in low-cut gowns or at home reading *War and Peace* (in the center of the sofa squatted a fat girl holding on her lap a thick object which consisted of a great many sheets of paper glued to a cardboard backing, and every few minutes she inserted two bare, fat fingers into it to reverse the sheet facing her, all the while giggling, snuffling, scowling, fit as a fiddle and ready for love). There must be witches.

Pierre too, destined for Natasha, is good rather than bad, a high-minded, naïve, and trusting person whom witches can lead by the nose so to speak into if you'll pardon the expression wedded bliss with that gorgeous pin-up Hélène; but class will tell, they can give him a license and lead him to the bedroom door but they can't make him relish for even a moment the prospect of perfectly legal love with his pneumatic spouse: "There is something nasty, something wrong, in the feeling she excites in me," he muses *before* the wedding, and forever afterward he feels nothing for her except virtuous loathing. (Earlier in the novel he goes to brothels during drunken sprees, but that's another matter.) As for Hélène herself (or Anna Pavlovna, or almost any other society woman in Tolstoy's fiction), Tolstoy takes such pains to keep her unvaryingly base, trivial, and dull that the reader of English novels is by contrast reminded of belles like Trollope's Lizzie Eustace or the signora Neroni, who are as socially daunting as Hélène but allowed to present themselves to us with a flair that indicates how their lives might seem not only to Snow White and Savonarola but to their lovers and themselves.

Tolstoy's moral anxiety, which is the prevailing tone through much of *War and Peace*, eventually screws itself up to a pitch of cannibal self-righteousness: for instance, the gratification with which he reports Hèléne's death (freeing Pierre for Natasha) "in agony" from a self-administered overdose of an abortion drug; above all, the description of Anatole's grossly phallic (doubtless Tolstoy wasn't attending to the image and would have been horrified) physicalness at the moment before it and he are cut off together:

> One large white plump leg twitched rapidly all the time with a feverish tremor. The man was sobbing and choking convulsively. Two doctors . . . were silently doing something to this man's other, gory leg. . . .
> The wounded man was shown his amputated leg stained with clotted blood and with the boot still on.
> "Oh! Oh, ooh!" he sobbed, like a woman. . . .
> In the miserable, sobbing, enfeebled man whose leg had just been amputated . . . [Prince Andrey] recognized Anatole Kuragin. . . .

So much for the dirty beast who wiggled our heroine's pedestal.

If there were no bad men around to tempt them, or if Tolstoy were around to rescue them from the bad men, all women might end as satisfactorily as Natasha: married and mindlessly devoted to a good sort like Pierre, quite under control and submerged in family life ("The old fire very rarely kindled in her face now"), incapable of being interested in ideas or the arts or society, matronly or even slatternly, valuing only "the company of those to whom she could come striding disheveled from the nursery in her dressing-gown, and with joyful face show a yellow instead of a green stain on baby's diaper . . ." (while working on *War and Peace,* still contented with his marriage of a few years and living the patriarchal life on his estate in the country, Tolstoy wrote to a friend that "I am lucky enough to be fettered by chains of rich liquid green and yellow children's shit to Yasnaya Polyana").

In the years before Sofya Andreyevna, the girl he had been most likely to marry was Valeriya Vladimirovna Arsenyeva, his letters to whom are a Bartlett's book of quotations from the anxious male: "As for what you call my cold feelings, I can tell you that they're 1,000 times stronger and better than your feelings, although I do keep them in check"; "I expect a great deal from our correspondence"; "wear a corset, and put on your stockings yourself"; "Don't despair of becoming perfect"; "Tell me everything that was, and is, bad in you"; "I'm also sending you Turgenev's *Tales,* . . . in my opinion, they're nearly all charming, but all the same come out with your opinion frankly, however absurd it may be"; "I know many women more intelligent than you, but I've never met one more honest"; "you will teach me to love, I will teach you to think"; "Your principal defect is weakness of character"; "the slightest faux pas destroys everything, and you can't regain a happiness that is lost"; "Nothing else matters as long as you love me and are as I wish, i.e. perfect"; "You are deluding yourself that you have taste [in clothing]"; "It's impossible for you to understand (perhaps you'll understand in time) the indescribably great pleasure one feels from understanding and loving poetry"; "you must talk less, so as to feel more"; "if Mr. Mortier [her piano teacher, of whom Tolstoy is jealous] were to write a love letter to my wife or kiss her hand, and she were to hide this from me . . . then if I loved my wife, I would shoot myself, or if not, I would get a divorce instantly and flee to the ends of the earth simply out of respect for her and for my name, and from disappointment over my plans for the future"; "*let us never speak* of religion. . . You know I'm a believer, but . . . this question should not be touched upon, especially by people who want to love each other"; "Religion is a great thing, especially for women"; "I'm *lecturing* again; but what can I do?"; "You're angry that *I'm only able to give lectures.* But . . . all these are the ideas and feelings most precious to me, and I write about them almost with tears in my eyes (believe me); but to you it's all *lecturing and boredom*"; and so at length to the uneasy brush-off letter with its unctuous goodbye and good luck: "Goodbye, dear Valeriya Vladimirovna, Christ be with you; you and I both have a long and splendid road ahead of us, and God grant it may lead you to the happiness you deserve 1,000 times over."

He begged off because he couldn't be sure: "I'm so afraid of marriage," he had written her two weeks earlier, summarizing the short course in Russian melodrama, "that I look at it too sternly and seriously. . . . I'm staking everything on this one card. If I don't find complete happiness, I shall ruin everything, my talent, my heart; I'll become a drunkard and a gambler; I'll steal, if I haven't the courage to cut my throat." He wrote the novella *Family Happiness* soon after breaking with Valeriya, who was the model for its heroine: an attempt to turn his anxieties and expectations about marriage into an account of their marriage as it might have been. The narrator is the girl herself (one of the very rare exceptions in Tolstoy's fiction to his customary choice of omniscience), and the point of view contributes a voyeuristic tinge to this sentimental, spiteful, self-pitying, and—to use a Tolstoyan epithet—impure male fantasy: An older man serves as father, uncle, guardian, priest, teacher, playmate, husband, and lover to a teen-aged girl, who after an extended bucolic honeymoon quite to his taste proves to be unworthy of him, compromising her blind and slavish devotion by learning to enjoy the big city, parties, even the flattery of other men; but at the end he condescends to a reconciliation back in the boondocks for the fading twilight of their life (she's about twenty-two now, he's thirty-five or so)—

> "Let all be as it was before! Surely that is possible?" I asked, looking into his eyes; but their gaze was clear and calm, and did not look deeply into mine.
> Even while I spoke, I knew that my wishes and my petition were impossible. He smiled calmly and gently; and I thought it the smile of an old man.
> "How young you are still!" he said, "and I am so old. What you seek in me is no longer there. Why deceive ourselves?" he added, still smiling.

Why indeed? but seldom has an important writer been more self-deceived: "'That's the truth, my dear one,' he said, drawing down my head and kissing it, not a lover any longer but an old friend," while outside on cue "the fragrant freshness of the night rose ever stronger and sweeter from the garden." The slightest faux pas destroys everything ("That day ended the romance of our marriage"), and you can't regain a happiness that is lost, except maybe by taking the six-week Masters-and-Johnson course in regaining lost happiness. What a splendid fellow! and how lucky she is that he doesn't cut his throat or shoot himself.

On October 1, 1862, married just a week, Tolstoy wrote to his sister-in-law, "I am now very drawn to writing a free work de longue haleine—a novel or the like," and he added, "Life is very, very good for me, and I flatter myself with the hope that it is for Sonya too." He was happy and confident, he felt he had staked everything on the fatal card and won (and therefore could put Valeriya and *Family Happiness* behind him; but, though he must have thought otherwise, he wasn't able to put the sex question behind him), soon he began writing, and for more than five years the long breath animated and sustained a "free work" that he himself insisted wasn't a novel (later he called *Anna Karenina* "my first novel"). He hadn't the patience for a novel, not yet anyway. The oddest fact about *War and Peace* is that, though fifteen hundred pages is a long breath all right, scarcely a scene in it breathes for longer than a moment. Not only are the chapters astonishingly and uniformly short, but Tolstoy almost never permits anything between the characters to expand dramatically, rather he will wrap it up with his own summaries and judgments or theirs (as if what people say or do is much less important than what it all means) or (as if enough is enough) will cut it off abruptly: "Next day Anatole left for Petersburg"; or "Every act of theirs, which appears to them an act of their own will, is in an historical sense involuntary, and is related to the whole course of history and predestined from eternity"; or—

> For a long time Pierre did not sleep, but lay with eyes open in the darkness listening to the regular snoring of Platon, who lay beside him, and he felt that the world that had been shattered was once more stirring in his soul with a new beauty and on new and unshakable foundations.

Tolstoy is so impatient with character and dialogue that he continually lapses into the most banal fictional shorthand (so that readers won't have to waste their time thinking): Prince Andrey has "firm clear-cut features" (not blurry irresolute ones); Speranski has "very plump, soft, and white hands" (cf. Anatole's "white plump leg" before Tolstoy brings down his retributory surgical saw); Natasha is "not pretty [pretty means sexy and out of control] but full of life." Because Tolstoy wants us to know at once, there are repetitions and changes and patterns and accidents but no surprises or developments. Only the wolf-hunt and (except when he's getting on with his laborious determinism) the military scenes seem to spring from sources outside his conscious and imperious need to control; but Pierre's and Prince Andrey's great moments, whether gazing into the blue sky of infinity at Austerlitz or finding the secret of life in Platon Karatayev, read nowadays like recruitment posters for the latest school of acupuncture. Revelations don't come off in *War and Peace* because all Tolstoy is sure of is what's doing, the relationships are clear and easy to follow and one keeps reading to see how they come out, but there's no moral coherence, there's a will but there isn't a way; he can't make out what it all means (babbling about green fields or blue skies or "new and unshakable foundations" or "the whole course of history" doesn't help), which is all that matters to him.

The meaning of *Anna Karenina*, on the other hand, is supplied by its subject: All for love against God and man. True, one suspects that the voice speaking the novel's epigraph—"Vengeance is mine; I will repay"—isn't God's but Tolstoy's, and that Anna and Vronsky aren't against God or man or even law and order but against the swarm of social parasites at Anna Pavlovna's soiree whose vileness Tolstoy was so delighted to memorialize in the opening chapter of *War and Peace*. Nevertheless he now has a scaffolding which will support a continuous and self-explanatory narrative. Something can therefore happen, but the fact that the heroine is Tolstoy's only completely sympathetic worldly woman and also one of the primary heroines of literature can hardly be accounted for by his choice of subject; there are no witches here but there is something like a miracle, for Anna is what she is, as in her *real* moment of truth: not when she reacts to Vronsky's love-making "with disgust and horror," but when she is so publicly unnerved by Vronsky's fall at the steeplechase that her husband feels obliged to lecture her (as Tolstoy lectures Yekaterina and Valeriya)—

> "I asked you once before to conduct yourself in Society so that evil tongues might be unable to say anything against you. There was a time when I spoke about inner relations; now I do not speak of them. I speak now of external relations. Your conduct was improper and I do not wish it to occur again."
>
> She did not hear half that he said, but felt afraid of him and wondered whether it was true that Vronsky was not hurt. Was it of him they were speaking when they said that he was not hurt but the horse had broken its back? She only smiled with simulated irony when he had finished; and she did not reply because she had not heard what he said. Karenin had begun to speak boldly, but when he realized clearly what he was talking about, the fear she was experiencing communicated itself to him. He saw her smile and a strange delusion possessed him. "She smiles at my suspicions. In a moment she will tell me what she told me then: that these suspicions are groundless and ridiculous."
>
> Now that a complete disclosure was impending, he expected nothing so much as that she would, as before, answer him mockingly that his suspicions were ridiculous and groundless. What he knew was so terrible that he was now prepared to believe anything. But the expression of her frightened and gloomy face did not now even promise deception.
>
> "Perhaps I am mistaken," said he. "In that case I beg your pardon."

—so that now at last she can tell Karenin the anxious husband (as well as Tolstoy the anxious father and suitor) all, and then, her soul suspended and too full for anything less than catastrophe, await her lover:

> "No, you were not mistaken," she said slowly, looking despairingly into his cold face. "You were not mistaken. I was, and cannot help being, in

despair. I listen to you but I am thinking of him. I love him, I am his mistress, I cannot endure you, I am afraid of you, and I hate you. . . . Do what you like to me."

And throwing herself back into the corner of the carriage she burst into sobs, hiding her face in her hands. Karenin did not move, and did not change the direction in which he was looking, but his face suddenly assumed the solemn immobility of the dead, and that expression did not alter till they reached the house. As they were driving up to it, he turned his face to her still with the same expression and said:

"Yes! But I demand that the external conditions of propriety shall be observed till"—his voice trembled—"till I take measures to safeguard my honor and inform you of them."

He alighted first and helped her out. In the presence of the servants he pressed her hand, re-entered the carriage, and drove off toward Petersburg.

After he had gone the Princess Betsy's footman brought Anna a note.

"I sent to Alexey to inquire about his health. He writes that he is safe and sound, but in despair."

"Then he will come," thought she. "What a good thing it is that I spoke out."

She looked at the clock. She had three hours still to wait, and the memory of the incidents of their last meeting fired her blood.

"Dear me, how light it is! It is dreadful, but I love to see his face, and I love this fantastic light. . .My husband! Ah, yes. . .Well, thank heaven that all is over with him!" [All the ellipses in this passage are Tolstoy's.]

Against poor Karenin, who deserves this as little as he deserves Anna, against the gawkers and gossips at the racetrack and even the stick Vronsky, whom Tolstoy can't or won't make vivid enough to justify Anna's passion as more than a necessary reflex of despair, and especially against Tolstoy himself, Anna is right.

The live ones in the novel are Anna and her brother, Stiva. Karenin the vulnerable bureaucrat is consummate to the last button and rather touching; Karenin temporarily irradiated by Christian love is too useful to the plot (and too like Tolstoy's occasional fond misconception of himself); Karenin the dupe of charlatans is a crude reduction. Levin and Kitty are retreads of Pierre and Natasha but more acceptable because less pretentiously childlike and given more space and leisurely detail, though Levin's communications with the soil or the firmament aren't any more apocalyptic than Pierre's or Prince Andrey's. Stiva Oblonsky, however, is, like Anna, an anomaly and a marvel for as long as Tolstoy lets him be himself (he is slighted and diminished after the first half of the novel): lavishly unfaithful to his likable and hard-pressed wife; a shameless sensualist and materialist; cheerful, helpful, kind, affectionate—Tolstoy's only sympathetic representation ever of a man of the world, to the point of even allowing him to be straight-arrow Levin's best friend! *Anna Karenina* is Tolstoy's generous and unintentional tribute and farewell to worldliness.

After *Anna* all of his fiction—with a single exception—is obsessive (nothing but sex and death) and minimalist (nothing but the truth), the work of a prodigious eccentric who has finally closed his mind with a bang: non-violent, non-alcoholic, celibate, vegetarian fiction with a mad gleam in its eye and a razor edge. (It all comes from the white-bearded apostle of love and of the free individual conscience, who writes to his chief disciple, Chertkov, denouncing contraception: "It's impossible to write about it and argue against it, just as it's impossible to argue against a man trying to prove that copulation with dead bodies is pleasant and harmless. A man who doesn't feel what elephants feel, that copulation generally is an act humiliating both to oneself and one's partner, and therefore repulsive . . . is on the level of an animal"; but where this logic leaves elephants remains to be seen.) It's decisive, energetic, steamroller fiction, as impossible to live with as the wife-murderer "hero" of *The Kreutzer Sonata*.

The exception is *Hadji Murad*. Tolstoy left it unpublished and was still working on it in his seventy-fifth year, when he addressed a number of questions to somebody who had known the historical Hadji Murad a half-century earlier (it isn't the old crank asking, it's the novelist: "Did he speak even a little Russian?"; "Did he limp noticeably?"; "Did the house where you lived upstairs, and he downstairs, have a garden?"; "What were the murids [followers] like who were with . . . him?"; "Did they have rifles on them when they escaped?"). A half-century earlier Tolstoy himself had spent three years in the Caucasus with the army (one of his letters mentions that "Shamil's number two, a certain Hadji Murad, went over to the Russian government the other day"): he was stationed in a Cossack village just across the Terek River from the mountain peoples whom the Russians were trying to drive back and subdue. As far as possible from Petersburg, Moscow, and Yasnaya Polyana, both the Cossack on this side of the Terek and the mountain tribesman on the other lived Tolstoy's buried life. Both *The Cossacks* (some of the writing of which was contemporaneous with *Family Happiness*!) and, fifty years later, *Hadji Murad* are tributes to unfussed-over lives—Only the unexamined life is worth living—from the man who young and old insisted on examining his life to the last discreditable millimeter: "all my nastiness, stupidity, depravity, and meanness," as he haughtily summed himself up to his biographer Biryukov (his favorite writer all his life was Rousseau, who he thought had done the best job ever of spilling the beans about himself). Tolstoy knew that neither the Cossacks nor the Chechens would have been impressed by Tolstoy the young self-seeker or Tolstoy the old crank; and he had always loved and envied their ways; so, writing about them, he was free to experience the moral feelings he elsewhere in his work could do little but make a case for: modesty and love.

Eroshka the old Cossack hunter tells the young soldier from Moscow, "I'll take you hunting and teach you to fish. I'll show you Chechens and find a girl for you, if you like—even that!"

"You, an old man—and say such things," replied Olenin. "Why, it's a sin!"

"A sin? Where's the sin?" said the old man emphatically. "A sin to look at a nice girl? A sin to have some fun with her? Or is it a sin to love her? Is that so in your parts? . . ."

That's how it is back in Moscow, but out here in Eden Olenin can rejoice in Tolstoy's only sympathetic—and lingeringly specific!—representation of a superbly physical woman in all of his writings:

> Olenin went on reading, but did not understand a word of what was written in the book that lay open before him. He kept lifting his eyes from it and looking at the powerful young woman who was moving about. Whether she stepped into the moist morning shadow thrown by the house, or went out into the middle of the yard lit up by the joyous young light, so that the whole of her stately figure in its bright colored garment gleamed in the sunshine and cast a black shadow—he always feared to lose any one of her movements. It delighted him to see how freely and gracefully her figure bent: into what folds her only garment, a pink smock, draped itself on her bosom and along her shapely legs; how she drew herself up and her tight-drawn smock showed the outline of her heaving bosom, how the soles of her narrow feet in her worn red slippers rested on the ground without altering their shape; how her strong arms with the sleeves rolled up, exerting the muscles, used the spade almost as if in anger, and how her deep dark eyes sometimes glanced at him. Though the delicate brows frowned, yet her eyes expressed pleasure and a knowledge of her own beauty.

Maryanka is as admirable as a man! and talks like one ("The girl was milking the buffalo-cow in the shed. 'Can't keep quiet, the damned thing!' came her impatient voice . . ."), and attracts the masculine epithets—"her virile upright bearing"; "her firm masculine tread"; "her beautiful powerful form"; "Her features might have been considered too masculine and almost harsh had it not been for her tall stately figure, her powerful chest and shoulders, and especially the severe yet tender expression of her long dark eyes." When Olenin thinks she may be watching he tries to show off, sitting his horse "with a slightly conscious elegance," smartly dressed, glowing with youth and health: "He thought himself handsome, agile, and like a brave; but he was mistaken." Try as he may in hunting, fighting, drinking, courting, he will never be one of them, he can only admire them and set down how they look and move, what they say and do, with a loving attention to the flow and detail of dailiness in this primitive outpost that recalls not only the subject but the modesty and strength of Pushkin's *The Captain's Daughter*.

As for *Hadji Murad*, apart from an episode in which Tolstoy makes sure we understand how contemptible Tsar Nicholas was ("the welfare and happiness of the whole world depended on him, and wearied though he was he would still not refuse the universe his assistance"), the author is even more remarkable than in *The Cossacks* for his self-effacement. Hadji Murad speaks for himself, as when he tells the Russian officer the story of his captivity and escape:

> ". . . Akhmet Khan did as he pleased. He sent a company of soldiers to seize me, put me in chains, and tied me to a cannon.

"So they kept me six days," he continued. "On the seventh day they untied me and started to take me to Temir-Khan-Shura. Forty soldiers with loaded guns had me in charge. My hands were tied and I knew they had orders to kill me if I tried to escape.

"As we approached Mansokha the path became narrow, and on the right was an abyss about a hundred and twenty yards deep. I went to the right— to the very edge. A soldier wanted to stop me, but I jumped down and pulled him with me. He was killed outright but I, as you see, remained alive.

"Ribs, head, arms, and leg—all were broken! I tried to crawl but grew giddy and fell asleep. I awoke wet with blood. A shepherd saw me and called some people who carried me to an *aoul*. My ribs and head healed, and my leg too, only it has remained short," and Hadji Murad stretched out his crooked leg. "It still serves me, however, and that is well," said he.

"The people heard the news and began coming to me. I recovered and went to Tselmess. The Avars again called on me to rule over them," he went on, with tranquil, confident pride, "and I agreed."

One of the most moving qualities of Tolstoy's last long work of fiction is his chivalrousness toward the *civilized* women out there, living their lives in the dangerous border country—intelligent, resourceful, charming, gallant, like the colonel's wife Princess Marya Vasilievna, "smiling the radiant smile of a happy woman":

Leaving Hadji Murad with his wife, Vorontsov went to his office to do what was necessary about reporting the fact of Hadji Murad's having come over to the Russians. When he had written a report . . . [he] hurried home, afraid that his wife might be vexed with him for forcing on her this terrible stranger, who had to be treated in such a way that he should not take offence, and yet not too kindly. But his fears were needless. Hadji Murad was sitting in an armchair with little Bulka, Vorontsov's stepson, on his knee, and with bent head was listening attentively to the interpreter who was translating to him the words of the laughing Marya Vasilievna. Marya Vasilievna was telling him that if every time a kunak [sworn brother] admired anything of his he made him a present of it, he would soon have to go about like Adam. . . .

"He is delightful, your brigand!" said Marya Vasilievna to her husband in French. "Bulka has been admiring his dagger, and he has given it to him."

Later, at dinner, "he hardly ate anything":

"He is afraid we shall poison him," Marya Vasilievna remarked to her husband. "He has helped himself from the place where I took my helping." Then instantly turning to Hadji Murad she asked him through the interpreter when he would pray again. Hadji Murad lifted five fingers and pointed to the sun. "Then it will soon be time," and Vorontsov drew out

> his watch and pressed a spring. The watch struck four and one quarter. This evidently surprised Hadji Murad, and he asked to hear it again and to be allowed to look at the watch.
> "*Voilà l'occasion! Donnez-lui la montre,*" said the Princess to her husband. Vorontsov at once offered the watch to Hadji Murad.[2]
> The latter placed his hand on his breast and took the watch. He touched the spring several times, listened, and nodded his head approvingly.

And the same old man who wrote that fire-and-brimstone letter to his son's mistress depicts with love, amusement, and admiration Major Petrov's mistress, "a handsome, fair-haired, very freckled, childless woman of thirty . . . the major's faithful companion . . . [who] looked after him like a nurse—a very necessary matter, since he often drank himself into oblivion":

> "Plucky fellow! He rushed at Arslan like a wolf! His face quite changed!"
> "But he'll be up to tricks—he's a terrible rogue, I should say," remarked Petrovsky.
> "It's a pity there aren't more Russian rogues of such a kind!" suddenly put in Marya Dmitrievna with vexation. "He has lived a week with us and we have seen nothing but good from him. He is courteous, wise, and just," she added.
> "How did you find that out?"
> "No matter, I did find it out!"
> "She's quite smitten, and that's a fact!" said the major, who had just entered the room.
> "Well, and if I am smitten? What's that to you? Why run him down if he's a good man? Though he's a Tartar he's still a good man!"

Hadji Murad dies, as he must, in battle:

> Another bullet hit Hadji Murad in the left side. He lay down in the ditch and again pulled some cotton wool out of his *beshmet* [undershirt] and plugged the wound. This wound in the side was fatal and he felt that he was dying. Memories and pictures succeeded one another with extraordinary rapidity in his imagination. Now he saw the powerful Abu Nutsal Khan, dagger in hand and holding up his severed cheek he rushed at his foe. . ., then he saw his son Yusuf, his wife Sofiat, and then the pale, red-bearded face of his enemy Shamil with its half-closed eyes. All these images passed through his mind without evoking any feeling within him—neither

---

[2] Not only Colonel Voronstsov; in *Hadji Murad* even the generals are allowed to behave like grown-ups. Only the Tsar is as stupid as all the commanders are in *War and Peace* except Tolstoy's unhistorical surrogate, Kutuzov, whom, revising *War and Peace*, Tolstoy turned from a senile weakling resembling the historical figure to a folk-hero resembling, in his notions at least, Tolstoy.

Father Knows Best

pity nor anger nor any kind of desire: everything seemed so insignificant in comparison with what was beginning, or had already begun, within him.

Yet his strong body continued the thing that he had commenced. Gathering together his last strength he rose from behind the bank, fired his pistol at a man who was just running toward him, and hit him. The man fell. Then Hadji Murad got quite out of the ditch, and limping heavily went dagger in hand straight at the foe.

Some shots cracked and he reeled and fell. Several militiamen with triumphant shrieks rushed toward the fallen body. But the body that seemed to be dead suddenly moved. First the uncovered, bleeding, shaven head rose; then the body with hands holding to the trunk of a tree. He seemed so terrible that those who were running toward him stopped short. But suddenly a shudder passed through him, he staggered away from the tree and fell on his face, stretched out at full length like a thistle that had been mown down, and he moved no more.

He did not move, but still he felt.

When Hadji Aga, who was the first to reach him, struck him on the head with a large dagger, it seemed to Hadji Murad that someone was striking him with a hammer and he could not understand who was doing it or why. That was his last consciousness of any connection with his body. He felt nothing more and his enemies kicked and hacked at what had no longer anything in common with him.

Afterward (though earlier in the story, because Tolstoy reserves Hadji Murad's death for the end) "shall I show you a novelty? You won't be frightened, Marya Dmitrievna?"

"Why should I be frightened?" she replied.

"Here it is!" said Kamenev, taking out a man's head and holding it up in the light of the moon. "Do you recognize it?"

It was a shaven head with salient brows, black short-cut beard and moustaches, one eye open and the other half-closed. The shaven skull was cleft, but not right through, and there was congealed blood in the nose. The neck was wrapped in a bloodstained towel. Notwithstanding the many wounds on the head, the blue lips still bore a kindly childlike expression.

Marya Dmitrievna looked at it, and without a word turned away and went quickly into the house.

Major Petrov, on the other hand, "looked long at it with drunken eyes":

"All the same, he was a fine fellow!" said he. "Let me kiss him!"
"Yes, it's true. It was a valiant head," said one of the officers.

Tolstoy gives Marya Dmitrievna the last angry outburst: "You're all cut-throats!" But they are all in it together, and the old novelist sees and feels it all.

Portnoy's Bachelor Uncle

In July 1916 Kafka was on vacation—really a trial marriage—with his fiancée in Marienbad, and it seems to have been the best time of his life. It had begun as badly as usual: "What kind of person am I! What kind of person am I! I am tormenting her and myself to death," he wrote to Max Brod.[1] (He was the kind of person who three years earlier, thinking about marrying Felice, noted in his diary, "Coitus as punishment for the happiness of being together"; who also, telling Brod he had to break with Felice though he loved her, confessed in anguish that "when I want to disgust myself I have only to imagine placing my arm around a woman's waist.") But this time was different, Felice didn't leave or give up, "the rat [he means himself] had been driven to its very last hole" (if you'll please pardon the expression, and how's that for a howler from a writer as watchful and scrupulous as Kafka who moreover, according to Brod, would never countenance the "dirty" or "vulgar"? but he had taken his eye off the words because, as the words confirm, nothing mattered for the moment except Felice whom he considered his last chance—he was thirty-three—for marriage and a family and ordinary life), no doubt he bared his little teeth but this time Felice couldn't be frightened or repelled. So he recklessly reported that "we arrived at a human relationship of a kind I had so far never known and which came very near . . . to the relationship we had achieved at the best periods of our correspondence," his side of which incidentally, during the four years since they had met, had consisted of deliberate, powerful, and convincing efforts to prove his incapacity for any relationship at all:

> Haven't I for months now been squirming before you like something poisonous? Am I not here one moment, there the next? Aren't you beginning to feel sick at the sight of me? Can't you see by now that if disaster—yours, your disaster, Felice—is to be averted, I have to remain locked up within myself? I am not a human being; I am capable of tormenting you coldbloodedly, you whom I love most, whom I love alone out of the entire human race (as far as I'm concerned, I have no relatives and no friends, am unable to have them, and don't want them), and cold-bloodedly allowing you to forgive the torments I inflict. Can I tolerate this situation when I am in a position to see it so clearly, have suspected it, find my suspicions confirmed, and continue to suspect it? If need be, I can live as I am, my rage turned inward, tormenting only by letter, but as soon as we lived together I would become a dangerous lunatic fit to be burned alive. . . .

---

[1] Franz Kafka, *Letters to Friends, Family, and Editors* (Schocken, 1977).

Now however in Marienbad he sounds like anybody else, like a hero of chivalry or an ordinary man: "Basically I have never had that kind of intimacy with a woman . . . but now I saw the look of trustfulness in a woman's eyes, and I could not fail to respond." Such sentiments occur nowhere else in the four volumes of his letters available in English. True, even here he has some characteristic recollections: "When she came toward me in the big room to receive the engagement kiss, a shudder ran through me," and "I have never feared anything so much as being alone with F. before the wedding"; but, in his most uncharacteristic summing up ever, "Now all that has changed and is good," and he concludes with a unique image of himself settled at last in the hitherto unimaginable toils of domesticity:

> an apartment of two or three rooms in some Berlin suburb; each to assume economic responsibilities for himself. F. will go on working as she has done all along, while I—well, for myself I cannot yet say. Should one try to visualize the situation, there is the picture of two rooms somewhere in Karlshorst, say, in one of which F. wakes up early, trots off, and falls exhausted into bed at night, while in the other room there is a sofa on which I lie and feed on milk and honey. So there the husband lolls about, the wretched and immoral lout (as the cliché has it). Nevertheless, in this there is calm, certainty, and therefore the possibility of living. . . .

When Felice went back to her job in Berlin, Kafka stayed on in Marienbad another week; and, as if circumstances were now going to arrange themselves for his pleasure and benefit, the Hasidic Rabbi of Belz happened to be visiting there: "He looks like the Sultan in a Doré illustration of the Münchausen stories which I often looked at in my childhood. But not like someone masquerading as the Sultan, really the Sultan. . . . One eye is blind and blank. His mouth is twisted awry, which gives him a look at once ironic and friendly. He wears a silk caftan which is open in front; a broad belt above his waist; a tall fur hat, which is the most striking thing about him . . .") but, though his followers assure the onlookers that when it's raining it always stops as soon as the Rabbi arrives to take his evening stroll, "this time the rain did not stop," in fact it poured and poured. Kafka's account to Brod is full of curiosity, skepticism, amusement, affection, delight, and envy:

> There are four . . . "intimates"—employees, secretaries. The highest of the four, according to Langer [a friend of Kafka's and one of the Rabbi's followers], is an exceptional rogue; his huge belly, his smugness, his shifty eyes seem to bear that out. However, one must not hold this against him, for . . . people cannot endure the continual presence of the rabbi without suffering damage. It is the contradiction between the deeper meaning and the unrelenting commonplaceness that an ordinary head cannot sustain.

This of course isn't what Kafka himself thinks but rather a synopsis of the stubborn piety of those rained-on followers; the "contradiction" is theirs, not his, and in what comes next he contradicts it instantly by going back to their clear and irrepressible source:

> [The Rabbi] inspects everything, but especially buildings; the most obscure trivialities interest him. He asks questions, points out all sorts of things. His whole demeanor is marked by admiration and curiosity. All in all, what comes from him are the inconsequential comments and questions of itinerant royalty, perhaps somewhat more childish and joyous. At any rate they reduce all thinking on the part of his escort to the same level. Langer tries to find or thinks he finds a deeper meaning in all this; I think that the deeper meaning is that there is none and in my opinion this is quite enough. It is absolutely a case of divine right, without the absurdity that an inadequate basis would give to it.

There is, then, no contradiction between the deeper meaning and the unrelenting commonplaceness not because an ordinary head can't resolve it but because to begin with there isn't a deeper meaning, which is what the pious think that for their own redemption they have to scratch and salvage out of all the commonplaceness, which on the other hand is what the master pays attention to because he suspects it's all there is, as when the Rabbi examines the New Bathhouse:

> Behind the building, which is where we go first, is a sort of ditch in which run the pipes for the steambath. The rabbi bends over the railing and cannot take his eyes off the pipes, concerning which various opinions and counteropinions are exchanged.
> The building is of a neutral and indefinable eclectic style. The ground floor consists of a sort of blind arcade with a window set in every arch, and each vertex ornamented by an animal head. All the arches and all the animal heads are uniform. Nevertheless the rabbi comes to a halt before each of the six arches of the building's side, studies them, compares them, and passes judgment on them, from close up and from a distance.
> We turn the corner and are now standing before the façade. The building makes a great impression on him. Golden letters over the door read NEW BATHHOUSE. He has the inscription read to him, asks why the building is called this, whether it is the only bathhouse, how old it is, and so forth. He repeatedly says with that characteristic East European Jewish wonderment: "A handsome building."
> All along he has been taking note of the rain gutters . . .

—and not necessarily because the imperturbable rain is still pouring down on this perfect tourist.

Marienbad faded; Kafka kept losing touch with the commonplace, which meaning kept trying to redeem; his work became more and more saturated with meaning till it crystallized into the late collections of aphorisms: e.g. "There is a goal but no way; what we call a way is hesitation." Advice for Hamlet, rapists, and murderers: what would the itinerant Rabbi have made of it? except, though he wouldn't have bothered, to turn it inside out like a glove that fits any occasion—There is a way but no goal; what we call a goal is meaning. Kafka envied the Rabbi's singleness and sometimes grew confident enough to claim it for himself. When Martin Buber was about to publish "Jackals and Arabs" and "A Report to an Academy" in *Der Jude*, Kafka asked him "not to call the pieces parables; they are not really parables. If they are to have any overall title at all, the best might be 'Two Animal Stories.'" Yet the first is a grim and shiny engine of meaning, nothing but pairs of terms (carrion and fresh meat, slaves and overseers, hope and custom) for the pious, a parable par excellence; the second does have some of Kafka's comic invention and some narrative impulse, but meaning leaks out at every seam.

Because the Rabbi of Belz is a Jew who can live in a world without meaning, he exposes Kafka's duplicity and even breaks it down for a moment in the momentary euphoria of Marienbad. But Kafka would say that this explanation contains a tautology, that to be a Jew (even if not a venerated rabbi) is it goes without saying to be able to live like a Sultan in a world without meaning; that Gentiles who reproach Jews for being "anxious," though they are right about Kafka, are wrong about Jews ("The strangest thing," in view of all the reasons Jews have for feeling nervous in Gentile communities, "is that in general the reproach does not fit"); that therefore Kafka isn't a Jew ("What have I in common with the Jews when I have scarcely anything in common with myself?"), he's a changeling in his father's house.

In which, notwithstanding, he has his own room and from time to time—for instance, here at the age of thirty—sounds like an early Philip Roth character coping with Mama:

> Later she asked me if I were going to write to Uncle Alfred, he deserved it. I asked why he deserved it. He has telegraphed, he has written, he has your welfare so much at heart. "These are simply formalities," I said, "he is a complete stranger to me, he misunderstands me entirely, he does not know what I want and need, I have nothing in common with him."
>
> "So no one understands you," my mother said, "I suppose I am a stranger to you too, and your father as well. So we all want only what is bad for you."
>
> "Certainly you are all strangers to me, we are related only by blood, but that never shows itself. Of course you don't want what is bad for me."

—and with Papa ("from your armchair you ruled the world," Kafka wrote bitterly in his *Letter to His Father*[2]):

> I spent most of the day in bed, and the only two, though terrible, adventures were caused by my father who gradually, and despite all resistance,

---

[2] According to the Publisher's Note in the bilingual edition (Schocken, 1953), Kafka "wrote this letter in November, 1919. Max Brod relates that Kafka actually gave the letter to his mother to hand to his father. . . . Probably realising the futility of her son's gesture, the mother did not deliver the letter, but returned it to the author." Thank God.

dragged me firmly out of my morning sleep back into this bleak world with his insane, monotonous, incessant shouting, singing, and hand-clapping, which he repeated over and over again to amuse a great-nephew, while in the afternoon he carried on in the same way to entertain his grandson. . . .

(Father, a big, strong, handsome, sarcastic man who ran a small business with an iron hand, was a butcher's son and indignantly disappeared behind his newspaper at the dinner table while Franz, a long solemn stringbean weighing 120 pounds, picked at his vegetarian plate. In his diary he noted "the whimpering of my poor mother because I don't eat"; or while he was writing to Felice she would interrupt him by coming "into my room crying . . . she caresses me, wants to know what's the matter with me, why I don't talk at meals." But there are problems even in Gentile families. Kleist was a writer whom Kafka not only greatly valued but, since he too had been unappreciated by his unintellectual family, felt a personal sympathy for: "On the 21st," begins the diary entry for November 23, 1911, "the hundredth anniversary of Kleist's death, the Kleist family had a wreath placed on his grave with the epitaph: 'To the best of their house.'" Some day Mama and Papa would be sorry.)

"In the next room," Kafka noted on March 24, 1912, "my mother is entertaining the L. couple. They are talking about vermin and corns. (Mr. L has six corns on each toe.) It is easy to see there is no real progress made in conversations of this sort." With close friends Jewish mothers would sometimes unburden themselves about domestic commonplaces: corns, bunions, varicose veins, bedbugs, cockroaches, mice. Later in the same year Kafka took the hint and began writing *The Metamorphosis* ("the bedbug story," his publisher called it), an animal story which isn't a parable because the interest is in what's happening, not in why it happens or what it all means. Misfortunes happen in the best of families: fathers have to stop working, daughters don't get married, sons wake up one morning transformed into gigantic vermin; keeping things clean, orderly, and cheerful is hard enough anyhow, and it doesn't help to criticize from the next room just because you crave privacy:

> His mother once subjected his room to a thorough cleaning, which was achieved only by means of several buckets of water—all this dampness of course upset Gregor too and he lay widespread, sulky and motionless on the sofa—but she was well punished for it. Hardly had his sister noticed the changed aspect of his room that evening when she rushed in high dudgeon into the living room and, despite the imploringly raised hands of her mother, burst into a storm of weeping, while her parents—her father had of course been startled out of his chair—looked on at first in helpless amazement; then they too began to go into action; the father reproached the mother on his right for not having left the cleaning of Gregor's room to his sister; shrieked at the sister on his left that never again was she to be allowed to clean Gregor's room; while the mother tried to pull the father into his bedroom, since he was beside himself with agitation; the sister, shaken with sobs, then beat upon the table with her small fists; and Gregor hissed loudly

with rage because not one of them thought of shutting the door to spare him such a spectacle and so much noise.

"Kafka is important to us," said Auden, "because his predicament is the predicament of modern man." This is the sort of pronouncement made about Kafka by numerous top names, and it would be interesting to know whether any of them actually believed that modern man's predicament is to love women but loathe sex; to love the idea of marriage and family but loathe his father, despise his mother, and feel like filth in their presence or proximity; to be a kind and decent person but have lurid and persistent fantasies about guilt, torture, and execution; to insist on explaining things to death as if his very life depended on it. (Psychoanalytic critics, who are wary of what people merely *say*, will remind us that Kafka was after all typical, *loved* his mother too, *loved* his father too, had *ambivalent* feelings that stemmed from . . . ; but they wouldn't have made much of an impression on Kafka, who believed that psychoanalysis had gone off the track when it began to imagine it was a branch of medicine rather than a mode of romance: "I consider the therapeutic part of psychoanalysis to be a hopeless error.") Sometimes Kafka could turn his private preoccupations into a comedy of barely disrupted domesticity, what happens when the commonplace has one screw loose or missing: the loathsome and irritable insect clinging to its memory of humanness; the underground creature of *The Burrow* that dedicates its life to manufacturing the world's safest hole in the ground—

> If only I had someone I could trust to keep watch at my post of observation; then of course I could descend in perfect peace of mind. I would make an agreement with this trusty confederate of mine that he would keep a careful note of the state of things during my descent and for quite a long time afterwards, and if he saw any sign of danger knock on the moss covering, and if he saw nothing do nothing. With that a clean sweep could be made of all my fears, no residue would be left, or at most my confidant. For would he not demand some counter-service from me; would he not at least want to see the burrow? That in itself, to let anyone freely into my burrow, would be exquisitely painful to me. I built it for myself, not for visitors, and I think I would refuse to admit him, for either I must let him go in first by himself, which is simply unimaginable, or we must both descend at the same time, in which case the advantage I am supposed to derive from him, that of being kept watch over, would be lost. And what trust can I really put in him? Can I trust one I have had under my eyes just as fully when I can't see him, and the moss covering separates us? It is comparatively easy to trust anyone if you are supervising him or at least can supervise him; perhaps it is even possible to trust someone at a distance; but completely to trust someone outside the burrow when you are inside the burrow, that is, in a different world, that, it seems to me, is impossible.

A consciousness that keeps eating itself up and always has something left over to chew on: like Dostoevsky's underground man, who boasts, "I have an explanation for everything, don't you worry"; who confides, "I should like to tell you . . . why I've never been able to become even an insect" (till Kafka, taking a hint from his mother, showed how); who describes himself as "an intensely conscious mouse" that whenever challenged scurries back to "its stinking, disgusting, subterranean hole"; who confesses that "though innocent I was guilty and, as it were, guilty according to the laws of nature." Dostoevsky declared that all of Russian fiction had come out of the sleeve of Gogol's *Overcoat* (though in fact only Dostoevsky's did); sometimes it seems unavoidable to infer that Kafka and his preoccupations crawled full-grown out of the "dark cellar" of *Notes from Underground*, where for example Dostoevsky's protagonist preëmpts the reader's right to squash him by exercising it conclusively himself:

> "But aren't you ashamed? Don't you feel humiliated?" you will perhaps say, shaking your head contemptuously. "You long for life, yet you try to solve the problems of life by a logical tangle! And how tiresome, how insolent your tricks are, and, at the same time, how awfully frightened you are! You talk a lot of nonsense and you seem to be very pleased with it; you say a lot of impudent things, and you are yourself always afraid and apologizing for them. You assure us that you are afraid of nothing, and at the same time you try to earn our good opinion. You assure us that you are gnashing your teeth, but at the same time you crack jokes to make us laugh. You know your jokes are not amusing, but you seem to be highly pleased with their literary merit. You may perhaps have really suffered, but you don't seem to have the slightest respect for your suffering. There may be some truth in you, but there is no humility. You carry your truth to the market place out of the pettiest vanity to make a public show of it and to discredit it. No doubt you mean to say something, but you conceal your last word out of fear, because you haven't the courage to say it, but only craven insolence. You boast about your sensibility, but you merely don't know your own mind. For though your mind is active enough, your heart is darkened with corruption, and without a pure heart there can be no full or genuine sensibility. And how tiresome you are! How you impose yourself on people! The airs you give yourself! Lies, lies, lies!"

Or, as Kafka describes himself in his *Letter to His Father*: "my cold indifference, scarcely disguised, indestructible, childishly helpless, approaching the ridiculous, and brutishly complacent, the indifference of a self-sufficient but coldly imaginative child, I have never found anywhere else; to be sure, it was the sole defense against destruction of the nerves by fear and by a sense of guilt. All that occupied my mind was worry about myself. . . ."

What Auden must have intended by "the predicament of modern man" is something like the following: that consciousness has no choice but to round on and tear at itself when it comes up against problems too large for solving or even facing— the death of God; the rise of totalitarianism (or of technology). So Kafka (having picked up quite a few pointers from Dostoevsky) suffers representatively for us all, and represents our suffering for all time in such epics of the modern predicament as *The Trial* (the r. of t.) and *The Castle* (the d. of G.); e.g. in *The Trial*:

> Here K. was interrupted by a shriek from the end of the hall; he peered from beneath his hand to see what was happening, for the reek of the room and the dim light together made a whitish dazzle of fog. It was the washerwoman, whom K. had recognized as a potential cause of disturbance from the moment of her entrance. Whether she was at fault now or not, one could not tell. All K. could see was that a man had drawn her into a corner by the door and was clasping her in his arms. Yet it was not she who had uttered the shriek but the man; his mouth was wide open and he was gazing up at the ceiling. A little circle had formed round them, the gallery spectators near by seemed to be delighted that the seriousness which K. had introduced into the proceedings should be dispelled in this manner. . . .

—or in *The Castle:*

> ". . . Is it really Castle service Barnabas is doing, we ask ourselves then; granted, he goes into the offices, but are the offices part of the real Castle? And even if there are offices actually in the Castle, are they the offices that Barnabas is allowed to enter? He's admitted into certain rooms, but they're only a part of the whole, for there are barriers behind which there are more rooms. Not that he's actually forbidden to pass the barriers . . . [etc. ad infinitum.]"

Now the point of such unendingly reverberant circumstantiality is that it has no point at all: quite unlike the realistic detail of such comedies as *The Metamorphosis* and *The Burrow*, it's a parody whether intended or not of the pretensions of realism: nobody ever does anything and nothing ever happens and the setting is nowhere and one explanation is as good or bad as another but, but, but meaning accumulates—e.g. authority is mysterious, scary, inaccessible, maybe nonexistent; appearances can't be trusted; guilt is inherent in consciousness; individuals are at the mercy of processes, bureaucrats, delays; personal relationships are impossible, personal encounters transitory and mostly unpleasant. Page after page of sawdust, and a hope—rapidly dwindling and at last unwarranted—of coming at last to something better than a rubber bone.

What's called for from the writer here isn't invention but illustration or filler as in S.F. or detective fiction, he starts with a scheme and works it out more or less efficiently or runs it into the ground or, as in *The Trial* and *The Castle*, can never quite decide how to carry it through to an ending—though for *The Trial* Kafka wrote an abrupt and helplessly melodramatic final chapter in which while somebody watches from a window ("Who was it? . . . Was it one person only? Or was it mankind?") K. gets knifed to death: "'Like a dog!' he said; it was as if the shame of it must outlive him." When in 1918 Brod was trying to sustain both his marriage of convenience and an intense affair, he wrote to Kafka for advice and consolation, and Kafka concluded his discreet, attentive, loving reply with a comment on "the vision you have, and have with such certainty—'calm, complete peace in eros'": it "is something so tremendous that you can't really swallow it; which fact should prove how untenable it is. I'd have some belief in it only if you called it by a less fancy name. But . . . because you do give it that name, it's likely to indicate a different conflict." *The Trial* and *The Castle* are such tremendous visions that Kafka can't really swallow them; he has something different and simpler in mind, as in his diaries and letters, as in his realistic fiction about baffled animals; and it may be that he was encouraged to attempt such outsize projects by his affinity with and derivation from Dostoevsky, a much more complex, more various, and more problematical writer.

Amerika, which was Kafka's first try at a novel, is very different from the later two—he had been reading Dickens, and he set out to write a Dickens-like novel of a boy's adventures that would avoid Dickens's weaknesses: "There is a heartlessness behind his sentimentally overflowing style. These rude characterizations which are artificially stamped on everyone and without which Dickens would not be able to get on with his story even for a moment." Kafka himself, though, hasn't the range and momentum without which a novel becomes episodic or disintegrates entirely (which for instance Dickens has, and which even against the inertia of those "rude characterizations" keeps his novels going). *Amerika* jolts and lurches and often seems merely odd, maybe not only because it wasn't completed but because Kafka's own rude characterizations aren't moved or motivated any more individually or independently here than they are in his later novels. Nevertheless it's the most uncharacteristic and the most inventive of Kafka's works as from the middle of Europe he recreates the Land of Promise: roaring traffic day and night (before the First World War!); an immense and mysterious "country house" outside New York anticipating Gatsby's; the adventures of a conscientious and hapless elevator operator; a political rally at which the candidate addresses the crowd while being carried about on the shoulders of a giant; the hundreds of women dressed as angels standing on pedestals and blowing long golden trumpets to recruit performers for "the Nature Theater of Oklahoma"; and fat, slothful, pampered Brunelda—

> For that must be your first consideration, Rossman. Brunelda mustn't be disturbed. Her hearing's very keen; it's probably because she's a singer that her ears are so sensitive. For instance, say that you're rolling out a keg of brandy which usually stands behind the trunks, it makes a noise because it's heavy and all sorts of things are lying about on the floor, so that you can't roll it straight out. Brunelda, let us say, is lying quietly on the couch catching flies, which are a great torment to her. You think she's paying no attention to you, and you go on rolling the keg. She's still lying there quite peacefully. But all at once, just when you're least expecting it and when you're making least noise, she suddenly sits up, bangs with both hands on the couch so that you can't see her for dust—since we came here I have never beaten the dust out of the couch; I really couldn't, she's always lying

on it—and begins to yell ferociously, like a man, and goes on yelling for hours. The neighbors have forbidden her to sing, but no one can forbid her to yell; she has to yell; though that doesn't happen often now, for Delamarche and I have grown careful. . . .

It's Dickensian all right, and it's original too and quite like Papa and the Rabbi of Belz. A very promising first novel by a writer who takes chances and isn't afraid to be funny.

Agèd Eagles and Dirty Old Men

Aside from his numerous wives and mistresses and at least one of his children,[1] very few people have a kind word for Bertrand Russell. Most of his illustrious contemporaries didn't and nowadays the reviewers don't. Certainly he's not only a genius but here or there and now and then everything they say he is, "complacent," "dogmatic," "wilful," "arbitrary," a flagrantly dissociated sensibility, "dry and passionate," doctrinaire and insinuating, stony pedant and unctuous sensualist (Gradgrind-cum-Pecksniff), an intellectual trifler and (in Santayana's *mot*) "a many-sided fanatic," a politician and what's more (according to Wyndham Lewis) "a born entertainer"—in short, a sitting duck for agèd eagles:

> . . . *Priapus in the shrubbery*
> *Gaping at the lady in the swing.* . . .
> *He laughed like an irresponsible foetus.*
> *His laughter was submarine and profound*
> *Like the old man of the sea's*
> *Hidden under coral islands*
> *Where worried bodies of drowned men drift down in the green silence.* . . .

In 1914, already the author of "Prufrock," Eliot had attended Russell's seminar at Harvard. Within the year, his doctoral studies in Germany cut short by the war, he arrived in London, encountered Russell again, courted and married an English girl, and tossed off the hissing squib against Mr. Apollinax—"I heard the beat of centaur's hoofs over the hard turf/As his dry and passionate talk devoured the afternoon"—that for all its skepticism didn't deter him from turning his wife and himself over to its target for guidance, solace, and salvation. Russell couldn't have been more solicitous (he probably ought to have been much less), he lent them his flat and gave them money, he was confidant to both of them against each other, on one occasion at Eliot's urging he took Mrs. Eliot away on vacation to a seaside resort (though their relationship, uniquely for Russell, appears to have been platonic), and as late as 1925 the author of *The Waste Land* and editor of *The Criterion* could write an eager and pathetic letter recalling and renewing his dependence on the irresponsible foetus:

---

[1] Ronald W. Clark, *The Life of Bertrand Russell* (Knopf, 1976). Dora Russell, *The Tamarisk Tree* (Putnam, 1975). Katharine Tait, *My Father Bertrand Russell* (Harcourt Brace Jovanovich, 1975).

> If you are still in London I should very much like to see you.
>
> My times and places are very restricted, but it is unnecessary to mention them unless I hear from you.
>
> I want words from you which only you can give. But if you have now ceased to care at all about either of us, just write on a slip "I do not care to see you" or "I do not care to see either of you"—and I will understand.
>
> In case of that, I will tell you now that everything has turned out as you predicted 10 years ago. You are a great psychologist.

As Eliot discovered, it was easy to be publicly skeptical about Russell but hard to keep from being privately charmed out of one's very pinfeathers by his interest and concern, his talent for persuasion, his wit and sense of fun, his companionableness,[2] his generosity with his time and money, the intensity of his need to be helpful.

Summarizing the friendship with Eliot, Clark waxes ironic at Russell's facility for falling in and out of "love" with bright young men:

> Their friendship gathered pace and was soon careering along the path that friendship with Russell often followed. A few years previously it was Wittgenstein who had been the disciple and Russell who described how he loved him. He continued to do so until, a decade later, the disciple struck out on his own and they agreed to differ. Relationship with Lawrence had followed a similar course. "I love him more and more and I wouldn't dream of discouraging his socialist revolution," he had declared before falling out with him on the means of social reconstruction. Now came Eliot and [Lady] Ottoline [Morrell] once again was reading. "I loved him like a son."

Maybe "love" isn't the right word. Nevertheless, it was with every evidence of attachment and good will that Russell did what he did for Eliot, who could still be full of trust after ten years, still respectful after thirty-five years to "one of the few living authors who can write English prose," and after fifty years still susceptible to "grateful and affectionate memories" of the old centaur with whom, "as you may know, I disagree . . . on most subjects, but I thought that you put your beliefs over in a most dignified and even persuasive way" (Eliot was seventy-six and Russell ninety-two!). As for Wittgenstein, nobody could have been more personally kind and more professionally useful over many years than Russell toward this archetype of the solitary, original, helplessly unworldly, bristling, unbudgeable mind: Clark's sneer at Russell's "love" for Wittgenstein is particularly unwarranted because the feeling despite changes of temperature sustained itself into old age, it never failed to respond at once and generously through a range of crises and difficulties, and it was quite unimpaired by Russell's modest and cheerful conviction—as early as the time when

---

[2] A friend of his, the soldier and explorer Francis Younghusband, who made the Atlantic crossing with him, remarked that "he did not carry his argumentative habit on to an Atlantic steamer. On board ship he was a . . . delightful companion. We had a small table to ourselves at meals; and we paced the decks together all day long; and there was no end to the subjects which interested him."

Wittgenstein was his pupil—that the pupil was far beyond the master and would go forward to do the work in the philosophy of logic which was beyond the master's reach. The only one of Clark's trio against whom Russell recoiled with violence, in fact with an extremely uncharacteristic lifelong hatred, was Lawrence; but Lawrence had just exploded into his most trying phase of irritable vaticination, and even a less inveterate rationalist than Russell might have been repelled by Lawrence's Delphic snottiness at the time. Anyhow, during three years (1911-1914) to have bound to oneself with hoops of love or friendship or mere mutual admiration three such various young men as Wittgenstein, Lawrence, and Eliot isn't bad for a born entertainer.

Besides, the term suits Russell less neatly than it suits one of his contemporaries: Shaw, with whom he was often associated in pacifist and libertarian agitation during the first decades of the century, and who like Russell was liable to mistake publicity and hurly-burly for influence. Wyndham Lewis may have carelessly lumped them together as they were lumped together by a generation of British feminists and political reformers, for whom they made up two-thirds of the secular Trinity, so the second Mrs. Russell reminds us in her autobiography—

> Shaw, Wells and Russell were the three great emancipators for my generation from Victorian orthodoxies, liberating thought from superstition and prejudice, the individual from the tyranny of the family system, woman from her traditional servitude, the worker from his chains. . . .

Also, Shaw and Russell both lived long enough to stop being funny and wither into superannuated scarecrows hurling low-voltage thunderbolts at the enormities of a world they had never made. This last period of Russell's life—the decade of the 'sixties—is what Solzhenitsyn must have been concentrating on when, in a recent BBC-TV interview (as reported in *The New Yorker* of March 15, 1976; and there are a couple of relevant footnotes in *Gulag Two*), he denounced Russell for the pusillanimity of the "better-red-than-dead" slogan of the anti-nuclear demonstrations. But Russell was almost the only Western liberal intellectual who from the outbreak of the Russian Revolution weighed its facts against its promises. His account of the Soviet reality, which he observed during a visit in 1920, isn't incompatible with *The Gulag Archipelago* as he describes "the sense of utter horror which overwhelmed me while I was there. Cruelty, poverty, suspicion, persecution formed the very air we breathed. . . . I felt that everything that I valued in human life was being destroyed in the interests of a glib and narrow philosophy, and that in the process untold misery was being inflicted upon many millions of people."[3] (Compare Shaw's unrestrained public flirtation with Stalin and his praise of the purges; anything for a laugh.)

---

[3] Clark publishes for the first time Russell's account in his Russian Journal of his interview with Lenin. Solzhenitsyn would be interested. "Nothing in his manner or bearing suggests the man who has power. He looks at his visitor very close, & screws up one eye. He laughs a great deal; at first his laugh seems merely friendly & jolly, but gradually, one finds it grim. He is dictatorial, calm, incapable of fear, devoid of self-seeking, an embodied theory. The materialist conception of history is his life-blood. He resembles

Russell never changed his mind about the Soviet tyranny, which as late as the last years of World War II he called "even worse than Hitler's"; indeed, as late as 1950, the slogan he favored was "better dead than red," when he very nearly advocated a preventive nuclear war against Russia: "The next war, if it comes, will be the greatest disaster that will have befallen the human race up to that moment. I can think of only one greater disaster: the extension of the Kremlin's power over the whole world." It took another decade or more—at ninety he remained an implacable public man who still felt the need to be useful to the world—before he let himself be persuaded by the Cuban missile confrontation and Vietnam, as well as by the opinionated and presumptuous young man who had moved in as his last disciple (an American in the mold of Rubin, Hoffman, and company), that the Americans were even worse than the Russians; but his record of the previous forty years on the Soviet issue oughtn't to be brushed aside.

Moreover, he was personally committed to social issues as the all-licensed jester Shaw never was. Russell didn't content himself with producing books and pamphlets and hortatory newspaper articles, or even with conducting energetic campaigns for Parliament: e.g. he had as was to be expected strong views on education, but also, like Tolstoy before him, when the opportunity came he insisted on putting his time and money where his mouth was. In their books his wife and his daughter have much to say about the Beacon Hill School, in which they were respectively co-director and student. It was founded in 1927, and run on principles that today sound as reasonable and practicable as in 1927 they must have sounded dangerous and outlandish. He gave it a good try. For five years whatever money of his he hadn't managed to hand out already in public and private benefactions, as well as whatever he earned from lecturing and royalties, went to the school; except for his financially essential lecture tours he devoted his time to directing and teaching at the school, and on the evidence he was patient, conscientious, enthusiastic, affectionate, and effective in both capacities; his participation ended only when his second marriage ended.

All his life he loved to be with children, not only in classroom situations. His youngest son, Conrad, recalled hill-climbing with him in Wales: "I remember him reaching the top of Cnicht when he was 77 and I was 11 and our climbing powers were approximately equal, and I remember him at 95, swinging over the steps to the balcony for the sheer delight of the view of Snowdon in the afternoon sun." According to his daughter,

> He was a perfect grandfather. He gave the children wonderful presents and grandfatherly bits of money, and talked to them intelligently about things that interested them, so that they soon ceased to be shy. And he told them all his best stories, the ones I had loved most as a child. I have a vivid memory of him sitting by the fire, ancient and wrinkled and strange, perhaps even a little frightening, telling them about Mysie with the golden leg.

---

a professor in his desire to have the theory understood & in his fury with those who misunderstand or disagree; also in his love of expounding. . . ."

> "There was once an heiress," he began, "a very rich young woman, who lost a leg in an accident. She was far too grand for a mere wooden leg, so they got her one made of gold. In due course, she married a handsome villain who cared only for her money. After he had spent all she had, he murdered her at night and ran off with the golden leg. Soon after, she came haunting him by night, as ghastly as ghosts usually are."
>
> Here he would lean forward in his chair, open his eyes wide and declaim, in a sepulchral Scots voice:
>
> "Mysie, Mysie, whaur's yer beautiful blue e'en?"
> "Mould'ring in the grave."
> "Mysie, Mysie, whaur's yer beautiful rosy cheeks?"
> "Mould'ring in the grave."
> "Mysie, Mysie, whaur's yer beautiful gowden hair?"
> "Mould'ring in the grave."
> "Mysie, Mysie, whaur's yer beautiful gowden leg?"
> "You have it, you thief!"—shouting suddenly, to make small listeners jump out of their skins.

Some of Mrs. Tait's book reads like a half-hearted attempt at a debunking: she says the school was bad for her because, after an idyllic childhood with two loving parents, once the school opened they decided to treat her without the slightest appearance of favoritism, and so she lost both mother and father in the mentors they necessarily became; furthermore, irrespective of the problems brought by the school, Russell's standard was usually too high for his children, and they suffered in unspeakable silence for not measuring up to it. Now doubtless Russell was naïve to think that everything could be talked out, and that a sensible education would prevent or cure the defects and miseries of children; but mainly what Mrs. Tait's touching book proves is that growing up is hard for anybody and growing up with a dazzling exemplar on the premises may be hardest of all. Then she concludes with a tribute that rings true:

> It was a long time before I thought of writing about him. I will tell the world what a great father he was, I said to myself, how wise and witty and kind, how much fun we always had. They mustn't think he was always a cold and rational philosopher. So I thought, and so I began to write, but it has not come out that way. The "but"s and complaints seized my pen and forced it to record them. "He loved truth, you know," they urged. "You cannot honor him with a lying memoir. You must set down all that was wrong, all that was difficult and disappointing, and then you can say: 'He was the most fascinating man I have ever known, the only man I ever loved, the greatest man I shall ever meet, the wittiest, the gayest, the most charming. It was a privilege to know him, and I thank God he was my father.'"

(This daughter of the world's champion atheist had turned to religion early and married a man who soon after quit his job to study for the ministry and be ordained, whereupon they went off to Africa together as missionaries—characters in an Eliot play! "The care that God provided included considerable financial assistance from my father, which prompted me to write to him that I thought God must be amused by the irony of the situation. He wrote back to say that he didn't know about God, but certainly the officials of the Bank of England, whose permission he needed to send us money, had been very much amused.")

Women adored him, no matter how badly things worked out. His second wife, more doctrinaire than the Pope, made the error of taking Russell's views on free love so literally that, having informed him of her project, she had a child by another man; what followed was not only divorce but bitter and protracted wrangling over custody of the two children she had had by Russell; yet her book questions nothing about him except his decision to leave her: "I loved Bertie with adoration and almost worship. He was lover, father-figure, teacher, a companion never at a loss for a witty rejoinder or a provoking bit of nonsense. . . . The joy of living side by side with Bertie was that he was never superior, he was always such fun. . . ."[4]

He married four times, had two mistresses with whom his relations were probably closer and more serious than with any of his wives, and innumerable casual affairs—for example with a young faculty wife (he was old enough to be her grandfather) when he returned to Cambridge in 1946: "although she was still in her twenties and he in his seventies, she could later speak of 'the peculiarly intense & complete nature of our very passionate feelings'" which continued off and on so to speak for years. Nobody could have predicted such a future from his first marriage, which was conventionally happy for seven years, suicidally miserable (and celibate) for the next nine, till he absconded abruptly in 1910 (his first wife loved him all her long life, and died a half-century later still hoping he would come back to her): Russell was thirty-eight, he had just completed with Whitehead, after a decade's terrible labor, his major philosophical work, *Principia Mathematica*; the only woman with whom he had ever had sexual relations was his wife, and not with her for the past nine years. In 1909 he met Lady Ottoline Morrell and in 1911 the dam broke: she became his mistress and, till her death in 1938, his most trusted confidante. In 1916 he met "Colette" (Lady Constance Malleson), the love of his life (he was old enough to be her father),[5] an actress, daughter of an Earl, an intelligent, brave, beautiful woman

---

[4] In his Autobiography Russell remarks that he "tried to preserve that respect for my wife's liberty which I thought that my creed enjoined . . . [but] my capacity for forgiveness . . . was not equal to the demands I was making on it." The prose is no fun at all, uncandid (he doesn't mention that there was already another woman on the scene), and typical. One reason for the prevailing chilliness toward Russell may be that readers have been deriving their impressions of him from the Autobiography, which is dry, scrappy, often evasive and misleading especially about the women in his life, written in a sniffy and remote donnish style, and consistently low-spirited: Clark notes that the first draft was done when Russell was "in one of his deep periodic troughs, at low ebb both personally and professionally." For readers who know Russell only through his Autobigraphy, the biography will—or at least should—be a revelation.

[5] When in 1918 he was in prison for seditious pacifism, she would go to bed early the night before the weekly visit she was allowed "anointed with Madame Helena Rubinstein's face cream, so's to look presentable for you tomorrow; if not the Lord's Anointed, anyway the Hon. Bertrand's." She was twenty-two.

who loved him selflessly and passionately—it's true, really!—till his death fifty-three years later:

> In his autobiography, Russell gives the impression that this was an *affaire* which ended when he abandoned Colette after five years; when, as she herself put it, she "woke up one fine morning in 1921 to find life finished." At its best, this is an urbane example of his ability to make the best [?] of his own story. The truth is very different. In the late 1920s, he renewed the relationship in a number of idyllic meetings in Somerset and Cornwall. More than a decade on, and after an ecstatic holiday together in Sweden, Russell had again become convinced, as he told her, that they "should never have parted." Yet the story was still the same, and the two persistent lovers parted for the third time, Russell perhaps fearing that marriage would ruin it all. But nearly twenty years later, in his nineties, he was still to be filled with love and affection at the regular arrival of Colette's red roses every birthday. And on the eve of Christmas 1968, she could still write to him, "Nothing on this earth could have given me greater delight than getting your dear letter of the 16th this very day. My thoughts are constantly with you. I send you all the most devoted love always and for ever."

He was seventy-six when they had their "ecstatic holiday" reunion in Sweden: "Colette had decked out his room with lilies-of-the-valley, violas and golden cowslips. He was wearing on his watch chain the small gold coin she had given him after the Lulworth reunion of 1919. She was wearing the dress, trimmed with his mother's lace, which she had made for his return from China in 1921. Did his wife know, she asked, that she was not only in the same city, but in the same hotel and with a bedroom on the same floor? Russell, with a lifetime's experience of turning dangerous corners, was unperturbed. 'I will make little of it,' he replied."

The following year she stayed with him in his cottage in Wales (his wife was away), and when he left on a trip to the Continent for more honors she wrote him the next morning so that he would have a letter waiting in Aix:

> But isn't it just another fleck of the irony which has always dogged our steps that what would have saved a number of shipwrecks in 1920 is out of place—or seems so—in 1949.
> I'll creep into your big bed tonight, to have the ghost of that kind of closeness as well as "the coldness of interstellar spaces." I expect that both will live on always in me, independent of everything.

Soon after, they met for the last time: "He knew that she was returning to Sweden and asked when she would be coming back. 'Never,' she replied—'unless you ask me.' He appeared astonished, repeating the one word, 'Never.'" But he lived another twenty years and never asked her. The swine.

Issues and Answers; or, If You've Tried It Don't Knock It

Writing to a friend who has a new book out, Edmund Wilson remarks that "I find it rather hard—which happens rarely with me—to judge it as a book"; but he's being modest, the case isn't rare, it's unique: among these letters[1] and his two dozen volumes, it may well be the only evidence that he is ever stumped, no other critic except Mencken has ever been so ready to produce a brisk and categorical judgment for anything at all that comes along. Sometimes, especially when what comes along is muddle-headedness or malice, he can be as exhilarating as the best of Mencken and more focused:

> It is appalling that Nabokov's little story, so gentle and everyday, should take on the aspect for the *New Yorker* editors of an overdone psychiatric study. (How *can* you people say it is overwritten?) It could only appear so in contrast with the pointless and inane little anecdotes that are turned out by the *New Yorker's* processing mill and that the reader forgets two minutes after he has read them. . . .

Wilson's correspondent here (in 1947) is the fiction editor of *The New Yorker*, and which of us during the past fifty years hasn't written this letter a thousand times in his dreams? Or here (in 1940) is Wilson reasoning with *Partisan Review* after both he and his wife have had commissioned articles turned down:

> You people are getting as bad as *The New Republic*. Dwight Macdonald was after me for that Lenin piece for months, constantly writing me and calling me up. I fixed it up for you when I was in New York at a time when you knew my book was coming out and what the piece would be like. At the same time you asked Mary [McCarthy] to do a piece on *Pinocchio* and *The Grapes of Wrath*, which she went to some trouble to see in order to be able to do the article on time. The next time you saw her, you told her that the piece was all off for what seems to me the fantastic reason that you wouldn't be able to make space for it—as if Sidney Hook's interminable articles wouldn't always be the better for cutting. Now you send back my Lenin with the suggestion that I do you a little something on the younger

---
[1] Edmund Wilson, *Letters on Literature and Politics* (Farrar, Straus and Giroux, 1977).

novelists. You are developing all the symptoms of the occupational disease of editors—among them, thinking up idiotic ideas for articles that you want the writers to write instead of printing what they want to write. . . .

Or bulldog Wilson sinking his teeth into the flabby haunch of the Modern Language Association—Wilson had proposed a series of complete editions of American authors in a convenient and inexpensive format like that of the French Pléiade editions, and the proposal had been approved for a Federal subsidy; but the MLA had pulled strings to have the subsidy canceled in favor of a Federally subsidized monopoly for its own grotesquely over-edited, overpriced, oversized, overweight editions (Wilson observes that *The Marble Faun*, "the masterpiece of MLA bad bookmaking," has 748 pages and weighs nine pounds in an elephantine format, whereas the Pléiade complete Montaigne has 1,791 pages in beautifully readable type and weighs two pounds in a shape and size feasible for reading), all these MLA projects to proceed at a pace which promises that the last volume of each will be extruded from the computer in time for the first manned flight to Alpha Centauri:

> a team of thirty-five scholars . . . are working on the Mark Twain papers. . . . It seems that eighteen of these Mark Twain workers are reading *Tom Sawyer* word by word, backward, in order to ascertain, without being diverted from this drudgery by attention to the story or the style, how many times "Aunt Polly" is printed as "aunt Polly," and how many times "ssst!" is printed as "sssst!"

Wilson's essay "The Fruits of the MLA" (reprinted in *The Devils and Canon Barham*), together with his letters on the issue, is the scholarly introduction to the cretins who run the MLA and the profession. Stirred to their muddy depths, they responded by publishing a collective rebuttal that began with a diatribe against "amateurs" and continued backward word by word with the usual parade of low-comedy lecture-note pig-Latin: "After all, Eliot revolted against the Romantics, of whom Blake was one." After all, even more revolting than Blake and Eliot are the literary professors, of whom neither was one.[2]

---

[2] Wilson accurately describes *PMLA* as a "periodical . . . which contains for the most part unreadable articles on literary problems and discoveries of very minute or no interest." If he had turned into a faithful reader, he would soon have noticed its limpetlike adhesion to any already moribund intellectual fad, e.g. structuralism—as in the Table-of-Contents "abstract" of an article in the March 1978 issue:

> A letter to the hero in *Daniel Deronda* offers an interpretation of George Eliot's novel, an account of its rhetorical principles: The Deronda plot discloses not "the effects of causes" but the "present causes of past effects." This metaleptic plot structure contradicts the linking of origin, cause, and identity affirmed in the story of Deronda's Jewish birth. The story must shift between constative and performative conceptions of language and must finally invoke the notion of an actual, nonlinguistic fact or act. The relevant referent is Deronda's circumcision, which the novel must occlude; otherwise the story of discovering identity could not unfold. The scandal of this referent is its status as an exemplary signifier, alluding to the divine pact with Abraham, a story of the institution of signification.

Issues and Answers; or, If You've Tried It Don't Knock It

Wilson doesn't play favorites, he's just as ready to take on even his friends if they too make a point of ignoring common sense and common decency—"What in God's name has happened to you?" he writes to Malcolm Cowley, who is still following the Stalin line in 1938: "In fact, you try to mislead the reader by one of those 'bedfellow' tricks in which the *Daily Worker* indulges. . . . I don't suppose you're a member of the C.P.; and I can't imagine any other inducement short of bribery or blackmail . . . to justify and imitate their practices at this time." But the last phrase—"at this time"—is important, because as late as 1935, when the Stalinist rewriting of history had been under way for a decade and the early purges had already occurred, Wilson didn't hesitate to defend the Stalin line with arguments that Cowley or *The Daily Worker* would have cheered to the rafters:

> I don't see any reason to disbelieve that they had a counterrevolutionary conspiracy backed by Germany on their hands, as they say they had. . . . It is surely a mistake, as [Robert Morss] Lovett said the other day, to assume that the victims were innocent because there were so many of them. . . .

Others—faint-hearted comrades and fair-weather friends—could hang on only by managing to doubt that death had undone so many, but straight-shooter Wilson didn't doubt and didn't mind. Anyhow numbers or innocence is overrated, in a much smaller country centuries ago Swift had already recommended the butchering of as many as a hundred thousand babies a year to serve the purposes of the cannibal elite, you can't make a Soviet omelette without breaking a million eggs, and, so Wilson opines in 1935, "Stalin is a convinced Marxist and old Bolshevik . . . working for socialism in Russia." (In 1938 he wrote to Muriel Draper: "I can't imagine that you believe that the Stalin administration has been trying to achieve the aims of Lenin.") Wilson at any moment ("at this time") knows what he knows, and insists on sharing it: in any however casual letter no issue is too difficult for his off-the-cuff unconditional judgment, e.g. (in 1952) judicial euthanasia—"the great reform needed is a law to authorize the chloroforming of imbeciles and hopeless psychiatric cases. Of course, mistakes would be made, and the people would have to be very carefully checked, but we already put a lot of other matters into the hands of Boards of Health, etc." Utopian omelettes from innocent cracked eggs.

With Wilson, though, it isn't malice or muddle-headedness or political opportunism or inhumanity, it's a compulsion to settle the issue (explain the book, solve the problem) once and for all, to classify it and dispose of it and make room for the next in line; but issues don't stay put, and few are simple. Wilson is a plugger, ambitious and indefatigable, he keeps up, he enjoys the work of close reading (most of all, the work required by this century's hard texts: "I have described . . . what actually takes place there [an episode of *Ulysses*] as I have worked it out"; but in 1965 he confides to

---

Circumcision is an emblem of the novel's allusive or citational mode: the narrative makes its starting point, not a subject, but a rhetorical operation.

Occluded circumcisions were all the rage just a few years back.

a friend, "parts of . . . [*Ulysses*] are just incredibly dull"), he enjoys the mechanics of language and the variety of languages (he had learned Russian and Hebrew late, he was learning Hungarian in his old age); but words, his own or others', are mainly meaning (when he learned Russian—and there is testimony, including his own, that he was no expert—he excitedly discovered untranslatable marvels in the very texture of Pushkin, Turgenev, *Doctor Zhivago* which somehow he too couldn't translate or even begin to give an impression of beyond mere meaning) because meaning, once he fits it in or works it out, leaves him with little feeling for the words in their particular vibrations—

> I have sometimes become so bored with the language in which I wrote articles—the monotony of the vocabulary and the recurrence of routine formulas—that I would find it a great relief to get away from this kind of writing and give myself a freer hand in a play or a piece of fiction in which I could make people talk as contemporary Americans did . . .

(but his plays and fiction are very much duller and less idiomatic than his criticism); the trouble is that ideas are mostly formulas, books are not life, people don't do what they're supposed to, history doesn't come out right ("Reading the newspapers, and even the world's literature, I find that I more and more feel a boredom with and even scorn for the human race"), common sense and good intentions are indispensable but limited, Freud and Marx and Symbolism don't take up the slack, dogmatic platitudes stream in from all directions and try to pass for discoveries and answers: "One cannot tell whether Mr. Carr is aware of the obvious connection between Bakunin's incurable impotence and his orgiastic passion for destruction"; Edna Millay's "Renascence" is "a great affirmation of the stature of the human spirit"; "*The Fall of the House of Usher* is not merely an ordinary ghost story: the house—see the opening paragraph—is an image for a human personality, and its fate—see the fissure that runs through the wall—is the fate of a disrupted mind"; *Lady Chatterley's Lover* is "something more than the story of a love affair: it is a parable of post-war England" (a book with ideas and meanings and the courage to say shit and therefore Wilson admired it; but otherwise, having read only *Lady Chatterley,* Wilson dismissed on hearsay evidence everything else by Lawrence and so missed something else he had written: "Books are not life").

It's less a passionate conviction than a bookish and—perish the thought—professorial certainty: the assignment for Monday is—, the meaning of this passage is—. Wilson is a kind of classroom showman whose daily disclosures come to look rather less sensational when they appear in print and outside the blackboard birdcage: "I have just done a very Freudian study of Ben Jonson, which I have a feeling . . . [*The New Yorker* is] not going to print," he writes anxiously to a friend; but it was duly printed, and turned out to be an account of the meaning of Jonson's work examined in the light of Wilson's discovery that Jonson was "an obvious example of a psychological type which has been described by Freud and designated by a technical name, *anal erotic* . . . [of which] the three main characteristics are . . . paraphrased from Freud as follows: '(a) orderliness . . . ; (b) parsimony . . . ; (c) obstinacy . . . '";

repressed, retentive, sluggish, and so forth, though nothing that can't be taken care of by a strong dose of salts: "But his habit of saving and holding back—did his Scotch ancestry figure here too?—had an unfortunate effect on his work" (The Scotch Marine went over the top/Because he heard a nickel drop). Probably Wilson's most widely read essay is "The Ambiguity of Henry James" (reprinted in anthologies of lit-crit as an example of how to do it), which rather than being about ambiguity—Wilson apparently doesn't understand the word—is another Freudian exposure of a writer's true meaning, taking off this time from Wilson's excited discovery (with the help of an earlier essay by somebody else) that *The Turn of the Screw* is a *trompe-l'oeil* and *tour de force* which *seems* to mean one thing but *in fact* means another (though years later, when James's notebooks were published and said the opposite, Wilson somewhat recanted and came to believe that there was more in what it meant and less in what it seemed to mean).

Gertrude Stein's derisive label for Pound—"village explainer"—sticks better to Mencken or Wilson, both of whom were Chautauqua rationalists who tended to clarify issues into unintelligibility; only, unlike Mencken, Wilson secretly believed he could change the world. For example, the professor with a platform at *The New Yorker* and a secure reputation as the leading American critic really believed, when he "published a little book on the subject of the Dead Sea scrolls" (for which his beginner's Hebrew was pressed into service), that it would make the Church totter:

> It seemed to me that the discovery in these pre-Christian documents of a doctrine, a ritual and a discipline very similar to those of Christianity, as well as of a "Teacher of Righteousness" who seemed in some ways to anticipate Jesus . . . might present an embarrassing problem to any theology based on the dogma that Jesus was the Son of God, a unique and supernatural figure . . . yet the scrolls have proved not to be [so] disturbing . . . as I had thought they were likely to be.

But then the world didn't measure up to his plans and expectations from as early as 1917, when he was twenty-two in an army camp waiting to be shipped overseas—

> You have no idea, seriously, how isolated and inward you become, surrounded by and dealing with people with whom you cannot talk the real language, whose habits and manners you detest, and with whom the only qualities which you have in common are the qualities which you would most willingly destroy forever. And yet *nihil humani mihi alienum est.* This is not the absence of charity on my part; it is only the reaction of intelligence.

—till a half-century later in his seventies when he charitably itemized the world's more recent defects:

> The policies of the lying governments; the inevitable standardization of what we assume to be "exotic" and "backward" peoples; the stupidity of

applied ideologies; the competition for "success" and "status"—and with all this, the inferiority, mental as well as physical, of the specimens of the human race that I see all around me in America.

We had better make one thing perfectly clear. Wilson can be as cutting as he pleases about his mental edge over us youth of 1966: we've disappointed him; we're sorry; but when he says that he and his contemporaries at Princeton and at camp among the alien humanoids and in the Manhattan of the 'twenties—that in short these dumpy people have a *physical* edge over us, he is going too far. A typical method of Wilson's when the grand manner seems called for is to describe in the voice of a tape-recorded museum tour an official portrait of somebody or other: "Let us take a last look at him [Michelet, in *To the Finland Station*] . . . with his mask of determined will, which seems always to have been straining, never relaxed—the long plebeian jaw, the self-assertive chin, the set mouth, the fine trenchant nose . . ." and so on. Wilson himself was five-feet-six, weighed two hundred pounds much of his life, and in the photo on the back of the jacket of the *Letters* is the spit and image of Sydney Greenstreet in *The Maltese Falcon.*

We grew up on Wilson's essays and collections, we waited for his next piece in *The New Republic* and later in *The New Yorker,* he was our polymath and our incorruptible, he tackled everything and we trusted him, he knew who the important writers were, he dosed us with Marx and Freud and *explication de texte* in just the right proportions and—presto! all the big books made sense; he had the right tone (revolutionary and down-to-earth, sardonic and millennial, reasonable and concerned), he was familiar and authoritative, he was easy good reading on the bus or in the college cafeteria. Pound had long since gone round the bend; Eliot was slippery, and his politics dismayed us; Leavis seemed—well, a mite touchy; Trilling sounded like Eliot after shock treatments; we didn't know Lawrence had written anything but novels: so we kept returning to Wilson with the feeling that, as long as those unequivocal bulletins kept coming out, we didn't have to worry about the life of the mind. Nonetheless, back in those halcyon days we couldn't help suspecting he didn't have the makings of a theoretical critic: whenever he took a deep breath he floated off into a sort of eternally revolving unintense inane—"what she wants other people to know she imparts to them by creating an object, the self-developing organism of a work of prose" (which means that novelists write novels; cf. an undergraduate's equally dizzying but much more direct approach to the zero degree of writing, as reported by Irving Howe: "The idea of character is fictitious"). Moreover, he always had too much petulance to be the flinty Jeremiah he latterly aspired to be: when in *A Piece of My Mind* or *The Cold War and the Income Tax* he denounced the world and the human race, he sounded like an eminent contemporary of his, Harold Rosenberg, another veteran of the apocalyptic 'twenties and 'thirties who, asked a half-century later why Marx's hopes and dreams for us hadn't come true, replied in thunder: "Because what he couldn't figure on was that the working class would turn out to be a bunch of bums!"

"When I call myself a journalist," said Wilson, "I mean that I have made my living mainly by writing in periodicals." He is of course trying to pull the rug out

Issues and Answers; or, If You've Tried It Don't Knock It

from under those who might argue he's a journalist in a different and less neutral meaning of the word—for instance if they said that his style is journalistic because its intention is to be clearer and more coherent and more general than the topic (any topic) allows, and because to reread him (or to read him carefully) is to be "bored," as he himself complains, "[by] the monotony of the vocabulary and the recurrence of routine formulas." His three "serious" books (not his collections or his fiction) are all efforts to make a grand design and lengthy synopsis or quotation and judgment, judgment, judgment do the work of style; but monotony and routine formulas are never merely a matter of style, and in *Axel's Castle* and *To the Finland Station* the endlessly assertive judgments and the monotony of the lists of the virtues and the vices of each of the characters—first enthusiastically pro, then deprecatingly con, then maybe five pages of pro again and back to con and then, thank God! a synthesis—get to be a trifle more exasperating than the not quite complex inexhaustible style:

> [Joyce's] work is prodigiously rich and alive. His force instead of following a line, expands itself in every dimension (including that of Time) about a single point. The world of "Ulysses" is animated by a complex inexhaustible life. . . . . '
>
> Joyce has as little respect as Proust for the capacities of the reader's attention; and one feels, in Joyce's case as in Prousts, that the *longueurs* which break our backs . . . are partly . . . [intended] to compensate by piling things up for an inability to make them move. . . .
>
> Yet even these episodes contribute something valuable. . . . . [Axel's Castle]

To the Finland Station introduces us to a well-known German philosopher and one of the seminal influences on Marx, a fellow named Hegel, "who had been swept up in his early years, before he had stiffened into a Prussian professor, by the surge of the French Revolution"; and just as depressing as the racy intercourse between these images are Wilson's usual (Hegelian?) last-ditch struggles to synthesize the pros and cons:

> if we are repelled by these traits [arrogance, mistrust, jealousy, vindictiveness, gratuitous malignity] in Marx, we must remember that a normally polite and friendly person could hardly have accomplished the task which it was the destiny of Marx to carry through . . . .

—but Marx "was closer than he could ever have imagined to that imperialistic Germany he detested. After all, the German Nazis too—also, the agents of an historical mission—believe [the book was published in 1940] that humanity will be happy and united when it is all Aryan and all submissive to Hitler." Thus, presumably, we oughtn't to be repelled by Hitler's unpleasant traits because without them he could hardly have accomplished the task which it was his destiny to carry through.

Wilson's most satisfactory book is *Patriotic Gore*—perhaps because for once he is dealing with impressive people who aren't a part of the intellectual's portable pantheon: in fact he has no alternative to inventing, for the purposes of his book, General Sherman, Alexander Stephens, Harriet Beecher Stowe and her husband, even Lincoln, out of their own voluminous and relatively unrifled documentation of themselves, which he quotes not only voluminously but effectively and surrounds with judgments that are fresh and sympathetic enough to do it justice. It's a pity, then, that the Introduction (written years after many of the chapters) is mostly irrelevant to the book and an example of the author in his unloveliest ill temper, and that the book itself goes on far too long, tries to cover far too much ground, and eventually bogs down and sinks without a trace among the minutiae of the innumerable minor and uninteresting post-Civil-War writers that Wilson has persuaded himself he needs to bring in for the sake of his grand design.

Or that he brings in simply because he can't resist doing a little lecture on almost anybody who writes books. What is evident from his letters as well as from the late and the posthumous memoirs is that he lived as literary a life as possible. He accepts it as a responsibility and a power; he is very generous with long letters full of careful and practical suggestions not only to writers who are friends of his—Dos Passos, John Peale Bishop, Fitzgerald—but to strangers who ask for encouragement and advice; he is an honorable and tactful editor, he enjoys discovering and helping new writers, he reads up on things, he likes to keep in touch. True, he isn't infallible, especially about the work of friends: for example he dotes on Alfred Kazin's *Contemporaries,* the standard mix of NY*TBR* puffs and snarls that stay news as long as the Sunday papers they come wrapped with; and as late as 1945 he can still say that Paul Rosenfeld is "the best writer on music we have—the only one who is really a writer," but, after a sampling of twenty years of Rosenfeld's prose in several of his books and a few volumes of *Modern Music,* it's hard to avoid the conclusion that Rosenfeld is the worst writer in the history of civilization, turning out on every page abstract stuff like this: "Never a poet endowed, say, in Stravinsky's degree with the instinctive capacity for the harmonization of expression and actuality, Hindemith seasonably showed himself responsive to the pace and rhythm of contemporary life"; and, describing a piece of music, concrete stuff like this: "peasants and 'little kids' [he means *children*!] sporting in the abandon and joy of wholeness. (Toughness and fecundity of earth, that lets the sharp teeth of her children bite into the real!)."

Wilson seems to have been at least acquainted if not on familiar terms with every American writer from Rosenfeld to Wilfrid Sheed and Erich Segal. Indeed gossiping about Eliot's private miseries, John Peale Bishop's Gorgon of a wife, Fitzgerald and Zelda misbehaving, Edna Millay taking men on like a Greenwich Village Messalina, Wilson is a more useful writer than in his public essays about the same writers: "Nabokov has suddenly written me a letter telling me that he values my friendship and that all has been forgiven. He has been told that I have been ill, and it always makes him cheerful to think that his friends are in bad shape. He was mourning for Roman Grynberg at least ten years before he died." The great love of Wilson's life was Edna Millay, yet his memorial essay about her is glum and sentimental: one of the events quickly passed over is an evening "John Bishop and I. . . spent. . . with her together . . . on our old high and positive basis" just before her first visit to Europe;

and the essay ends with an Ivory-Flakes image of Millay "running around the corner of Macdougal Street, flushed and laughing, 'like a nymph,' with her hair swinging. Floyd Dell, also laughing, pursued her." But in his journal (published in the posthumous memoir *The Twenties*) Wilson is more specific about that farewell evening: "After dinner, sitting on her day bed, John and I held Edna in our arms—according to an arrangement insisted upon by herself—I her lower half and John her upper—with a polite exchange of pleasantries as to which had the better share"; and though he still can't quite get down to details, this much of the truth is more useful than the high and positive basis he is sitting on in the public essay.

Thirty years later, in a chapter of *A Piece of My Mind* which he calls "Sex" (and for which a more accurate title would have been "Eugenics for Tiny Tots" or "The Fox and the Grapes" or "The Dog in the Manger"), he has come to understand that sex has no interest or "purpose" whatever except the improvement of the breed, that whether they know it or not lovers in modern literature suffer from "the basic biological bafflement of the failure to produce children," that Lawrence's "glorification of intercourse for its own sake" (though except for Connie and Mellors he hasn't read Lawrence) and Millay's "feminine promiscuity" are silly. Forty years later, in *Upstate*, "When I read even a love story that might once have moved me—instead of thinking that, except on the very lowest level, a principle of selection is at work: they are trying to improve the human breed—I think, Oh, it's just a man trying to get his penis into some woman"; and one day, in a theater on West 42nd Street, he sits through three hard-core pornographic films:

> I do not think that such films should be allowed. College students should not be encouraged to go in for drug-taking orgies, and the film about the rapist could be taken as demonstrating how easy it is to commit a rape: just follow the woman up a dark alley and give her a clout with a club.

—and furthermore he wants us to know that he has come to understand that the 'twenties, the decade of his young manhood, were in fact "a squalid period" of drunkenness and debauchery. So, as the sun sinks slowly in the west, we bid farewell to issues and answers and the rational roving reporter, who by now ("at this time") has doubtless quite forgotten all the undisclosed details and sensations of that fond farewell to his better half, so long ago, when (at *that* time) in concert with his best friend he was so delightfully attached not for eugenic purposes to "some woman" but for fun and games to the particular and irreplaceable love of his life.

The Smell of Mortality

ALLON Schoener's book[1] is dedicated "To my father, who was a Lower East Side boy, and to my mother, who, as I did, learned about the Lower East Side from my father." Schoener had been asked by The Jewish Museum to set up an exhibition on that great source and forcing-bed of twentieth-century American-Jewish life:

> I was born and raised in Cleveland; I never knew the Lower East Side until I went to college. When I came to New York on weekends from New Haven, I found myself roaming around Delancey Street and Second Avenue eating food that my mother had never cooked and trying to find the world of my father's youth. By the time I started to look, it was gone. The exhibition and book have permitted me to explore this vanished world in libraries and archives. . . .

It took only two generations for the Jewish Lower East Side to materialize as if by teleportation from Eastern Europe, flourish like the New Jerusalem, and disappear utterly into legend and now into archeology. (Jews don't stay put, they're here today and somewhere else tomorrow, pillar to post, fire to frying-pan, whether from Delancey Street to suburban split-levels and Park Avenue condominiums or at the turn of the century—the Cossacks' horses breathing down their necks in 661 devastated Russian ghettos during the black year of 1905-6—from Kishinev and all the *shtetlach* over the waves to Delancey Street. Till Hitler they had the habit of keeping one jump ahead.) To retrieve a sense of the milieu as it was, Manners's chatty account[2] concentrates less on the Russian-Jewish greenhorns in the tenements than on the rich, Americanized German-Jews from uptown who intercepted them just this side of Customs and at once began maneuvering (and spending!) to coax them out of the poverty, Russian radicalism, and especially Jewishness that were a scandal to the Gentiles. *Portal to America* is more panoramic, and Schoener's method, deriving from its origin in the exhibition he assembled, is documentary: to let the whole story be told, schematically at least, without explicit editorial comment, by the contemporary statements (mostly newspaper articles) and photographs he selects and arranges for the purpose. One of the pieces he includes is taken from Hutchins Hapgood's recently

---

[1] Allon Schoener, *Portal to America* (Holt, 1967).
[2] Ande Manners, *Poor Cousins* (Coward, McCann & Geoghegan, 1972).

reprinted[3] pioneer book on the New York ghetto (first published in 1902). Hapgood was a conscientious, sympathetic, and penetrating observer; he did the research and respected his subject, unlike a more famous American writer, who didn't scruple to practice his hit-and-run impressionism on a subject about which he knew nothing except that it frightened and repelled him.

Two years after the publication of *The Spirit of the Ghetto,* which would have been a useful book to seek out and ponder if one hadn't been an impressionist, Henry James came back home (on a ship that doubtless carried, seven decks below, a thousand refugees from the latest pogrom) and registered the impression that, while he sojourned all unaware abroad, the Jews had slithered in and taken over the Lower East Side. Words were called for. The appalled impressionist, dictating the New York section of *The American Scene* with one eye on his stockpile of vivid metaphors and the other on the Protocols of the Elders of Zion, had no choice but to bait the Jews for their Jew trick of coupling and *breeding* like bugs wherever, as in his cherished old New York, they happened, by the momentary inadvertence of the elect, to be allowed to live: "There is no swarming like that of Israel when once Israel has got a start, and the scene here bristled, at every step, with the signs and sounds, immitigable, unmistakable, of a Jewry that had burst all bounds."

It was a bitter scene and a yet more bitter prospect: "the Hebrew conquest of New York" (upward and outward from Delancey Street), and the Babel of "ethnic" accents that threatened the very spelling of the English language (the Jews with their "all-unconscious impudence" were "the agency of future ravage," the East Side cafés were "torture-rooms of the living idiom"). Luckily, though, this all-unconscious social cretin and political provocateur found Central Park so seductive that he was occasionally—"in the happiest seasons, at favouring hours"—able to suppress his shudder of revulsion at the mere idea of sharing its rustic pathways with a rubbish of "superfluous" sheenies:

> The strange thing, moreover, is that the crowd, in the happiest seasons, at favouring hours, the polyglot Hebraic crowd of pedestrians in particular, has, for what it is, none but the mildest action on the nerves. The nerves are too grateful, the intention of beauty everywhere too insistent; it "places" the superfluous figures with an art of its own, even when placing them in heavy masses. . . .

James, incapable of economics or religion, couldn't have had the ordinary motives for objecting to Jews; but, *grand seigneur* of literary milliners, he was all taste and condescension, nerves, and it wasn't only Jews who didn't measure up on the American scene, it was also "the Italians, who, over the whole land, strike us, I am afraid, as,

---

[3] Hutchins Hapgood, *The Spirit of the Ghetto* (Funk and Wagnalls, 1965). Harry Golden's preface and notes to this "new edition" are as cheerful and anecdotally informative as his writing usually is, as peripheral to the subject as, say, a nightclub routine by Sammy Davis, Jr., and, in their uncomprehending intrusions on Hapgood's sustained thoughtfulness an insult to the book they presume to extend and elucidate.

after the Negro and the Chinaman, the human value most easily produced" (scraped free of the customary Jacobite cholesterol, what James meant was that, just as the Jews had too much individuality to interest a man of taste, so such poor neutral creatures had too little). This man of taste who, as late as 1880 (in *The Portrait of a Lady*), could diagnose in three words the "bare, familiar, trivial" music of the organ-grinder Verdi may even have been moved, every blessed night before sleepy-poo, to whisper "kike, nigger, dago, chink" into his tall silk hat as he removed it tenderly from over his tucked-in jackass-ears.

"The Jewish quarter of New York," writes Hapgood in his Foreword to *The Spirit of the Ghetto*, "is generally supposed to be a place of poverty, dirt, ignorance and immorality—the seat of the sweatshop, the tenement house, where 'red lights' sparkle at night, where the people are queer and repulsive." Hapgood, however, wasn't an evangelist, a theoretician, or a man of taste:

> That the ghetto has an unpleasant aspect is as true as it is trite. But the unpleasant aspect is not the subject of the following sketches. I was led to spend much time in certain poor resorts of Yiddish New York not through motives either philanthropic or sociological, but simply by virtue of the charm I felt in men and things there. East Canal Street and the Bowery have interested me more than Broadway and Fifth Avenue. Why, the reader may learn from the present volume—which is an attempt made by a Gentile to report sympathetically on the character, lives and pursuits of certain East Side Jews with whom he has been in relations of considerable intimacy.

While he was writing the essays that eventually became the book, Hapgood worked as a reporter for Lincoln Steffens on the *Commercial Advertiser*. Another reporter on the paper, and a close friend of Hapgood's, was Abraham Cahan, already the author of the prototypic novel of Jewish immigrant life, *The Rise of David Levinsky*, later for many years editor of the *Jewish Daily Forward* and the most influential and most knowledgeable citizen of the New York ghetto. Steffens himself at the time, according to his *Autobiography*, "was almost a Jew. I had become as infatuated with the Ghetto as eastern boys were with the wild west, and nailed a mazuza on my office door; I went to the synagogue on all the great Jewish holy days; on Yom Kippur I spent the whole twenty-four hours fasting and going from one synagogue to another." So Hapgood, a young man from Harvard, had much encouragement and guidance; but he made the most of his opportunity.

His Foreword is misleadingly modest: "certain East Side Jews" turn out to be a large, various, passionate, and busily intellectual community of rabbis, philosophers, poets, playwrights, actors, journalists, writers of fiction, and eccentrics whom Hapgood writes about with the (indeed) "considerable intimacy" of no outsider at all but a member of the family, a colleague, a friend, a *landsmann*, and a distinguished critic and social observer. In *The American Scene* James mentions having shown up once, briefly, at a Yiddish play till he was driven off forever by the smell of the multitude—"a scent, literally, not further to be followed." Hapgood seems to have watched and studied for years every play and player in the endless repertoire of the three Yiddish theaters on the Bowery: his descriptions and distinctions are lively and evocative; moreover, he is able to persuade us that what went on in these theaters must have represented, consistently, a level of committed intelligence putting to shame the dilution of a dilution of a genteel Anglo-Saxon theater uptown that it was James's unfulfilled dream of glory to make good in.

The Yiddish theater could try anything because its audience was everybody—"the sweatshop woman with her baby, the day laborer, the small Hester Street shopkeeper, the Russian-Jewish anarchist and socialist, the ghetto rabbi and scholar, the poet, the journalist." Hapgood describes the actor Jacob Adler playing an idiot boy in Jacob Gordin's *Wild Man:*

> The poor fellow is filled with the mysterious wonderings of an incapable mind. His shadow terrifies and interests him. He philosophizes about life and death. He is puzzled and worried by everything; the slightest sound preys on him. Physically alert, his senses serve only to trouble and terrify the mind which cannot interpret what they present. The burlesque which Mr. Adler puts into the part was inserted to please the crowd, but increases the horror of it, as when Lear went mad; for the Elizabethan audiences laughed and had their souls wrung at the same time. The idiot ludicrously describes his growing love. In pantomime he tells a long story. It is evident, even without words, that he is constructing a complicated symbolism to express what he does not know. He falls into epilepsy and joins stiffly in the riotous dance. The play ends so fearfully that it shades into mere burlesque.
>
> This horrible element in so many of these plays marks the point where realism passes into fantastic sensationalism. The facts of life in the ghetto are in themselves unpleasant, and consequently it is natural that a dramatic exaggeration of them results in something poignantly disagreeable. The intense seriousness of the Russian Jew, which accounts for what is excellent in these plays, explains also the rasping falseness of the extreme situations. . . .

The *Russian* Jew. It's necessary to emphasize, as Hapgood's evidence reminds us often, that, apart from their religion, these Jews are almost as Russian as they are Jewish: their literary and theatrical mode is a realism that Anglo-Saxon gentility found indecorous, their literary models are Tolstoy and Chekhov (and very likely, though Hapgood doesn't name him, Dostoevsky); their politics is Russian anarchism and socialism, which they argue interminably in cafés over tumblers of Russian tea. But the special pathos of their culture is that it is all too Jewish—bound up in a Teutonic "jargon" with fifty-seven different varieties of pronunciation and words pilfered from everywhere, a language at home nowhere in the world outside the immigrant's house, and which cannot survive the vivacity and ambition of the children of those who will be the last to speak it as the language of their bosom. The pathos is summed up, as Hapgood points out, in the brief history of the Yiddish stage and in the career of one of its actors, Zelig Mogalesco. The Yiddish theater was founded in Rumania in 1876, and Mogalesco was the first Yiddish actor; now (in 1901), in his forties, he is the best comedian of the New York Yiddish theater. He has seen "the birth of the Yiddish stage and may survive its death." (In fact he predeceased it, and the Yiddish theater died off less dramatically than it might have.[4])

But pathos is for the theater. Out in the world the Jews' tradition of learning, if not their vernacular, is quite at home in the new country that invites them to master its language and allows them to enroll in its public institutions of learning:

> The public schools are filled with little Jews; the night schools of the East Side are used by practically no other race. City College, New York University, and Columbia University are graduating Russian Jews in numbers rapidly increasing. . . . Then there are innumerable boys' debating clubs, ethical clubs, and literary clubs in the East Side.

"Altogether," Hapgood concludes with the spectacular generosity of a man who has no scores to settle, "there is an excitement in ideas and an enthusiastic energy for acquiring knowledge which has interesting analogy to the hopefulness and acquisitive desire of the early Renaissance. It is a mistake to think that the young Hebrew turns naturally to trade. He turns his energy to whatever offers the best opportunities for broader life and success. Other things besides business are open to him in this country . . . ." as of course they were not in the old country. What brass to bring up the Renaissance! at the very moment when Henry James was still innocently lisping the pogromist slogans of Pobedonostsev the Chief Procurator of the Holy Synod of autocratic Russia.

But then James, his nose out of joint with the smell of mortality, didn't know Moses Reicherson, seventy-three years old, living in the ghetto as a teacher of Hebrew to children, an outstanding Hebrew grammarian of the time, translator into Hebrew of Lessing, Gellert, and Krylov, author of hundreds of articles for Hebrew periodicals, of an important work on Hebrew grammar, of a Hebrew commentary on the Bible in twenty-four volumes:

> "When the national language and literature live," he said, "the nation lives; when dead, so is the nation. The holy tongue in which the Bible was written must not die. If it should, much of the truth of the Bible, many of its spiritual secrets, much of its beautiful poetry, would be lost. I have gone deep into the Bible, that greatest book, all my life, and I know many of its secrets." He beamed with pride as he said these words. . . .

Or the old popular Yiddish poet Eliakim Zunser, author of sixty-five collections of poems, "hundreds of which are sung every day to young and old throughout Russia";

---

[4]Typical of Golden's editing is his five-page "footnote" on this chapter of Hapgood's book: he strings together a number of jokes and anecdotes, some of them funny, about the Yiddish theater, identifies Mogalesco as a "great comedian," and otherwise his lips are sealed. According to the *Encyclopedia Judaica* (Macmillan, 1971), XV, 1088, "Mogulesko" died in 1914. Twenty pages earlier in the same volume is a summary of the decline, if not quite the demise, of the Yiddish theater since World War I.

"the wedding bard . . . so famous in that capacity that he went to a wedding once or twice a day," whose "part at the ceremony was to address the bride and bridegroom in verse so solemn that it would bring tears to their eyes, and then entertain the guests with burlesque lines," music as well as verse extempore, after no more preparation than "a hurried talk . . . with the wedding guests and the relatives of the couple":

> His poetry seemed to him only a detail of his life. Along with the simplicity of old age he has the maturity and aloofness of it. . . . . His wife and children bent over him as he recited, and their bodies kept time with his rhythm. One of the two visitors was a Jew, whose childhood had been spent in Russia, and when Zunser read a dirge which he had composed in Russia twenty-five years ago at the death by cholera of his first wife and children—a dirge which is now chanted daily in thousands of Jewish homes in Russia—the visitor joined in, although he had not heard it for many years. Tears came to his eyes as memories of his childhood were brought up by Zunser's famous lines; his body swayed to and fro in sympathy with that of Zunser and those of the poet's second wife and her children. . . .

Or the Chekhovian sketch-writer S. Libin, "a thorough product of the sweatshop," who was "born in Russia twenty-nine years ago, and came to New York when he was twenty-two years old. For four years he worked as a capmaker in shops which were then more wretched than they are now, from sixteen to seventeen hours a day. While at his task he would steal a few minutes to devote to his sketches, which he sent to the *Arbeiterzeitung*. [Abraham] Cahan recognized in Libin's misspelled, illiterate, almost illegible manuscript a quality which worthily ranked it with good realistic literature." Or the twenty-year-old Jacob Epstein, whose first commissioned work was the illustration of Hapgood's volume with beautifully quiet "drawings from life."

The Americanized "cousins" who don't appear in Hapgood's or Epstein's sketches were nevertheless very much in the picture, and Manners's book makes clear that they had mixed feelings, if not worse, about the sudden mass immigration of East European Jews. Rabbi Isaac Mayer Wise, for example, had been painstakingly trimming away Orthodox Jewish ritual into a Reform Judaism that he hoped would be "strong enough to outlive the end of the 19th century";

> Everything in East European Orthodoxy ran counter to an element which both Reform and Conservative Jews believed essential to modern Judaism—propriety, decorum. . . . . *Davening*—the sing-song chanting of prayers in the Orthodox service, which few of the worshipers understood because they were in Hebrew—was done by the congregation at each person's individual pace and accompanied by his singular style of swaying back and forth for concentration. The overall impression was of a prayer race, the devout achieving a paradoxically sacred babel. But this approach to prayer simply reflected the East European's peasant relationship with God. Their everyday *shtetl* closeness to Him made for a boisterous uninhibited

heartiness. God was one of them; in His presence no esthetic airs were needed. Similarly, Reform Jews saw God in the image they sought to project, a genteel American image (with just a slight German accent); therefore, their service, of necessity, had to equal in refinement that of the American Protestant. . . .

To Wise, the torrent of crude, unworldly Russian Jews presented the only major obstacle to his fifty-year goal of Americanizing Judaism. . . . . "Count Ignatiev," he wrote feelingly in 1882, after Ignatiev's May Laws sent steerageload after steerageload of Jews to the United States, "ought to be hanged."

The lines were drawn. "'They are Jews,' declared Dr. Isaac Mayer Wise. 'We are Israelites.' And the Russian Jews said with equal assurance, We are Jews. They are goyim.'" When, after a decade of unchecked immigration, a committee of eminent American Jews "appealed to President Benjamin Harrison to remonstrate with Russia for enacting special laws which 'forced groups of its people to seek refuge in another country and that country our own,'" their motive wasn't purely humanitarian.

Yet in the worldwide Jewish crisis the record of the wealthy and influential Jews was full of instances of patience, concern, open-handedness, tenacity, as well as the immemorial Jewish reluctance to fight City Hall. Manners tells a specially touching anecdote about the Baron Maurice de Hirsch. This German-Jewish financier tried in 1888 to head off further pogroms by informing the Russian government that he would donate to Jewish agencies in Russia fifty million francs to establish technical and agricultural schools for "his unhappy Russian co-religionists"; the offer was rejected even though he paid a bribe of a million francs to the infamous Pobedonostsev; but he had no stomach for anything beyond toleration and survival:

> [The Zionist leader Theodor Herzl] suggested that Baron de Hirsch sponsor a contest for Jews in the major anti-Semitic countries for "deeds of great moral beauty, for courage, self-sacrifice, virtuous conduct, notable achievements in art and science . . . in short for everything great." When Herzl assured him that this would achieve "a general uplift among Jews," Baron de Hirsch interrupted, crying out piteously: "No, no, no! I do not want to raise the general level. All of our misfortunes come from the fact that the Jews want to climb too high. We have too much brains. My intention is to restrain the Jews from pushing ahead. They shouldn't make such great progress. All of the hatred against us stems from this. . . ."

In the land of the free, Rabbi Joseph Krauskopf opened the National Farm School in 1897 with the aim of turning ghetto boys into "a toiling class" of farmers. "When a young immigrant visited Dr. Krauskopf and asked for his help in continuing his medical studies at the Jefferson Medical College . . . Krauskopf brusquely told him, 'I can do nothing for you. We have too many doctors as it is.'" By 1905, one of the trustees suggested discontinuing the school because "Jewish boys are not willing to do what we want them to do"—i.e. become "farmers pure and simple"—and in 1918 the trustees acknowledged their failure by closing the school, which had turned out mainly "bacteriologists, plant pathologists, horticulturists, entomologists, farm economists and statisticians, teachers, veterinarians—even an editor of an agricultural journal."

Other benevolent and apprehensive American Jews (Rabbi Wise among them) tried to appease City Hall by virtually shanghaiing, with no preparation at all, trainloads of immigrants on tragicomic excursions to Louisiana, Kansas, Arkansas, Oregon, and Colorado to found farming communities, "because there was no better way to destroy the ignoble stereotype of the Jew as a peddler and petty tradesman than to make him a man of the soil." Manners quotes from a report by a young Cincinnati Jew, Charles K. Davis, in charge of a group of sixty men, women, and children bound for western Kansas; at a stopover in Kansas City, Davis was having trouble with Skwerski, Roseman, Braselawski, Sasewitz, Boxer, and Sussman ("the two latter are developing into first-class rascals"): "I want to hide their conduct from the people of Kansas City, especially the Gentiles, who have never seen Russians before, because I don't want them to form a poor opinion of our people.

. . . ." Meanwhile, in American magazines of the time, writers were explaining why Jews lived in tenements ("their in-born love of money-making leads them to crowd into the smallest quarters"); an expert on crime hazarded the opinion that "Most Hebrews commit their crimes for gain"; "the fact that 'some chiefs of police will not tolerate a Jewish prostitute in their city because they find it impossible to subject her to regulations' revealed to the sociologist the stubborn contentiousness of Jews and, to those who probed even more deeply, a covetousness which led Jewish prostitutes to refuse to pay police graft"; according to *World's Week* (in 1904), the reason that "No Jew has ever been tried for rape in the state of Ohio, which has a Jewish population of 150,000," may well be "the notorious Jewish dislike of struggle, of good hard physical labor." It's easy to understand why Charles K. Davis hoped to keep the malefactions of Boxer and Sussman out of the public eye.

Americanization was the aim. In the Educational Alliance (according to its president, "educational, humanitarian, philanthropic, and patriotic in the broadest sense"), which the uptown philanthropists established in the ghetto, nearly everything cultural was permitted except the speaking, reading, and writing of Yiddish. Imagine how the Orthodox, the socialists, and the Yiddish playwrights reacted to *that!* "In 1901, led by . . . Jacob Gordin, they organized their own settlement house, the Educational League," in celebration of which Gordin wrote a play called *The Benefactors of the East Side*. At one point "Ashley Jefferson Yoshke" (a takeoff on the philanthropist Jacob Schiff) declares that the benefactors, by "uplifting" the East Side Jews, will be in the tradition of Lincoln: "Of course the East Side is not black, but they are Rumanian. True, they are not Ethiopians, but they are Russians."

But Schiff and his partner in almost all his philanthropic ventures, the constitutional lawyer Louis Marshall, were strong, brave, intelligent men, capable of demanding to his face that President Taft abrogate a century-old treaty with Russia because it penalized American citizens who happened to be Jews, and then, when he refused, mounting a public campaign that forced him to change his mind; capable of demanding and receiving from Henry Ford a recantation and apology (which Marshall wrote and Ford signed) for Ford's seven-year rash of anti-Semitism in the Dearborn *Independent;* always ready, with whatever qualifications or ulterior motives, to give time and money and attention. It's the particular virtue of *Poor Cousins* that Manners's abundant, sometimes disorderly documentation goes to prove her entertaining thesis that, uptown and downtown, the Jews were a match for each other.

Portal to America has no thesis, its form is ampler and more exacting: the form coincides with Schoener's decision to trust the documentation itself, the very *Zeitgeist* speaking, time past as time present, before the valuable dust gets shaken out through the sieve of history. Here's a paragraph of a story ("Sweatshop Girl Tailors") from the New York *Tribune* of June 18, 1897:

> Miss Minnie Rosen, who is a young woman of the thinking kind, says that all the girls demand are living wages and fifty-nine hours work a week instead of the present system of one hundred eight hours work weekly on salaries ranging from $3 to $6 weekly, according to the size and age of the worker. Miss Rosen is a finisher and lives in a three-room flat on the top floor of No. 248 Monroe Street where she is assisted in providing the family living by a sister and two brothers, who make cigars and peddle around the tenement district. She speaks Yiddish with the usual gurgling sound and speaks English with her tongue, two most expressive hands, and a cultured shrug of the shoulders that says volumes and must eventually straighten the shoulders, now slightly rounded by the sewing machine. She says "vell" in a way that no linguist on earth can properly translate. If she says it about the contractor, it may mean anything; if she speaks of "the boss," it implies all manner of things; and if applied to herself, it means that there is no one like unto her in woe.

"Jew Babes at the Library," from the Evening *Post* of October 3, 1903, begins with an image of hunger ("Lines of children reaching down two flights of stairs and into the street may not infrequently be seen at the Chatham Square branch of the Public Library when school closes at three o'clock in the afternoon . . .") and ends with "English as she is spoken" by the children at the library:

> "Dasent" is used in more ways than an American would ever think of. "Those things dasent be touched," they will say. "He's a murder," will succinctly describe a disagreeable person, and "I have a mad on her" sufficiently depicts a slight difference of opinion. "He's come to be joined into the library" is the accepted form of introduction for a new friend. The installment plan seems graven in the nature of these infants. They wish to pay their fines a penny a day even when they have the whole amount in their pockets. "I might as well be getting the interest on this as you," said one boy frankly of a three-cent fine. Excuses for maltreated books give glimpses of

home life. "The baby dropped it in the herring" is the favorite explanation for a soiled cover.

Unabashed personal voices invent the suffragette and the American labor movement, as well as the Jewish conviction that books get into everything and have all the answers. A change in the quality of life occurs because the Bureau of Public Works replaces cobblestones with asphalt on the streets of the ghetto (New York *Tribune,* July 5, 1896):

> The smoothness is perhaps the chief element in their adaptability to the sports of childhood....
> ... The children being on the street, there is more room on the sidewalk for their elders. Chairs are brought out on the sidewalk, and the curbstones furnish seats for many. With the old paving materials, the gutters were more or less unclean and noisome, but the asphalt makes the curbstone really an attractive place to sit.
> When it is called to mind that a certain East Side block has 3,700 dwellers, it is easy to believe that these streets are crowded on summer evenings.... Someone has said that there is not standing room at one time on these East Side streets for all the people that live in them....

The report of The Tenement House Committee to the New York State Legislature (New York *Times,* January 18, 1895) notes that Sanitary District A, of the Eleventh Ward (populated almost entirely by Jewish immigrants), contained on June 1, 1894 as many as 986.4 persons per acre; the next most densely populated area in the world for which there was any record being a district in Bombay, which in 1881 contained 759.66 persons per acre. (The major influx of Jewish immigration didn't come till after 1903, with a corresponding impact on the population density of the East Side.)

East Side youths congregate nightly in candy stores (or, summers, on the sidewalks just outside, as the story fails to add) for talk, cards, and general socializing (New York *Tribune,* April 22, 1900):

> A counter along the length of the store decked with cheap candies and perhaps with cigars, some shelving behind filled with cigar and cigarette boxes, and invariably a soda water fountain make up the entire furniture of the store, if we except a few cigarette pictures on the wall. Usually the proprietor lives with his family in the rear of the store. Some stores, making a pretense to stylishness, have partitioned off a little room from the store to which they give the elegant name of "ice cream parlor," a sign over the door to that effect apprising you of its existence. One or two bare tables and a few chairs furnish the "ice cream parlor." But this little room is very useful as a meeting place for a small club for boys or as a general lounging room....

The newspaper items range from a description of the compulsory shower baths for all the immigrants at Ellis Island, through every political, economic, educational, and social issue involving the immigrants, to a bouquet of the heartfelt Letters to the Editor ("Bintel Briefs") of the *Forward,* in which a worker confides his verdict on a fellow-worker ("Nothing in the world interests him. He hates music, the theater, and socialism"), or a sufferer sums up with brevity and vigor the accumulated miseries of mankind:

February 27, 1906

Dear Mr. Editor of the *Forward:*
  I read the troubles of family life in your "Bintel Brief" each day very attentively. But my own troubles are so great, so enormous, that I would not even ask you for your permission to print my few words in your paper, as others do, but simply, I ask you right on the spot: Help!

Your Constant Reader

What the newspaper items don't cover, the photographs do. Art photographs of an angled slab of a power plant, posed portraits, frames of Old Faithful or the Leaning Tower are imitations of paintings or mere reminders. But snapshots of people and lived-in places, trapped in the light of the past, age into a fearful irrecoverable clarity even in the most predictable instances. The instances that Schoener chooses are without exception transitory and important, and the sheaves of photographs are the prize of his wonderful book: Hester Street in the light of day, tenements, awnings, pushcarts, bearded men with hats on, long-skirted women walking; an Armenian Jew with unbelievable direct bright eyes, at Ellis Island; a cluster of Italian boys, grinning and clowning for the camera, on Mulberry Street; families of garment-workers at their "homework"; a shoemaker on Broome Street; a sly-looking Lothario-type among other men and boys in a sweatshop in 1889; the last meeting of the Garment Workers' Strike in 1913 (the sign held up among them is in Yiddish); victims of the Triangle Fire laid out side by side in their coffins; a boy in a littered tenement hall filling a pan from a communal tap; a middle-aged man with a full square black beard, sitting in what looks like the corner of a wooden shack, at a table holding an unbroken loaf of twist bread, "Making Ready for the Sabbath" in 1890; a bathtub stuck forever in an airshaft between two tenements. They were all here; and here they are.

II
Scholars: The Soft Recesses of Uneasy Minds

The Blind Men and the Elephant

CHAUCER is a darling, he lacks the majestic testiness of most of the world's geniuses, he pays attention, has the common touch, seems as receptive and unthreatening as a baby; surely like you and me and John Gardner he was once a baby himself and experienced all the humanizing pristine postnatal sensations including of course—nosy little beggar—smells: "little Geoffrey," it says here,[1] reveled in sights and sounds and especially smells, "his big stepbrother's funny smell, the fierce, slightly frightening animal smells of his father and uncle Tom, the smell of his mother as wide and sweet and otherworldly as a meadow" (though this last smell may well have been the family cow's). Postnasal drips like Gardner come and go, but little Geoffrey ripened and ripened for half a century into the good gray poet who wrote a poem about a bad smell, dedicated to any dozen past and future psychobiographers: *The Summoner's Tale,* which concerns the duodecimal distribution of an old man's fart.

Not satisfied with inventing Chaucer's life,[2] Gardner turns psychocritic and in his second book of the week[3] invents Chaucer's poetry, e.g. as it was affected by the politics of the time. Gardner keeps prompting us to draw the right inferences—i.e. his—from the fact that Chaucer was a government functionary during the reign of Richard II: "It should hardly surprise us," he asserts, radiating self-assurance, "that every one of the [Canterbury] tales in fragments II-V, written when Richard's near tyranny and the barons' disloyalty was on everyone's mind, is a tale which comments directly or indirectly on the interrelated ideas *constancy* and *patience* . . ."; but most of these tales have nothing to do with constancy or patience (one is *The Summoner's Tale!*), there's no evidence which closely dates any of them or indeed separates them by date from any of the other Canterbury tales, there's no evidence that anything at all was "on everyone's mind" at the time, there's no evidence that the themes of Chaucer's poetry were skewed or determined by the politics of the time.

Still, since psychocriticism works hand in glove with psychohistory, it should hardly surprise us that the psychocritic doesn't distinguish between what on the evidence actually happened, what may be reasonably inferred to have happened, and what for his self-aggrandizing purpose ought to have happened. It's Gardner's purpose to show us how susceptible he is to the stunning insights which can be induced by the wealth of specialized information he shares with other medievalists; but he has to do a lot of filling in and faking ("using the tricks of a novelist") around the information because there isn't much of it that helps explain Chaucer, and because for Gardner mere fact isn't in any case vivid enough to induce stunning insights. So, looking scholarly, Gardner argues—what wouldn't have occurred to modern readers if he hadn't argued it—that writing a medieval poem which seems to modern readers wholly innocuous could be a very risky political act: Chaucer having written *Troilus and Criseyde,* his sympathetic and loving poem about love, Gardner commends him for having had the grit and pluck to come out with a humane love story at a moment in English history when, if the commendation is to mean something, armed bands must have been roaming the streets of London exclaiming that if they had horses they would horsewhip the first poet they saw who wrote humane love stories: "The humane and forgiving position Chaucer takes and justifies [in *Troilus and Criseyde*] was not an easy one to take in the mid-1380s, when Gloucester's star was rising and Chaucer and many of his friends were in trouble"; but Gardner's portentousness is as usual a barrel of horsefeathers, there's no evidence that Chaucer was "in trouble" during the mid-1380s or any other fraction of a decade, "Gloucester's star" hasn't even been astronomically identified let alone seen rising, *Troilus and Criseyde* was written by Richard II, black is white, and it's unlikely that Gloucester or Richard or Attila the Hun would have reprimanded a poet for writing a humane and forgiving poem about love-struck Trojans (Richard might on the other hand have been irked by "Lack of Steadfastness," a poem in which Chaucer advises him to pull himself together and behave like a proper king; but mere fact or reasonable inference doesn't interest Gardner).

Donald R. Howard is another medievalist who knows from the inside just which political and social pressures were hardest to resist during any particular medieval period, and just which moral reactions poets couldn't avoid having to them. It seems that during the period when *The Canterbury Tales* was being written (a longish stretch lasting fifteen years or more through all sorts of public vicissitudes, which may now and then have been overshadowed by private and unpolitical notions and feelings in the minds and hearts of poets as well as peasants)—during all this time Chaucer read the morning papers with anxiety and foreboding, and every afternoon and evening

> experienced such distressing events in the English court, such enormous changes in the society, and such insecurity about the future, that it affected the idea of his work. The idea was a sufficiently moral and religious one, but the style appropriate to that idea made it impossible to scold or to despair. His response was secular and pragmatic within the limits of a Christian ethic: the work was a book about the world—its values and manner, its style, had to be "worldly." In "Lack of Steadfastness" and "Truth" he made it plain that he believed man in this world could follow reason, "do law," and serve social justice. This would be man's bulwark against the world's decline. And he expressed that belief with the metaphor which gave to *The Canterbury Tales* its distinctive form: "Here is non home, here nis but wildernesse: /Forth pilgrim forth! . . . ./Hold the high way."[4]

How could Chaucer have got any of his feelings or notions except by reacting to the turbulent world around him? The Gardner-Howard line is that the world shouted and Chaucer jumped; but the evidence indicates that Chaucer kept his counsel and kept his head, lived his private life, and may have been less worried and less combustibly moral about public affairs than modern medievalists make him out to be. It's for instance a fact that the only extant poem by Chaucer in which he explicitly reacted to a political event, "Complaint to His Purse," is a good-natured and playful appeal to the new king, Henry IV, for a continuation of the pension Chaucer had long ago been granted by the deposed and murdered Richard. True, Chaucer's mode of addressing Henry—"O conquerour of Brutes[5] Albyon"—obviously recalls that earlier usurper of the English crown, William the Conqueror; but it's possible to admire bold usurpers, Chaucer seems to admire Henry for having boldly emulated his great ancestor and perhaps for offering the prospect of a more stable reign than Richard's, there's nothing in the tone or argument to suggest that Chaucer was agitated or dumbfounded by an event which doubtless he considered the gravest political event of his lifetime. According to the Gardner-Howard line, though, Chaucer must have felt just awful about it ("Complaint to His Purse" therefore has to be ironic dissimulation or time-serving sycophancy), must have immediately begun revising *The Canterbury Tales* to feature an idea that could never have crossed his mind before—the mutability of created things.

The point of their hallucinations (the thorn in the flesh of these free spirits) is that Chaucer wasn't *free*, did what he did against the grain or in reluctant conformity or by reacting bravely or cravenly to forces much lordlier than himself—thus yet another medievalist

> brings out a real irony in Chaucer's situation as a court poet. The son of a bourgeois is placed in an equivocal position when he writes for a courtly audience, and especially when he confronts his audience, as we know Chaucer did, by reading his works aloud. If he is to be a poet according to the ideal conception of the artist, he must impart wisdom to his audience, and they are bound to look up to him as an authority. Yet, since he comes from an inferior class and acts in the ordinary business of life as their servant, he is expected to defer to their taste and judgment. If he wants to instruct his audience, he must do so without ever seeming to forget his place. He is not free to write what he pleases but must choose those forms and subjects most acceptable to his audience.[6]

Chaucer was, so they say, often under the influence or under the thumb of somebody or other, for example the Italians: "The crowning architectural pleasure of Chaucer's tour [in 1372 to Italy, about which nothing is known except that he made it], a work that cannot help having influenced his artistic vision, subtly moving him toward his late, so-called realistic style . . . was Giotto's campanile [which hadn't been completed by the time of Chaucer's tour] . . ."; and the unimaginable Gardner plunges ahead to explain how Chaucer, probably while picnicking on the so-called Arno with the *Commedia* open in his left hand and a goblet of Valpolicella clenched in his right, discovered not only the feeling of compassion but its literary uses—"It is largely Dante's compassionate view of the sinful that makes possible Chaucer's similar compassion toward people undone by love, like Troilus" (observe the reasoning: Dante's compassion toward sinners, whom incidentally Dante himself has judged and found wanting and consigned to Hell, teaches the notorious grouch Chaucer to feel compassion toward broken-hearted lovers). Such sweaty derivativeness, known to psychocriticism as the anxiety of effluents, accounts no doubt for Chaucer's failure to achieve "coherence," which

> would remain to the end of Chaucer's career not a product of his whole soul's conviction (like the coherence in the poetry of Dante or Goethe) but dramatization with the poet's judgment mostly suspended. Chaucer takes, that is, exactly the nominalist stance of philosophers like Roger Bacon, for whom truth is, outside doctrine, finally unknowable. When the Italian influence had deepened in him, strengthening his confidence in realism, Chaucer would create characters like the Wife of Bath, the Nun's Priest, and the Canon's Yeoman, who could so infuse their own personalities into the stories they told us as to create what Poe would call unity of impression. But for all the brilliance of his characterizations—his mimickry [sic], if you like—Chaucer was never a man like Shakespeare, or like his own less philosophical contemporary, the *Gawain*-poet, who "saw life whole."

(Chaucer sawed life in half and out tumbled hundreds of unpremeditated lives, because he didn't have the cast-iron grid of *a priori* coherence that makes reading Goethe, Shakespeare, or Dante an exercise in searching for signs of life among the conventions, compulsions, self-justifications, proofs, wise saws, simple but powerful messages, and poetry. All the same, lacking the total hindsight of his betters, Chaucer was better off than his own Arcite, the unhappy lover in *The Knight's Tale* who according to Gardner saw life even less than half, "believing, in his maniacal nearsightedness, that no man ever suffered or will suffer as he does." In the kingdom of the blind, the maniacally nearsighted wear dark glasses.) Howard, however, is more charitable than Gardner toward Chaucer's shortcomings and believes that, though subject to many foreign influences, the poet probably worked out his ingenious idea for *The Canterbury Tales* by taking Howard's advice on how to write dialogue:

> Chaucer did not make a representation of contemporary life or a portrait gallery or a framed series of tales, but a representation of memories and stories, a record of experience. It is mimetic, but that mimesis takes as its object a world within the mind. How did Chaucer learn this? From the dream-vision, perhaps. From medieval esthetics, perhaps. But I believe he may have learned it by learning to write dialogue. . . . Now writing dialogue is an extraordinarily hard knack to get, and many still believe that the writer must listen and then imitate on paper the speech he hears people speak. But this is not so. . . .

And Howard proceeds to list everything we always wanted to know but never dared to ask about dialogue. At all events, Chaucer got the knack, and so learned how to represent "a *group*. Like any group it is made of individuals, but it has a dynamics of its own based on interpersonal and social relationships. Like any group, it is a society in little." As for those readers who aren't sure how well an amateur like Chaucer understood "group dynamics," Howard's businesslike footnote on page 155 (no kidding, it's really there, check it out yourself) directs them to the authorities:

> On group behavior see George C. Homans, *The Human Group* (New York: Harcourt, Brace and World, 1950); Howard S. Becker, *Outsiders: Studies in the Sociology of Deviance* (New York: Free Press, 1963); Philip E. Slater, *Microcosm: Structural, Psychological and Religious Evolution in Groups* (New York, London, Sydney: John Wiley, 1966).

Howard has a fund of jazzy generalizations, as when he defends the dull Parson against the fascinating Pardoner: "If goodness is dull in literature—if Milton's Satan is more interesting than God, Iago more exciting than Desdemona—this is a fact not about goodness or about literature but about ourselves. Take someone to the zoo and he wants to see the snakes." But it doesn't occur to him that nothing in life or literature is more interesting and exciting than goodness: that Troilus, Criseyde, and Pandarus are all both good and wonderfully interesting; so too Elizabeth Bennet, Anne Elliot, Sophocles' Antigone, Pushkin's Tatyana, Trollope's Plantagenet Palliser, Lawrence's Tom Brangwen; so most of all the character Chaucer in Chaucer's poems, who is the best human being on record and marvelously interesting. And when someone takes *me* to the zoo I want to see the swans.

Howard has a thesis, something about *The Canterbury Tales* as "unfinished" but "complete." He believes that emitting any banality, commonplace, crude mistake, crude neologism ("bookness," "voiceness," "paperness"), lump of jargon, flower of rhetoric with loop-tape repetitiveness transforms it into an idea:

> I suggested earlier [and several hundred times] that we need to see *The Canterbury Tales* in two ways at once—on the one hand as a series of tales within an encompassing tale, on the other hand as an inexhaustible world of stories among which the story of the pilgrimage is only another pilgrim's tale. Such a double perspective characterizes the topos of the flower: the "rose" design represents order, perfection, and permanence, yet it represents as a part of such order the facts of change, flux, and transience which were symbolized by the wheel. John Leyerle has drawn attention to this combination of *rosa* and *rota* . . . .

—and Howard believes that everything including the plain sense of the text must be sacrificed to his concatenated binary principle:

> If one takes such a binary structure and makes a concatenation, so that the second part of one pair becomes the first part of the next, and so on, one has the beginning of an interlaced narrative structure. It opens the possibility of interrupting an episode with a new episode, then returning to the

interrupted episode. It has a "grammar" of its own, and the morpheme of that grammar is not the "episode" but the diptych structure: narrative unit + juncture + narrative unit. This concatenated binary principle is evident in *The Canterbury Tales*. The General Prologue presents a picture which is altered when we have read the tales; and the story of the pilgrimage—the General Prologue and the world of tales it generates—presents a picture which is altered when we have read the Parson's Tale and Retraction. It is the same within the series of tales: the ideas we have in mind when we have finished the Knight's Tale are thrown into a different light by the Miller's Tale. When Chaucer says we can "turn over the leaf and choose another tale" I believe he has this effect in mind: we turn from one tale to another without forgetting the first, but the second adds something to our experience, and if the tales touch upon a common theme it alters something. If we choose to skip a tale we miss something. . . .

Ignore for a moment Howard's "idea" that the effect of the tales is—who would guess?—cumulative and retrospective (don't think about the Donovan Professor of English at Johns Hopkins presuming to impose on us a 400-page book of unbearably muscle-bound Laocoön-like squirmings in celebration of such a novelty); just concentrate on the fact that, coming upon the passage in which Chaucer apologizes for the "cherles [churl's] tale" the Miller is about to tell—

> *For Goddes love, demeth nat that I seye*
> *Of yvel entente, but for I moot reherce*
> *Hir tales alle, be they bettre or werse,*
> *Or elles falsen som of my mateere.*
> *And therfore, whoso list it nat yheere,*
> *Turne over the leef and chese another tale;*
> *For he shal fynde ynowe, grete and smale,*
> *Of storial thyng that toucheth gentillesse,*
> *And eek moralitee and hoolynesse.*
> *Blameth nat me if that he chese amys.*
> *The Millere is a cherl, ye knowe wel this;*
> *So was the Reve eek and othere mo,*
> *And harlotrie they tolden bothe two.*
> *Avyseth you, and put me out of blame;*
> *And eek men shal nat maken ernest of game.*

—reading this transparent passage, the most helpless Hopkins freshman understands he is reading the funniest, cleverest, soundest, and most disarming argument against censorship ever set down (It's no fault of mine that the Miller doesn't talk like a parson, if you can't put up with a dirty story turn the page and you'll find a clean one, there are plenty of clean and classy ones coming along, don't make a Federal case out of a little fooling around); moreover the freshman will soon learn by reading the annual honors list for faculty that to say Chaucer is saying quite the opposite (Be sure you read every one of the tales because each is a comment on all the others) is to commit a deed of maniacally nearsighted thesis-diddling for which the penalties are a major research grant, a sabbatical year in London, and elevation to an endowed professorship.

"In literary criticism," remarks Alfred David, "one tends to steer away from the obvious and press harder and harder after some elixir to multiply the meaning of the text": the metaphors are mangled, but the point is well taken, and (as if Gardner and Howard don't suffice) David illustrates it himself, for instance in his deeply moved reading of Chaucer's Retraction:

> For myself, the Retraction, especially when taken in conjunction with the Parson's Prologue, is a deeply moving statement of the limitations of art, and one that is very difficult to answer. The justification of poetry is by no means a peculiarly medieval problem although the Christian Middle Ages give it a religious form. Plato had banished poets from his Republic. A legend has it that Virgil wanted the *Aeneid* destroyed. Tolstoy wrote a tract in his later years rejecting his great novels. Kafka asked that his literary remains be burned. The luxury of literature and the study of literature have never been easy to justify in a world torn by harsh necessity, wars, and relentless social struggle.
>
> It is in this broader context that we must place the Retraction. In retracting his works Chaucer does not deny their right to exist, but he wants to warn us about the limitations of poetry lest they be misused, and he wants to be forgiven for the venial sin of having created something of such equivocal worth....

And here is the relevant part of Chaucer's Retraction at the end of *The Canterbury Tales*:

> Wherfore I biseke yow mekely for the mercy of God, that ye preye for me that Crist have mercy on me and foryeve me my giltes;/and namely of my translacions and enditynges of worldly vanitees, the whiche I revoke in my retracciouns:/as is the book of Troilus; the book also of Fame; the book of the xxv. Ladies; the book of the Duchesse; the book of Seint Valentynes day of the Parlement of Briddes; the tales of Caunterbury, thilke that sownen into synne;/the book of the Leoun; and many another book, if they were in my remembraunce, and many a song and many a leccherous lay; that Crist for his grete mercy foryeve me the synne....

In sum, checking David against Chaucer, one discovers that David can't read any better than Gardner or Howard: because (1) the Retraction isn't difficult to answer it's impossible to answer if one is a medieval Christian on one's deathbed or at any other moment of terrified or agonizing contrition, (2) the Retraction is otherwise unnecessary to think about at all except for such light as it may shed on Chaucer's feelings late in life, (3) it isn't for a "venial sin" but for his not necessarily venial "giltes" that Chaucer hopes to be forgiven, (4) he condemns his poems not conditionally as "something of equivocal worth" but unequivocally as "worldly vanities," and (5) it's for no other reason whatever than to "deny their right to exist" ("the whiche I revoke in my retracciouns") that he gives the names of the poems he condemns. But David is, as he might say, in the homestretch of his book steering away from the obvious and pressing harder and harder after some elixir that will metamorphose him for his smash ending into a medieval Goliath six cubits and a span high, with eyes like laser beams, wearing a pair of sandwich-boards that read in letters of fire: "Remember the deeply moving limitations of poetry!"

Such noodling philosophasters have taken Chaucer over by default because for five hundred years his English has looked like Dutch to the common reader, and because the literary channels of the language were soon choked up by Shakespeare's pathos and rhetoric. The assumption that literature is a knotty string of metaphors to be worked out with footnotes and commentaries isn't eternal truth, it's a legacy from Shakespeare; so is the assumption that for literary purposes life is less a pilgrimage of souls than a tribunal crowded with victims, malefactors, tears, and judgment. Shakespeare is as political and nervous as Gardner-Howard would like Chaucer to be: Shakespeare worries about dynasties and successions, public and private disorder, villains; about women, who are habitually getting out of line themselves or vamping men out of line; as for the women he favors, he doesn't so much idealize them to the level of Artemis or Aphrodite as domesticate them to the level of Mrs. Grundy's finishing school, so that an Imogen or Ophelia or Desdemona is as pretty as a picture and as likely to have thoughts or feelings inconsistent with the headmistress's expectations; or at any moment, grand master of the big bang, he can obliterate the merely personal—"You sulph'rous and thought-executing fires,/Vaunt-couriers of oak-cleaving thunderbolts. . . ."

Shakespeare is the bad conscience of the language; Chaucer is the alternative, the road not taken except by the colloquial language. When Cassandra interprets for Troilus his ominous dream of betrayal, she concludes with a characteristically versatile Chaucerian pun—

This Diomede is inne, and thow art oute.

—the home truth about Criseyde and her new lover that figuratively and literally defines Troilus's terrible loss. Chaucer writes for the human voice, whether it belongs to the prophetess Cassandra or the character Chaucer or such loving and unceremonious friends as Pandarus and Troilus:

"How hastow thus unkyndely [unnaturally] *and longe
Hid this fro me, thow fol?" quod Pandarus.
"Paraunter* [perhaps] *thow myghte after swich oon* [such a one] *longe,
That myn avys* [advice] *anoon may helpen us."
"This were a wonder thing," quod Troilus.
"Thow koudest nevere in love thiselven wisse* [manage]:
How devel maistow brynge me to blisse?"

(As for *Troilus and Cressida*, Shakespeare's contemptible debasement of the same story, it is short on home truths, human voices, and common decency but teems with poetry, misogyny, and campaign speeches.) The power of the colloquial language to express the full range of experience has been exercised in literature only by Chaucer—most intensely in *Troilus and Criseyde*, a book about friendship and love and common decency, the greatest book in the world; most variously in *The Canterbury Tales*, in which everybody sooner or later runs into everybody else, as when in *The Pardoner's Tale* the three scoundrels, pursuing "this false traytour Deeth," encounter the mysterious old man:

"*. . . Why artow al forwrapped save thy face?*
Why lyvestow so longe in so greet age?"
This olde man gan looke in his visage,
And seyde thus: "For I ne kan nat fynde
A man, though that I walked into Ynde,
Neither in citee ne in no village,
That wolde chaunge his youthe for myn age;
And therfore moot [must] *I han* [have] *myn age stille,*
As longe tyme as it is Goddes wille.
Ne Deeth, allas, ne wol nat han my lyf!
Thus walke I, lyk a restelees kaityf [wretch],
And on the ground, which is my moodres [mother's] *gate,*
I knokke with my staf bothe erly and late,
And seye, 'Leve [dear] *mooder, leet me in!*
Lo, how I vanysshe, flessh, and blood, and skyn!
Allas! whan shul my bones been at reste? . . . "

The Pardoner, telling this supremely moral story of the three scoundrels, is himself a blasphemous scoundrel who as he boasts tells it in every country church to astound and swindle the poor and ignorant at the very altar, and tells it here on the pilgrimage to impress with his special talent an audience of respectable citizens who as he knows are themselves, most of them, in their different ways no better than they have to be and just as eager as anybody else to impress the world with their talents. We're all in the same boat, he would say; he sings bawdy songs with his chum the Summoner and drinks like a "good felawe" (but Chaucer the pilgrim remarks, "I trowe he were a geldyng or a mare"); his only mistake is to undervalue his talent and underestimate the effect of so tremendous a parable told by such a scoundrel ("For though myself be a ful vicious man,/A moral tale yet I yow telle kan"), when at the end of it he tries to ease this company of Christians back to earth by maybe making a joke of offering them his false relics and final absolution—

"*. . . Looke which a seuretee is it to yow alle*
That I am in your felaweship yfalle,
That may assoille [absolve] *yow, bothe moore and lasse,*
Whan that the soule shal fro the body passe.

> *I rede* [recommend] *that oure Hoost heere shal bigynne,*
> *For he is moost envoluped in synne.*
> *Com forth, sire Hoost, and offre first anon,*
> *And thou shalt kisse the relikes everychon* [every one],
> *Ye, for a grote* [small coin]! *Unbokele anon thy purs."*
>   *"Nay, nay!" quod he, "thanne have I Cristes curs!*
> *Lat be," quod he, "it shal nat be, so theech* [so may I thrive]!
> *Thou woldest make me kisse thyn olde breech,*
> *And swere it were a relyk of a seint,*
> *Though it were with thy fundement* [backside] *depeint* [stained]!
> *But, by the croys which that Seint Eleyne fond,*
> *I woulde I hadde thy coillons* [testicles] *in myn hond*
> *In stide of relikes or of seintuarie* [reliquary],
> *Lat kutte hem of* [off], *I wol thee helpe hem carie;*
> *They shul be shryned in an hogges toord!"*

The Pardoner demands too much, and something—for instance, the Host's professional good-fellowship—has to give; but sooner or later it will all be knitted back together again:

> *This Pardoner answerde nat a word;*
> *So wrooth he was, no word ne wolde he seye.*
>   *"Now." quod oure Hoost, "I wol no lenger pleye*
> *With thee, ne with noon other angry man."*
> *But right anon the worthy Knyght bigan,*
> *Whan that he saugh* [saw] *that al the peple lough* [laughed],
> *"Namoore of this, for it is right ynough!*
> *Sire Pardoner, be glad and myrie of cheere;*
> *And ye, sire Hoost, that been to me so deere,*
> *I prey yow that ye kisse the Pardoner.*
> *And Pardoner, I prey thee, drawe thee neer,*
> *And, as we diden, lat us laughe and pleye."*
> *Anon they kiste, and ryden forth hir weye.*

The pilgrims don't hesitate to make summary judgments of each other: "He was," pronounces the Friar, "if I shal yeven hym his laude *[due]*,/A theef, and eek *[also]* a somnour, and a baude"; but no living souls are excluded from Chaucer's pilgrimage, not even Friars, Summoners, Pardoners, and Chaucerians.

Twenty-Three Stone-Deaf Theologians

There aren't many things in the world less electrifying than the ten, six, or four latest Shakespeare books.[1] "It is clear," says Ralph Berry with undue confidence,

> that . . . [the situations in *Much Ado*] amount to variants of a single central situation: the problem of knowing. This problem is carefully delineated in *Much Ado;* the metaphysical probings of *Hamlet* are, I believe, nowhere hinted at. The concern of the characters in *Much Ado* is to determine from behavior the feelings and attitudes of the other characters. All other aspects of the problem are excluded.

No Danish pastry, then; nothing but daily bread: "the simple word 'know'—so banal, so profound--" which "in all its forms . . . occurs 84 times in *Much Ado*"; not Who am I? but the basic Shakespearean catechism:

> Claud. (or *Oth.* or *Leon,* or *Post.*) Who was that lady I seen you in bed with last night?
> Bora. (or *Cas.* or *Pol.* or *Iach.*) That was no lady, that was your wife.

"'Know' is the conceptual principle" of *Much Ado About Nothing.* "'Eye,'" on the other foot, "is easily the main motif in *A Midsummer Night's Dream;* it occurs in that form 20 times and in compounds and plurals a further 48 times": Demetrius and Lysander "are subjectivists who advance their retinal impressions as objective and rational justifications for their conduct." In *The Comedy of Errors,* with its two pairs of twin brothers, "the theme that emerges is the quest for identity." It's rash, though, to conclude that Berry, because he hasn't the ghost of an idea and lacks a way with words, lacks a way with "words": "Words compose the central symbol of *Love's Labour's Lost,*" in which the word "'word' (and its plural) occurs 48 times." Retinally, words are mere print and seldom mean what they say, so that when in *Much Ado* Beatrice commands Benedick to "Kill Claudio,"

---

[1] Ralph Berry, *Shakespeare's Comedies* (Princeton University Press, 1972). Thomas MacFarland, *Shakespeare's Pastoral Comedy* (University of North Carolina Press, 1972). Ruth Nero, *Tragic Form in Shakespeare* (Princeton University Press, 1972). Howard Felperin, *Shakespearean Romance* (Princeton University Press, 1972).

Several points converge in this terse imperative other than the purely theatrical. It is a version of "If you love me, *then* prove it." Moreover, the issue is symbolic. "Kill Claudio" is to kill the Claudio in oneself—to kill the force of distrust. It is to yield to the value of trust, formed on a sufficient appraisal of another, and implicit faith. In a word, it is to love. . . .

In a word, nothing's right or left but antic word-slinging makes it so:

> The writing of *The Comedy of Errors* is distinguished by a rigid concentration on the work in hand. It contains at least two major seams that ask to be mined: the ideas of gold-credit-value, and the situation of law infringed. But the iron demands of a comedy solely based on mistaken identity mean that these temptations (as surely they must have been) are suppressed. Those rich seams would have been incompatible with the development of this play. An ironic analysis of mercantile values . . . .

and so forth. Ironing out such paronomastic flypaper shouldn't distract us, however, from the deep gloom of Shakespeare's comedies: *The Comedy of Errors* is "pregnant with tragedy"; "The season of death ends . . . *[Love's Labour's Lost], as the news of death had stilled the Worthies";* in *As You Like It* Rosalind is ominously snippy to poor Phebe; *Twelfth Night* "implies a sour awareness that the real winter is to come."

Even more of a drag than the comic Shakespeare and his saucy transvestites is Thomas McFarland, who opens *Shakespeare's Pastoral Comedy* with the proposition that "Every work of art . . . is a consolation for the nothingness of our lives." As if nothingness isn't bad enough, McFarland goes on to assemble some preliminary evidence in behalf of the claims of sexual paranoia:

> The reason for . . . [Leontes'] molten torment may seem, to an industrious and mechanical scholar, sitting comfortably in his study, to be only a matter of dramatic license or Jacobean convention; it will not seem so to those whose misfortune has been actually to experience such agony. For the probabilities in such situations all too often support the fact of guilt. "There have been," says Leontes in recognition of the world's way, ". . . cuckolds ere now;/And many a man there is, even at this present,/Now while I speak this, holds his wife by th' arm/That little thinks she has been sluic'd in's absence,/And his pond fish'd by his next neighbor, by/Sir Smile, his neighbor." . . . .
>
> Such are the dramatic probabilities, and such too are the probabilities in lived experience. A newspaper report (and perhaps the more ephemeral the document, the more depressingly timeless the statistic) on the day this page is being written, estimates that in America "60 per cent of all husbands and 35 to 40 per cent of all wives cheat on their spouses." . . . .

"The most persistent theme in all Shakespeare," says McFarland (correctly), ". . . is that of human faithlessness. It is the very substance of the history plays, the most tormented preoccupation of the tragedies, the chief ingredient of the bitterness in the middle and late comedies, all haunted by the theme of sonnet 92: 'Thou mayst be false, and yet I know it not.' Othello's suspicions, like those of Leontes, are in the instance unjustified, but they derive motive power from the high probability of a young wife's betrayal"—i.e. about 35 to 40 per cent. (Yet McFarland quite misses the plain meaning of Shakespeare's most beautiful mad song of sexual anxiety, the Spring song at the end of *Love's Labour's Lost,* and blissfully declares that "The final songs of spring and winter . . . reinforce the mood of mutual happiness.")

For a literary scholar face to face with the nothingness of our lives as well as other high probabilities, one consolation is art, and another is the fast shuffle of index cards:

> Much of human desire is and always has been a longing to animate the inanimate. We need discuss neither anthropological formulations such as Tylor's animism, nor the speculations of philosophers: Strato's hylozoism, Leibniz's monadology, or, with reference to the separation of thought and thing, Sartre's *pour soi* and *en soi,* or Coleridge's persisting question, "what is the difference or distinction between thing and thought?" We need not invoke such matters because the realization of the difference between thought and thing, and the desire to animate the inanimate, are part of the fabric of all men's awareness.

True, we need not and should not.

This effect as of a debate among twenty-three stone-deaf theologians pervades the book, in the course of which authorized pronouncements get made about the nature of pastoral, the nature of comedy, the nature of pastoral comedy, and the nature of each of the five pastoral comedies considered (the quality of the pronouncements isn't misrepresented by McFarland's chapter subtitles: "The Playfulness of *Love's Labour's Lost*"; "The Happiness of *A Midsummer-Night's Dream*"). So it's pleasant to add that the Appendix is a fine indignant unauthorized defense of Falstaff, in which, having elaborated an interesting comparison between Falstaff and Socrates, McFarland denies that the rejection scene is "both right and necessary" or even "a required public demonstration":

> Required? By whom? To conform with what moral teaching? Now it may be that a youth should not consort with the likes of Falstaff; but if he does accept such a man, he also accepts the responsibilities of friendship. All human meaning depends upon such a fact. The whole agony of Hamlet testifies to the moral horror of precisely such breaches of human contract, express or implied. . . .
>
> To argue, as do some commentators, both here and in broader contexts, that the moralities of human interaction suggested by Shakespeare's presentations either should be seen as the result of stage conventions, or . . . are enslaved to perversely naive popular conceptions supposedly dominant at the time, or, still again, can be explained by Shakespeare's inability satisfactorily

> to transmute his source materials, is, I contend, to reveal fundamental misunderstandings of the nature of his art and its relationship to life. It is subtly to patronize Elizabethan experience; to postulate, in reckless exaggeration, existential differences (as opposed to those of the surface) between our own humanity and that of Shakespeare's time, which after all, was a mere five or six lifetimes ago. The attitudes crystallized most clearly in the work of Stoll, which have lain so heavily on Shakespeare studies, must be rejected once and for all—in his own books and whenever they appear in the work of his spiritual kindred and progeny. They discount Shakespeare's genius and reduce his humanity. . . .

Still, there are defenses and defenses. McFarland's here reads like a friend's, whereas much of Ruth Nevo's book reads like a closing statement for the accused, now and then even like a signed testimonial:

> The contrast with Brutus' speech could not be greater, and indeed the pair of speeches are a dramatic, as well as a forensic, tour de force. In each case the style is the man. and the projection of personality through contrasted devices of rhetoric is so consummately skillful, demonstrates so unerring a linguistic insight, as to make one yield to a fantasy of regret for the treatise *De Poetica* that Shakespeare never wrote. . . .

If only Shakespeare had written a *book*!

Tragic Form in Shakespeare is long and very busy: strenuously got up, carefully put together, tirelessly argued. Nevo takes the five-act division of the tragedies (she says nothing about the five-act division of the non-tragic plays) to be not a convenience or scaffolding but the very tissue and articulation of each work: "the structure of a Shakespearean tragedy is to be apprehended as an unfolding five-phased sequence, continuous, accumulative, and consummatory, rather than as a simple up-down movement, or even as more complex thesis-antithesis-synthesis." The five phases she calls (1) Predicament, (2) Psychomachia, (3) Peripeteia, (4) Perspectives of Irony and Pathos, and (5) Catastrophe; and her explications of the tragedies are designed to prove the conformity of these phases with the corresponding acts of each of the tragedies. Though the peripeteia (reversal of intention) occurs invariably in Act III, the tragic deed itself—what the hero does to make the reversal irreversible—can occur at almost any point in the five-phased sequence, very early as in *Lear* or *Macbeth*, very late as in *Othello* or *Coriolanus*, with corresponding modifications of proportion and effect. For the tragic deed she chooses Aristotle's term "error" in an attempt to play down moral and pious implications:

> it is the passage of character to self-discovery . . . . , and not a providential distribution of rewards and penalties, that constitutes the axis of development in Shakespearean tragedy. I place the emphasis therefore upon the act of erroneous choice, rather than, though not necessarily in exclusion of,

Pauline sin or Bradleyan flaw, the use of which terms invites a moralistic view of the development of events.

But, whether or not missionary zeal or Pauline sin or Bradleyan flaw is relevant to the tragedies, Shakespeare does have a Manichaean or Sadean or merely melodramatic fascination with the image of helpless innocence threatened and overthrown: Macduff's children, Ophelia, Desdemona; babes in the wood fit to be tied—an image that didn't appeal to Sophocles or Aeschylus and that isn't any more tragic than a human-interest front-page story about an eight-year-old falling down a well. Nevo's structural hypothesis is like all the other hypotheses in ignoring this aspect of Shakespeare. Moreover, like all the others, it's a facade for the same old devotion to Shakespeare's peerless verse and infallible psychological realism, which together are supposed to authenticate everything: for example, treating *Richard II* as a proto-tragedy, she remarks on the "high vein of prophetic patriotism," the "utmost seriousness," the "impressive dignity "of the following passage:

> *For that our kingdom's earth should not be soil'd*
> *With that dear blood which it hath fostered;*
> *And for our eyes do hate the dire aspect*
> *Of civil wounds plough'd up with neighbours' sword,*
> *And for we think the eagle-winged pride*
> *Of sky-aspiring and ambitious thoughts,*
> *With rival-hating envy, set on you*
> *To wake our peace, which in our country's cradle*
> *Draws the sweet infant breath of gentle sleep....*

To the common reader, however, this sort of thing seems the stock-in-trade of any Elizabethan hack: the galumphing lead-footedness of the verse, the banality of the images, the somnambulistic allotment of a single, usually redundant adjective per noun, the banal and redundant hyphenated adjectives. "Shakespeare always speaks for his kings," says Tolstoy, "in one and the same inflated, empty language": the comment is rude but not unfounded; Shakespeare's verse and diction for ceremonial occasions improve with age, but a certain fee-fo-fum persists among the image-clusters. (In *Shakespearean Romance* Howard Felperin observes cautiously that "Public moralizing in Shakespeare is often sententious.")

Nevo enjoys scoring points against T. S. Eliot:

> No character in drama has produced more powerful an impression of spontaneity, of lifelike unpredictability, than Hamlet. T. S. Eliot abandoned the enterprise of interpretation altogether, judged the play "an artistic failure," and diagnosed its cause as Hamlet's "domination by an emotion which is inexpressible, because it is in excess of the facts as they appear," and this because Shakespeare was under some mysterious "compulsion to attempt to express the inexpressibly horrible." Whatever problems can or cannot

be solved by an appeal to a dramatist's entirely hypothetical psychology, it might be observed that "the facts as they appear"—a faithless mother, a murdered father, a usurped inheritance, a venal and hypocritical court society—could provide, for spirits less fastidious than T. S. Eliot's, sufficient grounds for a quite considerable measure of dismay....

But Hamlet the hero of European literature and poltergeist of the Western mind *is* a mystery, he isn't explained by "the facts as they appear," he fathers innumerable mysterious progeny like Clarissa's Lovelace, the Marquis de Sade, Manfred (both Walpole's and Byron's), Pechorin, Eugene Onegin, Heathcliff, Stravrogin, Byron himself, and impresses nearly everybody except the Shakespeareans as the prototypical outcast hero, the man without a context, dominated by "an emotion which is inexpressible, because it is in excess of the facts as they appear," an emotion which can drive him to such an extremity of moral distemper that a man as wise and good as Dr. Johnson is obliged to judge it satanic: "This speech [when Hamlet happens on Claudius praying], in which Hamlet, represented as a virtuous character, is not content with taking blood for blood, but contrives damnation for the man that he would punish, is too horrible to be read or to be uttered [i.e. Eliot's "inexpressibly horrible"]." Or one may give up and settle for Nevo's flippant "commonsense" reliance on the exigencies of the plot: "No delay, no play"; maybe what she sees as Hamlet's "lifelike unpredictability" is only Shakespeare's practical need to keep pushing a dead plot (Tolstoy argues that Hamlet is nothing but a package of mutually conflicting, moment-by-moment theatrical expediencies; that the secret of Hamlet—gigantic cipher—is that he has no character at all). Nevo thinks she's justifying Shakespeare when she says that the delay is "the basic *donnée* of the play"; though of course a *donnée* isn't something given, it's something taken, and Shakespeare, anxious to turn out another hit or even another potboiler, is as responsible for the implausibilities as for the opportunities of Belleforest, Kyd, or the *ur-Hamlet*. At any rate, Hamlet has his reasons on the stage, and Shakespeare has his reasons at the boxoffice; but Nevo's quarrel about Hamlet's character isn't with Eliot, it's with Western civilization.

"His mother," she says, "has predisposed him to believe in women's perfidy, has produced in him a revulsion from sex and the stratagems of sex." This bonneted little toddler of a Hamlet recalls another spirit too noble to do some rudimentary thinking about women's perfidy, or to die without a public speech of self-absolution: so Nevo bridles at another comment of Eliot's, that Othello in his last speech is "cheering himself up"—a "notorious stricture" she condemns for its insensitivity to the technique of "self-dramatization," the very technique which as she believes "accounts for the realism of the great characters of realistic drama." "So-called 'self-dramatization' is the medium of existence of dramatic characters. They enact themselves, they unfold themselves; they have no *other* mode of being of which the dramatic representation is proxy"; and, anyhow, the "words [of Othello's last speech] are, in fact, despite the perplexities they have caused to literal-minded critics, the plain and lambent truth." But Nevo is answering a question Eliot didn't ask: the question has nothing to do with "truth" (verifiability); it has to do with propriety, and perhaps consistency, and possibly the Shakespearean high style as an instrument of pathos. Tolstoy, for instance, contends that Othello's suicide (Shakespeare didn't find it in Cinthio, as Tolstoy points out), "however [theatrically] effective . . . quite destroys the conception of his firm character":

> If he really suffers from grief and remorse then, when intending to kill himself, he would not utter phrases about his own services, about a pearl, about his eyes dropping tears "as fast as the Arabian trees their medicinable gum," and still less could he talk about the way a Turk scolded a Venetian, and how "thus" he punished him for it! So that . . . our conception of his character is constantly infringed by false pathos and by the unnatural speeches he utters.

The old Tolstoy was quite a scold himself, and his angry scolding of Shakespeare is generally ignored as an intercultural embarrassment; but at least one ought to pay attention when the supreme master of realistic fiction decides to speak out on the subject of the writer universally considered the supreme master of realistic drama. When Tolstoy says that Iago is "a complete villain, a deceiver, a thief, and avaricious; he robs

Roderigo, succeeds in all sorts of impossible designs, and is therefore a quite unreal person"; when, having synopsized the first scene of *Lear*, he says that "the reader or spectator cannot believe that a king, however old and stupid, could believe the words of the wicked daughters with whom he had lived all their lives, and not trust his favorite daughter, but curse and banish her; therefore the reader or spectator cannot share the feeling of the persons who take part in this unnatural scene"—when he says such shocking, artless things, we recognize their "truth" (verifiability) before ascending into a cloud of symbols, myths, image-clusters, and basic *données*. Likewise, when Tolstoy names the "false pathos and . . . unnatural speeches" in Shakespeare's ultimate tidying up of Othello, we recognize a pair of truths for which we might prefer friendlier names.

Pathos, genuine or false, isn't restricted to Nevo's fourth-act "Perspectives of Irony and Pathos," it's the typical mood of the Shakespearean catastrophe, whether Othello and Hamlet pleading to be understood, or Lear fumbling with a button, or Cleopatra gorgeously playing the role of queenly constancy for the benefit of her awestruck attendants, or Macbeth on the way out like a brave warrior fighting. Nevo thinks of the catastrophe as a moment of tidying up into "self-discovery," when the protagonist, albeit unused to the melting mood, fiddles away at it with swelling orchestral accompaniment to persuade the spectators that he or she isn't a gullible wife-murderer, or a bedeviled teen-age procrastinator, or an ill-tempered old fool, or a mere *femme fatale*, or a self-serving political assassin. The Shakespearean catastrophe does seem to aim at eliding all the imbecilities, miscalculations, and crimes into a conclusion that soars above mere fact; not much self-discovery, but floods of self-admiring tears from the awestruck spectators: What language! O, the pity of it! Iago himself has no power to rob Othello of *that*.

When, on an earlier stage, Creon enters at the end of *Antigone,* another father bearing the body of his dead child, he speaks without evading the fact of his guilt:

Nothing you say can touch me any more.
My own blind heart has brought me
From darkness to final darkness. Here you see
The father murdering, the murdered son—
And all my civic wisdom!
Haimon my son, so young, so young to die,
I was the fool, not you; and you died for me.[2]

And the very different Creon of *Oedipus Rex,* having listened to self-blinded Oedipus lament the fate of his children, cuts him short: "Enough. You have wept enough. Now go within."

Oedipus	I must, but it is hard.
Creon	Time eases all things.
Oedipus	But you must promise—
Creon	Say what you desire.
Oedipus	Send me from Thebes!
Creon	God grant that I may!
Oedipus	But since God hates me . . . .
Creon	No, he will grant your wish.
Oedipus	You promise?
Creon	I cannot speak beyond my knowledge.
Oedipus	Then lead me in.
Creon	Come now, and leave your children.
Oedipus	No! Do not take them from me!
Creon	Think no longer That you are in command here, but rather think How, when you were, you served your own destruction.

"Exeunt into the house all but the Chorus," whose brief admonitory summary concludes the play. No violins here; and Creon's severe, watchful irony helps hold Oedipus back from the flights of Shakespearean self-dramatization that Eliot regards as self-deception, Tolstoy as impropriety and melodrama, but Nevo as the very means of the tragic catastrophe, as indeed identical on the radar screen with the flights of angels that sing those sweet princes all the way to the boneyard.

---

[2] From the translation by Dudley Fitts and Robert Fitzgerald, in Sophocles, *The Oedipus Cycle* (Harvest Books, 1949).

So it's rather stunning to turn up a critic who may well believe that his own new synthesis can accommodate Eliot, Tolstoy, and Nevo together: the first two are right because Shakespeare's tragic hero is really a romantic hero; and the latter is right because the tragedies are great (if preliminary). Howard Felperin ranges himself among those latitudinarian theologians who grant everything to the skeptic if only the skeptic will grant that even when God nods He's not one smidgen less divine:

> Shakespearean tragedy characteristically places its heroes in situations which require nothing less than a radical transformation of the self. Othello's failure to remake himself is typical of most of the tragic heroes. In his final speech, whether or not he is trying simply to "cheer himself up," he recollects a deed of derring-do from his past to resurrect and validate his conception of himself as a brave and noble hero of romance, a role whose inadequacy at this point is dramatically obvious to everyone except him. One reason critics are tempted to "redeem" Shakespeare's tragic heroes is that most of them try so hard to redeem themselves.

Shakespeare's tragic hero is, in short, as self-deluded at the end as he was at the beginning: "Hamlet, Othello, and Lear are desperate for redemption in their closing speeches . . . to the point of falsifying their experience to attain some semblance of it"—an ultimate condition which Eliot, Tolstoy, and Nevo would consider disastrously unresolved, but which doesn't bother Felperin at all because it's an index of Shakespeare's capacity for dreaming up another universe even while (or if) he nods. If the tragedies (great, of course) are, without necessary prejudice to their own structure, incipient romances that lack only some arbitrary external redemptive force to turn back the clock and cancel the misery, it's hard to see how Felperin could object to the Nahum Tate *Lear* except, perhaps, on the ground of style. But the problem doesn't occur to him; and, since romance (incorrigible self-deception, stage trickery, implausibility, benignant deities descending from the flies) is transparently a good thing, he insists on admiring anything he can call romantic, till in a gesture worthy of a Unitarian Pope he goes so far as to embrace the New York Public Library: "To the extent that all literary experience involves a journey into another world inherently removed from present time and place, all literature is fundamentally romantic."

Felperin has a habit of admitting the worst in the course of asserting its claim to be the best:

> *The Tempest* is finally intolerant of all attempts to allegorize or idealize experience, whether they be ours or those of the characters within the play. Prospero's scenario is a noble one to be sure, born of the loftiest ideals and aspirations of the Renaissance mind, and if he could successfully stage it, he would no doubt deserve the titles of god and superman, philosopher-king, and ideal Christian prince that critics have bestowed on him. But *The Tempest* is as much about the limitations of the idealizing imagination as it is about its power, and of this Prospero seems to grow increasingly aware.

Why, for example, does Prospero persist in referring to his art as a "vanity" and a "rough magic"? Why does he feel that he has to abandon it at all? And finally, just how successful is his art in producing his stated objectives?

And Felperin goes on to include Hamlet himself, with his "self-righteous euphoria characteristic of stage 'revengers'" among the "histrionic" figures for whom Shakespeare shows "a healthy mistrust." Felperin's own self-righteous euphoria doesn't for a moment entertain the possibility that Prospero's nihilism may be getting out of hand (*The Tempest* is "finally intolerant" all right, and as gloomy as Ralph Berry's hilarious reconstructions of the comedies), or that Shakespeare may agree with the obsequious lackey Horatio in thinking Hamlet as princely a fellow as most of Western civilization has thought since; that in any case both plays are full of shadowy corners unrelated to the overt action.

As for Posthumus and Leontes, Felperin is more than ready to offer up such fall guys on the altar of the irreproachable Master:

> There is more than a touch of Cloten's sexual brutality and Iachimo's dirty-mindedness about Posthumus until both are finally purged by his ordeal of repentance, and in the peculiar logic of romance, his reformation is reflected in that of Iachimo, who has spent a night in Imogen's bedroom and wears her ring. Propsero will also purge by a similar kind of symbolic substitution whatever taint of Calibanism resides in Ferdinand by making him perform Caliban's role of log-bearer. The point is not that the ageing Shakespeare has grown puritanical as is sometimes said, but that love is what binds the universe of romance together and faith is what makes it live, and the romancer who understands the form must come down hard on all perversions of love and betrayals of faith. In *Pericles* these perversions take the form of incest and prostitution; *Cymbeline* and *The Winter's Tale* present that sexual unhealthiness and immaturity which see only adultery and betrayal in the most unwavering faith.

Doubtless Posthumus and Leontes behave very badly (unless it can be proved that they are motivated by basic *données*); doubtless love and faith, not to mention fatherland and motherhood, ought to be defended if they happen to be attacked; but one would like to know why "the romancer who understands the form must come down hard on all perversions of love and betrayals of faith." When Chaucer writes romances—*The Knight's Tale, The Clerk's Tale, The Franklin's Tale,* even *Troilus and Criseyde*—he doesn't come down hard on perversions or even betrayals; when Mozart and Schikaneder collaborate on the romance-opera *The Magic Flute*, they take love and faith pretty much for granted and deal mainly with the trials and ceremonies of both; and the list of other exceptions to Felperin's First Law of Romance is endless. The question is, then, not why in the romances Shakespeare insists on disapproving of perversions and betrayals, but why he treats them at all; and an answer is implicit in the fact that Shakespeare treats them at length, over and over again, in many of his non-romance plays besides as well as in most of his non-dramatic poems. The answer may be that these are subjects Shakespeare feels driven to treat ("Thou mayst be false, and yet I know it not"), that something one may fairly call obsession compels him to seek them out and redefine them again and again in situations and images—the sonnets', Posthumus', Hamlet's, Lear's—of pathological extremity. The point isn't that the ageing Shakespeare grew puritanical: his obsession with what might be going on behind closed doors was lifelong, he nursed it early and carried it to the end of the line; and critics who imagine unprecedented philosophical serenity and summits of reconciliation in the romances are taking Prospero's pipe-dreams more seriously than Prospero does.

Critics at work on the romances labor under a special difficulty, because they have to show that the last plays of the supreme dramatist breathe the air of some barely accessible peak or other. Felperin quotes Henry James observing enthusiastically that in *The Tempest* Shakespeare's "human curiosity . . . surrender[s] to the luxury of expertness": i.e. ingenious fable, marvelous verse, very few characters, almost no relationships—whether or not James means this much, a strong case could be made out for it. But Felperin isn't satisfied to found a book on such a case. So about *The Winter's Tale* he swallows hard and says that "No play of Shakespeare's (I venture to say not even *Hamlet* or *Lear*) creates a world of greater amplitude and variety"; and. discussing *Pericles,* he tosses into the fire that dry chestnut the "power and universality" of "the religious drama of the Middle Ages":

> The peculiar power and universality of *Pericles* and the subsequent romances, it seems to me, has less to do with their "conventional" or "mythic" or "archetypal" dimension than with their medieval dimension. Or perhaps the two are finally inseparable and the same, to the extent that the apparent crudeness and naivete of such plays is the condition of their power and universality. Because virtually everything in such plays is subordinated to a didactic purpose: they begin not in the middle of an action but at the beginning and proceed linearly to the end; they frankly announce and reiterate their designs on the audience; and their characters are simplified types rather than complex personalities. They may strike us as technically crude, yet there is an important sense in which they hold the mirror up to nature as faithfully as the most sophisticated of plays, which we mistakenly equate with naturalistic [sic].

While waiting for Felperin to explain (he never does) the "important sense" in which the romances do this or that as faithfully as other plays do, thousands of exasperated readers shout that crudeness and naïveté—even taken as a singular noun, even qualified by the weasel-word "apparent"—"isn't" the condition of anything except the crude and naïve: and the half-assed, tail-end scholars, critics, and commentators who have been lately discovering that the miracle and mystery plays compete with Sophocles and Shakespeare are like the art dealers and collectors who set themselves, everything else having zoomed out of reach, to heating up the prices of nineteenth-century American primitives. If Felperin would like to demonstrate that Shakespeare's romances are, as he seems to think, an improvement on the tragedies, he'll have to do better than the ludicrous quasi-anthropological condescension about those quaint Chaucerian peasants out of whose catholic hearts and bowels came the smoking raw stuff of literary greatness. After all, it was Chaucer who wrote *The Miller's Tale;* no ploughman wrote *Sir Gawain and the Green Knight*; and if *Pericles* reclaims the crudeness and naïveté that Chaucer and the Gawain poet were pleased to ignore or parody, then so much the worse for *Pericles.*

The First World Shakespeare Congress was held in Vancouver in August 1971, and a volume of its proceedings has been published.[3] Among much boondoggling is an essay by Jill Levenson, titled "What the Silence Said: Still Points in 'King Lear,'" the tone and content of which indicate that Shakespeare's identification with the Almighty is nearly complete. Miss Levenson notes that Cordelia's silence when her father asks the kingdom-splitting question "resonates like the silences of the Bible, fairy-tale and folk ritual, analogous moments that need reflecting upon." (Okay. I'm reflecting. I'm *reflecting!*) More, "A remark by the composer John Cage about silence suggests what we might find in Cordelia's: 'Keeping one's mind/on the emptiness,/on the space/one can see anything can be in it, is, as/a matter of fact, in it.'" Miss Levenson moves on to Abraham's dialogue with God as interpreted by Erich Auerbach, the dismissal from Eden, Noah (of the Ark), Joseph and his brothers, Moses, Jonah and the whale, Job ("The week-long silent reception of Job's calamity speaks for itself"), the Marys, Martha, and Salome; "But"—significantly—"it is Christ himself whose silence resounds most forcefully in each of the gospels." Evidently, this First—Pauline?—Congress is the modest inauguration of a new religion, and by about the tenth time will have come for a majority of "delegates" to ratify the Virgin Birth of Holy Willie. Elucidating the silence in *Lear,* Miss Levenson takes thirteen pages and sixty-four footnotes: seventy-seven to zero; about the proper ratio between commentary and Scripture. When she gets to the actual words of the play, she may be ready to undertake a new *Patrologia*. Atheists had better keep an eye on Vancouver.

---

[3] Clifford Leech and J. M. R. Margeson (ed.), *Shakespeare 1971* (University of Toronto Press, 1972).

III
Operators: If They Don't Like It Here Why Don't They Go Back Where They Came From?

Adorable Ideas and Absent Plenitudes

THE beauty part is that when I come right down to it I'm nobody's baby but my own! says the book. Writers are obsolete, man is fading fast, semes and bytes are in the saddle, everything reads like a bad translation from the French. Last year Northrop Frye became the first structuralist President of the Modern Language Association and in his Presidential Address launched his mission to the home folks: welcomed the "suggestion" by "some critics" that "the unconscious . . . is linguistically structured"; hailed without naming its foreign perpetrator the Barthean "zero degree of writing" and deciphered it with unscrupulous inaccuracy into something warmly familiar (French-Fryed Blake—"where the literary and all its conventions disappear and only the pure prophetic vision is left"); saluted "the authority of the word speaking for itself"; and disclaimed his books, royalties, academic salary, and Presidential Address. None of it would have happened if one day Rimbaud hadn't wearied of explaining his poems to tourists and said, "*Je' est un autre*": "'I' is another." "You *is*?" cried Verlaine in a jealous rage as he drew his revolver and opened fire. "'I' *ain't*," retorted Rimbaud, gone in a flash and rematerializing on the next boat-train to Africa where he spent the rest of his life dancing chic to sheik. Unfortunately his careless remarks were overheard by a professor who started a religion whose votaries at this very moment commandeer the lecterns like mad custodians announcing on campus platforms everywhere that "we" is the zero degree of absolutely nowhere:

> The human sciences, which begin by making man an object of knowledge, find, as their work advances, that "man" disappears under structural analysis. "The goal of the human sciences," writes Lévi-Strauss, "is not to constitute man but to dissolve him." . . . Michel Foucault argues . . . "that man is only a recent invention, a figure not yet two centuries old, a simple fold in our knowledge, and that he will disappear as soon as that knowledge has found a new form."[1]

"Subjectivity," says Roland Barthes, "is a plenary image . . . whose deceptive plenitude is merely the wake of all the codes which constitute me, so that my subjectivity has ultimately the generality of stereotypes"[2] (though I *resembles* plenitude I is really all platitude): in short, man (if Barthes may be considered representative) is boring and outmoded if not defunct; and Jacques Derrida, worry wart extraordinary, frets

---

[1] Jonathan Culler, *Structuralist Poetics* (Cornell University Press, 1976).
[2] Roland Barthes, *S/Z* (Hill and Wang, 1974).

himself into a Yeatsian pipe-dream that not only man but even structuralism is on the brink of being superseded by the slope-sided glitch:

> we are only glimpsing today the *conception,* the *formation,* the *gestation,* the *labor.* I employ these words, I admit, with a glance toward the business of childbearing—but also with a glance toward those who, in a company from which I do not exclude myself, turn their eyes away in the face of the as yet un-nameable which is proclaiming itself and which can do so, as is necessary whenever a birth is in the offing, only under the species of the non-species, in the formless, mute, infant, and terrifying form of monstrosity.[3]

When the French get heavy, they make the Germans look like ballerinas.

"Paris is terrorized by its intellectuals," writes Jane Kramer in her Letter from Paris in *The New Yorker* of July 4, 1977. "Roland Barthes has just written an alphabet of love called 'Fragments d'un Discours Amoureux,' and Parisians are busy discussing the plenitude of absence and the idea of the adorable. Michel Foucault is two volumes into a five-volume disquisition on the categories of sexuality which, with luck, should take him several years." What is sex but a recent invention? a simple fold in our knowledge? the formless, mute, and infant form of fashion? A decade ago Barthes published a structuralist study of fashion called *Système de la Mode*; and Jonathan Culler, self(if you'll pardon the expression)-appointed Anglo-American protégé and epigone of these operators, reverently summarizes its argument, which to anybody who has never in his life looked at a fashion ad in *The New Yorker* or anywhere else might come as a surprise:

> Reflexive verbs make the garments themselves agents of their stylishness (. . . *Dresses are becoming longer; Black mink asserts itself*). The arbitrary decisions about what shall be fashionable are concealed by a rhetoric which does not name the agents responsible, which takes effects and, concealing their causes, treats them as facts that have been observed or as phenomena which develop in accordance with some independent and autonomous process. . . .

In other words the writer of fashion ads, whose personal presence in the ads is so obvious that his efforts to conceal it have to be noticed even by a structuralist, proves to be a structuralist himself who treats his texts exactly as Barthes treats literary texts, as for example Barthes treats Balzac's *Sarrasine* with stupefying charm and repetitiveness in S/Z, where the arbitrary decisions about what shall be literature are concealed by a rhetoric which does not name the agent responsible, which takes the novella's effects and treats them as phenomena developing in accordance with some independent and autonomous process ("the authority of the word speaking for itself"), and which couldn't fool even an ad-writer. So *Système de la Mode* may have been Barthes's

---

[3] Richard Macksey and Eugenio Donato (eds.), *The Structuralist Controversy* (The Johns Hopkins University Press, 1972).

premature confession that he's jiving us and man isn't dead after all but only hiding out on Madison Avenue behind Foster Grant shades and a Sassoon hair-styling. Meanwhile an ambitious novice like Culler is encouraged by the hullabaloo to try to conceal his harrowingly obvious personal presence behind the independent and autonomous process of literature no less (because what human being would be responsible for such stuff?): "To recognize that there is in this respect a continuity within the novel—between Flaubert and Robbe-Grillet, between Sterne and Sollers—does not free us to abandon the notion of *jouissance* as a rapture of dislocation produced by ruptures or violations of intelligibility."

For structuralism asks us to bear in mind while Culler violates his ruptures that the critic isn't just a critic, he—or it—is equally a creator (Barthes: "we have today a new perspective of consideration which . . . is common . . . to the creator and the critic, whose tasks . . . are beginning to interrelate, perhaps even to merge"; President Frye: "perhaps the real motivation in literary scholarship is . . . some sense behind it of an identity of criticism and creation, . . . of the search for knowledge and the production of vision"). Criticism, which has been known to originate in envy of the novelist or poet ("the Author—. . . that somewhat decrepit deity of the old criticism," says Barthes), sometimes ends in competition: "the seme [of Wealth] is 'cited'; we," says Barthes plurally, two for the price of one, new critic plus decrepit deity, "would like to give this word its tauromachian meaning: the *citar* is the stamp of the heel, the torero's arched stance which summons the bull to the banderilleros." "Wow!" exclaims *tout Paris,* marveling at the plenitude of bull. Time wounds all heels. Cynosure of roaring thousands, suavely poised with arched eyebrows at the center of the logomachian arena, Barthes's bull-thrower awaits forever the moment of truth.

S/Z intends to sink the pretensions of the "classic text" by subjecting an instance of it, Balzac's *Sarrasine,* to the full battery of structural analysis.[4] Barthes detests the "classic text"—all fiction written earlier than Robbe-Grillet and Company—because it "impose[s] a dense plenitude of meaning or, if one prefers, a certain redundancy, a kind of semantic prattle typical of the archaic—or infantile—era of modern discourse, marked by the excessive fear of failing to communicate meaning . . . whence, in reaction, . . . our latest—or 'new'—novels . . . [which] state the event without accompanying it with its signification." As for *Sarrasine* in particular, it's a trivial and well-made mystery-story with an enormous number of clues (which Barthes mistakes for meanings) and one ultimate solution (which Barthes mistakes for meaning): castration, which gets mentioned on almost every page of Barthes's commentary and which probably represents the plenitude of absence. The mystery-writer's bag of tricks is, then, the master-critic's clue to the deficiencies of the classic text:

> A classic narrative always gives this impression: the author first conceives the signified (or the generality) and then finds for it, according to the chance of

---

[4] Very technical, full of marks and abbreviations, like a railroad timetable: (305) "*Come.*"
She led the Frenchman along several back streets * ACT. "Route": 1: to set out ** ACT. "Route": 2: to walk along. *** REF. Mysterious and romantic Italy (back streets).

his imagination, "good" signifiers, probative examples; the classic author is like an artisan bent over the workbench of meaning and selecting the best *expressions* for the concept he has already formed. For instance, *timidity*: one selects the sound of a champagne cork, a story of a snake, a story of highwaymen. However, the signifying imagination is even more profitable if it fills a double function; it then endeavors to produce doubly articulated signs, committed to that solidarity of notations which defines the readerly; for instance, *impiety*: one could be content to represent the subject playing games in church, but it is a greater art to link impiety to the child's vocation (by showing Sarrasine whittling licentious pieces during Mass) or to contrast it with La Zambinella's superstition (which makes Sarrasine laugh); for sculpture and pusillanimity belong to different narrative networks, and the closer and better calculated the anastomosis of the signifiers, the more the text is regarded as "well written."

Here, for example, is Balzac describing Sarrasine's childhood: "When a fight broke out between him and a friend, the battle rarely ended without bloodshed. If he was the weaker of the two, he would bite"; and here is Barthes's gloss: "Femininity (*to bite*, rather than to use the phallic fist, is a connotator of femininity)." Barthes sees nothing here but meaning (though there isn't even meaning, only clues). No doubt he would see nothing but meaning (or clues) in still another story about a Mediterranean temperament with teeth, those connotators of femininity and the *vagina dentata* if not of uninhibited masculine aggressiveness or of the artist fixing his unsemely byte on the phallic plenitude of the world:

> Not only the musical phrase that came out different from what he expected upset him: *anything* that wasn't as he expected it to be upset him. Once, in a temper, he dug his hands into the pockets of his jacket so violently that he tore them away. He made a tremendous effort to control himself, turning his back to us and saying: "No, Toscanini, no! *Calmo—calmo—calmo!*" Then he began to conduct again; but the passage went no better; and in renewed anger he started to dig his hands into his pockets again, but found they weren't there, since he had torn them away. This new frustration made him so furious that he began to tear the jacket itself to pieces. Another time he attempted to break his stick; but this one only bent and wouldn't break; and this made him so angry that he began to bite it. . . .[5]

But the musician's anecdote has nothing to do with Barthes's meanings and clues, it's the manifestation of a presence, in this case historical and documented, a presence as pristine as the great fictional presences that Barthes hasn't a clue to and that Balzac's novella with its linear suspense and didacticism doesn't seem to have heard of.

---

[5] Fred Zimmermann, quoted in B. H. Haggin, *The Toscanini Musicians Knew* (Horizon Press, 1967), p. 47.

These demon readers profess to ignore mere referents (Barthes jeers at the "totalitarian ideology of the referent") for the sake of sticking with the very word; but in practice they are all explainers and interpreters, as satisfied with stamped self-addressed messages as any Yale professor. The first approved "critical interpretation" that Culler quotes at length in his structuralist manual is Harold Bloom's Eng-Lit 1 unriddling of "Ah! Sunflower" ("Blake's dialectical thrust at asceticism . . . ."), by the poet who has just the right credentials—joy, love, nakedness, symbols, dialectical thrusts at asceticism—for attracting the attention of academics who may never have heard of structuralism but are into crossword puzzles and hydrotherapy. Riddles are more fun but the very word will do if it fits into twenty-three across. As for Barthes, he gets as far from words as fast as he can: in *S/Z* distinguishes five "codes" comprising the complete inventory of platitudes that he brings to his reading ("I is not an innocent subject, anterior to the text. . . . . This 'I' which approaches the text is already itself a plurality of other texts, of codes which are infinite or, more precisely, lost . . . "), codes that he finds reflected in every text he reads; and much the most important for him is the "hermeneutic" (lit-crit as Easter-egg and jellybean hunt), the unriddling or problem-solving code, the code that cracks the code of the story and shatters all the words for the sake of answers, solutions, referents, meanings (though he has a separate code of "semes"—"meanings"—to which he consigns what might be more properly listed under some such rubric as Mention the First Word that Pops into Your Head When I Say the Following: e.g. "to bite" suggests "Femininity"; "the clink of gold" suggests "Wealth"; and on and on with comparable *trouvailles*).

Hermeneutic, protatic, proairetic, aphanisis: the structuralists are obliged by their scientific consciences to use what they regard as a technical language (technical languages are by definition painstakingly referential, but that's another problem), but they all hanker after the lost paradise of "ordinary language"—"All technical languages can be translated into ordinary languages, but ordinary language can never be translated into a technical language" (Jean Hyppolite, quoting Hjelmslev, in *The Structuralist Controversy*); "there is no meta-language. . . . You cannot teach a course in mathematics using only letters on the board. It is always necessary to speak an ordinary language that is understood" (Jacques Lacan). But it doesn't occur to them that "ordinary language" is another way of saying "literature"—i.e. language that can never be translated into a technical language, theirs or anybody else's. Literature exchanges confidences with literature only, and scientific criticism is for the birds.

One of the obstacles to discussing these high-flyers is their incapacity to think straight, so that it's essential to do some surreptitious tidying up before it's possible to say what or even whether they think. Barthes doesn't know what meaning is (though he oracularly intones, "The meaning is as follows . . . "), but as between word and meaning he'll take the word every time (whatever *that* means). But, "interpreting" *Sarrasine*, he provides a flagrant and book-length *explication de texte* (of course he explicitly denies it's an *explication de texte*, for which, if they weren't all doing it, he'd be drummed out of the club) which consists of nothing but meanings as he conceives them (i.e. clues and solutions): "To read is to find meanings," and the more meanings the better. But the many meanings of the classic text are too *domestic:* it is "replete: like a cupboard where meanings are shelved, stacked, safeguarded . . . ; like a pregnant female. . . ." But the trouble with *Sarrasine* and all other "classic texts" (*Clarissa, Pride and Prejudice, Barchester Towers, Madame Bovary, Great Expectations, The Idiot, Anna Karenina, Sons and Lovers*) is that they don't have *enough* meanings (their "pluralism" is "limited"); they are like "classical music," which is limited by tonality but which, especially *Italian* classical music, is "like seminal fluid" and offers "the liquid plenitude of pleasure" and—therefore?—inspires Barthes to a veritable coloratura aria (which, it may not be seemly to suggest, may or may not suggest the counter-seminal seme of Castration or Femininity):

> What stands out, what flashes forth, what emphasizes and impresses are the semes, the cultural citations [:*citar*:torero's arched heel coming down like cymbal (symbol)-crash on bull-pats:paronomastic tauromachian anastomosis] and the symbols, analogous in their heavy timbre, in the value of their discontinuity, to the brass and percussion. What sings, what flows smoothly, what moves by accidentals, arabesques, and controlled ritardandos through an intelligible progression (like the melody often given the woodwinds) is the series of enigmas, their suspended disclosure, their delayed resolution: the development of an enigma is really like that of a fugue; both contain a *subject*, subjected to an *exposition*, a *development* . . . .

—for verily the classic text is "a *tonal* text. . . and its tonal unity is basically dependent on two sequential codes: the revelation of truth and the coordination of the actions represented: there is the same constraint in the gradual order of melody and in the equally gradual order of the narrative sequence. *Now, it is precisely this constraint which reduces the plural of the classic text."* Take a deep breath after that barrage of italics (at the climax of the Italian aria) and then get this: "The classic text. . . is a multivalent but incompletely reversible system. What blocks its reversibility is just what limits the plural nature of the classic text. These blocks have names: on the one hand, truth; on the other, empiricism: against—or between—them, the modern text comes into being."

Atonal music has more notes than Mozart; untruthful and anti-empiric, numerical and infinite, Robbe-Grillet or Sollers (who wrote a book called *Nombres*) or Sarraute or Butor has more meanings, which all of a sudden turn into more *voices* (which may mean no meaning and no voices), than Saint-Simon or Flaubert:

> Who is speaking? . . . The more indeterminate the origin of the statement, the more plural the text. In modern texts, the voices are so treated that any reference is impossible: the discourse, or better, the language, speaks [Heidegger: "Language speaks, not man"; but Barthes doesn't have to quote or acknowledge because they're all of one mind]: nothing more. By contrast, in the classic text the majority of the utterances are assigned an origin, we can identify their parentage, who is speaking . . .

—and this identification is klutzy and uncool because voices or no voices or discourse or language is better than persons because persons or centers of consciousness or presences don't exist or at least not on paper as the classic text pretends they do or at least have no authority in the new Nietzschean world of free play and infinite possibility, where we can discard such delusions of "bourgeois ideology" as "reality" and "life" ("'Life' then, in the classic text, becomes a nauseating mixture of common opinions, a smothering layer of received ideas . . . the army of stereotypes"), where Sarraute and Robbe-Grillet[6] are better (more plural, more meaningful, less meaning-full) writers than Dickens and Tolstoy, where Purcell and Schubert have to step aside for Milton Babbitt.

In 1966 a symposium entitled "The Languages of Criticism and the Sciences of Man," funded by a grant from the Ford Foundation, was held at Johns Hopkins. "Over one hundred humanists and social scientists from the United States and eight other countries gathered. . . . The symposium inaugurated a two-year program of seminars and colloquia which sought to explore the impact of contemporary 'structuralist' thought on critical methods in humanistic and social studies"; and "the papers and discussions collected in . . . [*The Structuralist Controversy*] constitute . . . [its] proceedings." Biogenous international lightning had struck the primal ooze of American literary scholarship. Barthes was there, and his paper is all in the title: "To Write: An Intransitive Verb?" In the discussion we learn without amazement that he has "a very high opinion of *La Jalousie*"; and Paul de Man wonders why Barthes's literary criticism is feeble and his literary history false:

> I have been somewhat disappointed by the specific analyses that you give us. . . . But more seriously, when I hear you refer to facts of literary history, you say things that are false within a typically French myth. I find in your work a false conception of classicism and romanticism. When, for example, concerning the question of the narrator or the "double ego," you speak of writing since Mallarmé and of the new novel, etc., and you oppose them to what happens in the romantic novel or story or autobiography—you are simply wrong. In the romantic autobiography, or, well before that, in the seventeenth-century story, this same complication of the ego (*moi*) is found, not only unconsciously, but explicitly and thematically treated, in a much more complex way than in the contemporary novel . . .

—to which Barthes's rejoinder is a lofty and mythical snarl:

> It is difficult to reply because you question my own relationship to what I say [i.e. you've got the gall to tell me I'm wrong]. But I will say, very recklessly and risking redoubled blows on your part, that I never succeed

---

[6] "What I found of some, but not inexhaustible, interest in the avant-garde of a few years ago was the exploitation of minutiae of sensibility in a man alone and immobile." "Stravinsky at Eight-Five: an Interview," *The New York Review of Books*, VIII, No. 10 (June 1, 1967), p. 15.

[however little I try] in defining literary history independently of what time has added to it. In other words, I always give it a mythical dimension. For me, Romanticism includes everything that has been said about Romanticism [including what I've just said about Romanticism, which makes what I've said about Romanticism unassailable]. . . .

Jacques Lacan, founder of l'École Freudienne de Paris, delivers a remarkably idiosyncratic lecture that aspires to combine metaphysics, mathematics, and psychoanalysis ("Of Structure as an Inmixing of an Otherness Prerequisite to Any Subject Whatever"): "in a universe of discourse nothing contains everything, and here you find again the gap that constitutes the subject. . . . The question of desire is that the fading subject yearns to find itself again by means of some sort of encounter with this miraculous thing defined by the phantasm . . . what in French we call the *sujet de la jouissance*"; and Angus Fletcher is exasperated:

> Freud was really a very simple man. . . . He didn't try to float on the surface of words. What you're doing is like a spider: you're making a very delicate web without any human reality in it. For example, you were speaking of joy [*joie, jouissance*]. In French one of the meanings of *jouir* is the orgasm . . . why not say so? All the talk I have heard here is so abstract! . . .

Jacques Derrida reads a touching and anguished and quite irrefutable paper on the impossibility of arguing the very case they are all there to argue:

> We have no language—no syntax and no lexicon—which is alien to . . . [the history of metaphysics]; we cannot utter a single destructive proposition which has not already slipped into the form, the logic, and the implicit postulations of precisely what it seeks to contest. To pick out one example from many: the metaphysics of presence is attacked with the help of the concept of the *sign*. But from the moment anyone wishes this to show, as I suggested a moment ago, that there is no transcendental or privileged signified and that the domain or the interplay of signification has, henceforth, no limit, he ought to extend his refusal to the concept and to the word *sign* itself—which is precisely what cannot be done. For the signification "sign" has always been comprehended and determined, in its sense, as sign-of, signifier referring to a signified, signifier different from its signified. If one erases the radical difference between signifier and signified, it is the word *signifier* itself which ought to be abandoned as a metaphysical concept. When Lévi-Strauss says . . . that he has "sought to transcend the opposition between the sensible and the intelligible by placing [himself] from the very beginning at the level of signs," the necessity, the force, and the legitimacy of his act cannot make us forget that the concept of the sign cannot in itself surpass or bypass this opposition between the sensible and the intelligible. *The concept of the sign is determined by this opposition* . . .

Following Derrida's *cri de coeur*, the lead-footed sociological critic Lucien Goldmann (who says that in the seventeenth—and presumably every other—century "the *society* decided which were the valid solutions" for writers of the time) makes a joke to the effect that Derrida is not only royalist but Merovingian in the extremity of his propositions and poor Derrida's feelings are hurt "because it defines me as an ultra-royalist ... whereas I have a much more humble, modest, and classical conception of what I am doing." Everywhere else in the world and here too, the metaphysics of presence prevails over the concept of the sign: there's nobody here but us chickens: Derrida's anxious and melancholy presence is even more irrefutable than his argument against that apocalyptic annihilation of presence which he otherwise insists ought and is just about to happen; Lacan is doubtless an inept wizard down on his luck, having inmixed a few too many othernesses between the fading gaps of desire; Goldmann eats butterflies for breakfast; and Barthes is a redoubled and intransitive jerk.

Only two of the papers in *The Structuralist Controversy* are intentionally anti-structuralist: Neville Dyson-Hudson's and Georges Poulet's. Dyson-Hudson, an anthropologist, raises pointed questions about Lévi-Strauss as an anthropologist rather than as a culture-hero, and manages incidentally to brush off "the expected inanities" of those public nuisances the weekly reviewers: George Steiner's peristaltic name-dropping, which derives Lévi-Strauss from Broch, Baudelaire, Mallarmé, Rilke, Valéry, Sartre, Camus, Hegel, the Cambridge Platonists, Montaigne, Gide, Leibniz, Vico, Jung, Marx, Bacon, Bruno, La Bruyère, and others; "the faintly hysteric ignorance" of Susan Sontag, complaining that "Anthropology has always struggled with an intense, fascinated repulsion towards its subject" and discovering its savior in none other than the one-and-only, "the man who has created anthropology as a total occupation." As for the blessed Poulet (just one of us chickens), he is an old-fashioned literary critic who does a nostalgic piece in defense of presence and consciousness:

> whenever I take up a book, and begin to read it . . . I am aware of a rational being, of a consciousness; the consciousness of another, no different from the one I automatically assume in every human being I encounter, except that in this case the consciousness is open to me, welcomes me, lets me look deep inside itself, and even allows me, with unheard-of license, to think what it thinks and feel what it feels . . .

—and answering Goldmann, who has asked how the sympathetic and unscientific Poulet would be able to judge a statement by one of his *bad* students: "What would Poulet do with a bad student of Poulet? . . . I would try to identify with my bad student, and I would not be able to do it." Barthes's ears must have been tingling at that electric moment.

Mad Dogs and Anglo Shrinks

For such a gathering of wide-eyed puffs and blurbs—Coles's usual item is three to five pages of unsparing praise of still another non-epoch-making recent book—this is a very cryptic title[1] (followed by a Table of Contents that favors cryptic and reversible chapter headings: "The Artist as Psychoanalyst," "Faith as Doubt," "Piaget as God"). But then Coles isn't content to be (what he is) a working psychiatrist and an unavoidable contributor of five hundred easy pieces on psychiatry to the liberal magazines; he intends to be also a writer who can handle ideas and perspectives, a thinker or, if not, at least the thinking man's psychiatrist.

Consider the last two and most ambitious of the pieces. Both are essays rather than reviews, both are long, both treat the same undeniably solemn subject (the socialization of children); most conspicuously, each opens with a startling historical analogy designed to strike us dumb with the author's originality, range, and boldness. "Children and Political Authority," for example, begins by citing Simone Weil on the similarities between ancient Rome and Nazi Germany, in either case "a ruthless military machine, harnessed to 'a centralized state'" that threatens to destroy all the good little independent countries; and it goes ahead to propose—from here Coles is on his own—that today's Rome or Nazi Germany is of course America, in the face of which blacks and Hopis and Navahos are today's good little independent countries:

> Rather like the Rome which Simone Weil portrayed, America is for a few thousand Hopis not only an enormous empire, but with respect to the smallest details of everyday life, a constant presence. Sometimes anthropological descriptions of a particular kind of Indian culture (Navaho, Hopi, Pueblo) manage to convey successfully the philosophical and psychological distinctiveness of a given people, as against the ways and assumptions of the "dominant culture," yet fail to account for the inevitable mix of two worlds that comes about—the point, for instance, in a child's mental life where he is not only a Hopi, but a Hopi who lives in the state of Arizona, one of the fifty United States. Unlike their white middle-class counterparts, the Hopi boys I have met don't draw missiles, don't crave airplane models,

---

[1] Robert Coles, *The Mind's Fate* (Little, Brown, 1975). Georges Bernanos supplies the title and the epigraph, one of those wingless flights in which the French make like philosophers: "The mind's fate is, after all, a person's fate. We are drawn along by our private visions, but beyond them stretch almost infinitely for each of us the vast and compelling mystery of chance and circumstance." (In this translation, presumably by Coles, "stretches" would be correct, but what the hell.)

don't collect scary "horror" statues, luminous Frankensteins, and on and on. They don't even play "war": Hollywood notwithstanding, there are no feathers on their heads, no bow and arrow encounters, no effort to defy invisible cowboys. They do play—a version of hide-and-seek is popular; they also help herd sheep, and they walk and run and climb. They are not averse to teasing and taunting, however "peaceful" they are taught to be; and very important, they learn, thereby, that they are Hopi and American, however incongruous the combination.

Which, after a dozen perplexed reperusals, seems to boil down to an assertion that teasing and taunting are unknown in primitive cultures, are indeed the first of the poison fruits imported from "the dominant culture." At any rate on pastoral uplands hark! while the young brave speaks with unforked tongue about the dominant-cultural neo-Nazi bullyboys of the jingo U.S. (i.e. us):

> "Anglo kids, they won't let you get away with anything. Tell them something, and fast as lightning and loud as thunder, they'll say, I'm better than you, so there! My father says it's always been like that. My grandfather remembers the Anglos and their horses; they had them for the soldiers. They'd ride through our reservation. Now they have Air Force bases in New Mexico, all over, and they have their atom bombs stored in the mountains. You go near the places where they do their atomic tests, and they'll tell you to get away fast. . . ."

How seamlessly the native American tells the Anglo shrink's portable Sony what it aches to hear! White America has much to answer for, not least the waxworks patness of the evidence that white Americans like Coles solicit against it.

In "The Outer and Inner World," Coles's opening analogy isn't quite so grand as the Roman-Nazi-Anglo Axis but it's just as vulgar and alarmingly more aberrant. Black or Chicano or Indian or Appalachian children are, he says, to white bourgeois America as Freud and his followers were to *fin-de-siècle* bourgeois Vienna: an oppressed "minority group" ("Freud had to endure not only social rejection but constant economic insecurity over a significant stretch of his life"), a band of "outsiders"—

> I do not wish to belabor [he means "labor"] a comparison which has only a limited value [Coles has an uneasy feeling that he'd better protect himself against the mad dogs in the audience], but I think there is a good deal in the history of psychoanalytic psychiatry that ought to make us especially sensitive to the way children who belong to our so-called "minority groups" grow up and come to feel about the world they so often have to take on against great odds. . . .

True, Coles doesn't mention the name of the street gang Freud joined at puberty (The Beautiful Dreamers) or young Sigi's hassles with the fuzz on Saturday nights in the

Wienerwald or his inability to turn up an honest job during the Austrian recession of 1867-85, but all the other resemblances between hawks and handsaws get a vigorous if incoherent airing:

> How does an outsider deal with a world he both lives in and feels separated from? How does an outsider keep his head up . . . ?
> Those questions are not new or surprising [No kidding! growl the mad dogs out front]. . . . Still, for black children . . . [they] are not of only casual interest. Certainly they are not asked rhetorically or philosophically, any more than Freud was indulging himself or being frivolous when he established the Psychological Wednesday Society, a prelude to the Vienna Psychoanalytic Society, and took pains to estimate from time to time how far along toward acceptance and respectability psychoanalysis had come. . . .

Coles's mistreatment of analogy is matched by his mistreatment of direct quotation. In the course of the essay he quotes at length from what is ostensibly a single statement made to him on a single occasion by an eight-year-old black boy in Mississippi; it's a statement as perfectly ideological, and therefore as pat to Coles's purpose, as the Indian's about atom bombs; but, after uninterrupted pages of it, the field investigator pauses for a moment to remark that it was "pulled together from several conversations and put into 'our' (grammatical, if often less expressive) language." (Are the Hopi and Pueblo statements in the other essay "pulled together" in the same way? No comment from Coles, but they too are grammatical and inexpressive.) So it isn't the eight-year-old black boy after all, and exactly how it isn't or who he really is we'll never know. Probably Coles himself doesn't know or care: his humaneness is general (*such* a nice man!) and before the fact; he already has what he needs, and everything else just goes to show; those stacked cassettes on the investigator's shelves are like the psychiatrist's raw files, none of the layman's business.

"Whenever I feel bad," says the hero of Walker Percy's novel *The Moviegoer*, "I go to the library and read controversial periodicals. . . ."

> Down I plunk myself with a liberal weekly at one of the massive tables, read it from cover to cover, nodding to myself whenever the writer scores a point. Damn right, old son, I say, jerking my chair in approval. Pour it on them. Then up and over to the rack for a conservative monthly and down in a fresh cool chair to join the counter-attack. Oh ho, say I, and hold fast to the chair arm: that one did it: eviscerated! And then out and away into the sunlight, my neck prickling with satisfaction.

As at criminal trials each side even has its own (if you'll pardon the expression) committed psychiatrist. In the conservative journal Percy's hero will be savoring the ironic and rebarbative Thomas Szasz (*so* hard-nosed!), in the liberal journal the grave and compassionate Robert Coles (*so* quietly strong!), and in either writer he will find a world of such dreamlike unity and immunity that his gratitude will stop at nothing.

It's a world in which partisanship is the game and everything that scores a point is permitted. When, for instance, Coles is stuck for a last paragraph to put his unusually messy and helpless piece on prisons out of its misery ("We still do not know why one man falls sick and another stays reasonably well, why one person's violence becomes a disaster for all of us and another's can be channeled into useful forms of expression" such as ice hockey), when for the harassed part-time writer routine closes in and the deadline is breathing down his neck, then nothing is sacred and even religion—which usually belongs in the *conservative* journals—isn't out of the question. Here's how it's done: the liberal psychiatrist, having failed to make any sense out of prisons or prison reform, slips an irrelevant and spiritual quotation in from where but *Crime and Punishment* and for the sake of an ending pretends to have found, of all things! God in those seminal words of Dostoevsky's ("I fucked a bear for the FBI and found God")—

> I suppose such words can be dismissed [by mad dogs] as embarrassing sentiment, the prerogative of soft, muddleheaded visionaries—which brings to mind an added embarrassment. We are fast approaching the year 2000 [this was written in 1970, when we were all moving at a terrific speed though we've come to a screeching halt since], which will again remind us how long ago it was that a child was born whom others eventually scorned, arraigned, and punished with the harshest penalty, only to find the man revealed as God Himself.

Aside from this last-paragraph tribute to the Father and the Son in his otherwise nonsectarian prison piece, Coles's most reverent performance is a review of Erik Erikson's *Insight and Responsibility*. Coles seems to idolize Erikson and one hopes he'll be inspired to turn out a clear and sensible sentence or two; but nothing doing, he rapidly tramples any hope of lucidity: "In the way . . . Erikson discusses Freud's friendship with Fliess, and in the way he tells about the relevance of psychoanalysis to other fields, he emerges with a lucidity qualified only by its respectfulness not only to Freud but to all who seek after knowledge." Common decency precludes a close analysis of this sentence; but Coles does seem to be saying that respect precludes lucidity. He also calls to our attention "the haunting title of 'Identity and Uprootedness in Our Time,'" a title that is hauntingly all jargon and no light, doubtless as pristine and opaque as the Holy Ghost. He also declares that Erikson's "Human Strength and the Cycle of Generations" is "as daring a piece as one will ever find in this jargon-filled era," for "Who else, I really wonder, on this confused planet is now writing about such matters as what makes for man's stamina and vitality, and how his qualities of mind and spirit are nourished and transmitted over the centuries?"; but Coles doesn't really wonder, because he knows that he himself and the thousands of others who manufacture the public-spirited jargon of our confused planet are writing about such matters day in and day out, unmercifully, with the heedless and presumptuous respectfulness that strangles lucidity in its cradle: "For some, such terms are the hackneyed soporifics of sermons. For others they are self-consciously or even militantly shunned in favor of ideas and words hardly as graceful and often simply a crying bore. To breathe new life into words like Love is no easy job in our sometimes perversely complicated intellectual climate. . . ." Even Coles's Navahos talk better English.

"I remembered," writes Coles in his Introduction,

> a remark I had heard from William Carlos Williams years earlier: "If I had it over, I might try psychiatry." He was quick to reverse himself, to say he didn't think he had the patience, the "knack," he put it, for such a specialty; but he was vastly interested. At the time I was far more interested in Dr. Williams' poetry (about which I wrote my undergraduate thesis) than psychiatry; if I eventually chose one of his two professions, I had scant information [sic], when I did so, of following his advice. (The remark about what *he* might do if another medical life were permitted him was, I now realize, offered me as tactful advice.)

The reader has scant information of giving Dr. Coles any advice except to avoid poetry and other mental disciplines like the plague, and to entertain the possibility that what Dr. Williams meant was what he said.

A Thrust in the Hand Is Worth Two in the Bush

Hilarious, maybe that's the kindest word for this book,[1] which in behalf of public order had better be taken as a hoax. Sometimes the style is abstract: "The ethical is superior to aestheticism, in that the self-concern of the fancy and willfulness is replaced by a more objective vision of the self, a vision that goes beyond self-conception and potential being toward actual performance"; and sometimes the style is concrete: "In the 1350s, with his hair gray and his remaining years visibly short, Petrarch acutely senses how limited is his time and is equally determined not to waste or spare a moment." (The reviewer, his remaining hair visibly short, is likely to be interrupted here and told that all he ever talks about is *style*.) Sometimes the style is blankly versical: "Man's victories are measured not in time . . . "; "But even here there is no resting place." Sometimes obesely allusive: "as in *Hamlet* or *Lycidas,* or in the philosophy of Martin Heidegger . . . "; "Lear's position, similar to that of Alfred North Whitehead in the *Function of Reason,* is that man has desires and needs which differ from those of simple survival. . . . [Lear] . . . feels the need for kindness, respect, and reverence, for generosity reciprocated and acknowledged, for attention being paid [Willy Loman, Arthur Miller, Marilyn Monroe], for still being somebody, although he has lost the power to command." Sometimes precise: "for Petrarch, for Rabelais, for Shakespeare, and for Milton, it is precisely this new sense of time . . . "; "precisely what is lacking . . . "; "Precisely the society to develop this new time sense . . . " (all within twenty-one consecutive lines of zero-zero intelligibility).

If typical scholarly theses are nets to catch the wind, Quinones's thesis is a stupendous vacuum into which rushes the accumulated hot air of ten thousand graduate seminars: "Curiously enough, given this century's own fascination with time—the century of Proust and Mann and Joyce, of 'West-Running Brook,' 'The Directive,'[2] and the *Four Quartets*—there exists no comprehensive and organic study of time in the literature of the Renaissance. This gap is more surprising when one considers . . . "; though "I am of course not suggesting that the study of time in the literature of the Renaissance is virgin territory." Virgin or territorial, comprehensive or unintelligible, organic or sprayed, Quinones's bag is time; his texts are merely Dante, Petrarch,

---

[1] Ricardo J. Quinones, *The Renaissance Discovery of Time* (Harvard University Press, 1972).
[2] The title of Frost's poem is "Directive."

Rabelais, Montaigne, Spenser, Shakespeare, Milton; and characteristic Quinonian propositions read as follows:

> True to its form, Shakespeare's argument of time exhorts response.
> Spenser begins with myth containing strong suggestion for personal apprehension.
> Society's development is doomed when ignorant armies clash in the very heart of the family.
> Such maximum exploitation of time in writers like Rabelais and Petrarch is introduced so as to forget time.
> But the important attitude to which Petrarch came most clearly and abundantly in the 1360s is somewhere in between activism and nothingness.
> Milton resists the incontinent need to show fruit.
> Spenser complains that the hyphenated ideal of Sidney has been ruptured.
> Even time, as we have seen in contrast with the sure acquisition of enduring goals, is reduced to its proper insubstantiality.
> Through the growth in the order of society, success has been negated by being prepaved [sic].
> There is no death-wish in Robinson Crusoe, no overreaching ambition; unseemly moments of hysteria, fear, and retching are blandly ignored or repressed from his account.
> The cry of alarm is natural to the argument of time.
> The dangers of blurred sight and the benefits of clear vision run throughout Petrarch's expostulations over time.

(That last one could be forgiven as the topic sentence of a letter to *PMLA* from a deranged optometrist.)

Time is clocks, schedules, routines, life, death, children, fame, foresight, hindsight, eyesight, blindness, succession, regression, past, present, future, fear, hope, apathy, ambition, love, hate, secularity, prophecy, horizontality (as opposed to verticality), caution, rashness, motion, suspension, anything else. Precisely. In Petrarch's poetry and prose, which are virtually immortal, "time is practically omnipresent." At every performance of Dr. *Faustus* it's the audience's responsibility to be "driven wild by the inevitable movement of time." (Douglas Bush calls *The Renaissance Discovery of Time* "a ripe product of active thought and insight"; Harry Levin praises Quinones's "important contribution to comparative literature, to the history of ideas, and indeed to his readers' perspectives on human experience.") *Macbeth*, which is about the dangers of blurred sight and the benefits of clear vision, teaches the lesson that it's a mistake to be wrong. The "famous speech shows . . . [Macbeth's] awareness that he has fallen into the common fallacy of always looking to a tomorrow"; and at this point Quinones advances to the positive side of the rostrum; "Basically . . . the speech is nihilistic; it does not take account of the restorative and healing powers in life, the possibilities for growth, of all the satisfactions, successes and even wisdom available to historical man," not to mention the possibility of moving to another country and setting up in business again with a few new murders. Quinones vividly distinguishes, *en passant,* between the bodies politic of *Macbeth* and *Lear*: in the former, "A gash has been made (in *King Lear* we think of the state as being gored, but in *Macbeth* it is a gash) and now the wound is closing" and "all the chickens [are] coming home to roost." Macbeth, up to his navel in blood and poultry, reminds us of another reprobate, Milton's Satan, who plumbs the abyss of Quinonian tautology: "His opposition to what is best in the nature of things commits him to negation and self-destruction." On the other hand, Samson (of *Samson Agonistes*) seems to Quinones quite likable. As for Milton himself, he "can be allied," according to Quinones, "with . . . Rousseau" among those who would like "more of the May Day spirit permitted that existed before the iron glove of Puritanism. . . . Against the stern rigors of Puritanical consciousness and relentless high seriousness . . . [Milton] suggests the virtues of small talk, easiness, the casual moments of pleasure . . . ": evidence, if there were one word of truth in it, that Milton himself was quite a likable chap too. Yet the living frabjous end is love, careless love, in all three of its dimensions: "Petrarch, perhaps because of his children born out of wedlock, frequently felt guilt at such penetration into human experience," but those "quick bright things" Romeo and Juliet, erectly vertical if not protuberantly horizontal, demonstrate that "love makes up in height for what it lacks in length."

Quinones can get pretty explicit in his anxiety to measure up as a dingdong daddy: "[Hamlet] . . . fully characterizes [?] one large thrust of the Renaissance response to time"; "patience before man's inherent incapacities in a changing world is only occasionally lightened by the sought-for thrusts of grace"; "a major thrust . . ."; "any temporal thrust . . . "; "issues which, given more thrust . . . "; "the thrust of these cantos . . . "; "Richard II . . . possessed no real thrust." When this edgy and dynamic scholar isn't being congested by nominal thrusts, he's being harried by adjectival roots: "in the face of life's root mutability. . ."; "still a root difference inheres"; "A root irrationality inheres in the working out of things"; "This root confidence . . ."; "more fundamentally . . . joined together by root similarities"; "a root imperfection in the world"; "a root individualism that . . . devours York's own house [an allusion to the deadly, invasive house-eating root, *Radix devorans* ssp. *quinoniensis,* a native of Patagonia]." The root thrust of all thrusts is "God's own creative thrust," which frolics like Moby Dick among the lesser tumidities: "the mysteries of God's higher hand [*hired* hand? handled herd? hare and hound?] . . . "; "Denied normal extension to their desires, the lovers . . . contract experience, bringing together in a terrible way, the womb and the tomb, the penis and the asp [sic]"; "Out of the entrails of the play itself there is no active force which we follow that leads to rejuvenation" (though this complex image may be peristaltic rather than genital); "While, like Dante, Shakespeare has a remarkable sense of the propensity of physical matter to run down, to lose its early fire, so, too, in Troilus and Hamlet, in the sonnets, and in any number of heroines, he introduces qualities which, if allowed [?], would give horizontal enlargement to the vertically aspiring will." Or Quinones ends the Montaigne chapter with a bang by turning up an unexpected shocker from his author: "'When I dance,

I dance; when I fuck, I fuck.' This is the ungentle Montaigne's sense of life with bite and reality[?]." The startled reader, unable to recover this particular explicitness from his own memory of Montaigne's text, turns to the footnote—printed, as university presses prefer, at a distance of three hundred pages from the text—and learns that "Of course Montaigne's actual words are here only roughly approximated. He in fact wrote, 'Quand je dance, je dance; quand je dors, je dors.'" For Quinones, then, sleeping "roughly approximates" fucking, and explicitness has gone approximately as far as the mind can boggle.

"No bromide this!" exults Quinones on another page, having emitted another bromide. No stuffed shirt he! Sex jingles like loose change in the pockets of his imbecile metaphors. As for offhand misrepresentation, it's as easy as pleasing a university press, one merely goes ahead and does it and buries the truth in a footnote. Nor could just any run-of-the-mill scholar season the graver claims [gravy stains?] of scholarship with newsy and colloquial touches, student-cafeteria scoop about youth, women, politics, psychology, and the other popular arts; but, with-it as a year-old videotape of Walter Cronkite, this is the cat that can: "A kind of 'domino theory' is operative . . . [in Spenser]"; "the stifled cry of the bored suburban housewife, 'Is it just enough [?] not to be bad?'"; "time . . . presents not a choice but an echo"; "Requited love in Shakespeare is an introduction to a sane reality, lending support to the banner, 'Make love not war'"; "The cutting from one force to another [in *Richard III*], the montage effect, as in *High Noon,* increases the dramatic suspense"; "Like every busy father . . . [Manoa] tries to exploit his pull with City Hall to get his son relieved"; "By removing his watch, and trying to regain a more natural sense of the time of his life, the young person of today actually returns to the Renaissance conception"; "Falstaff . . . courts disappointment when he seeks to insert himself between the father-son relation" (a daringly psychoanalytic and illiterate evocation of the homosexual sandwich). Between his own up-to-the-minute teacher-student relation this Falstaffian swinger inserts the prick of social conscience, the sought-for thrust of prepaved [sic] editorial razzmatazz that, ramming its fruitful tidings into the reader's ear on page 283 ("the contemporary American scene . . . where the explosive demands of the unjustly deprived challenge the order of a beleaguered establishment"), is later given horizontal enlargement as well as vertical aspirin by an almost verbatim stanifran on page 405 ("the confrontation of a beleaguered establishment with the destructive demands of the unjustly deprived").

It isn't every firebrand who's as grateful as Quinones: "A fine critic has recently . . . "; "Consequently, A. S. P. Woodhouse is right . . . "; "Burckhardt is right . . . "; "Oliver Elton was right . . . "; Professor Benjamin is also right . . ."; "E. E. Stoll is right to declare . . . "; Harry Levin is "the scholar's scholar and the critic's critic"; "With his usual synthesizing clarity Douglas Bush in his Claremont lectures" manages to say something or other. Yes yes yes yes oh my God yes.

Quinones has literary opinions, which tend to be simultaneously conventional, uninteresting, and bizarre. We have already heard about Milton as Queen of the May. Some professor with his usual synthesizing clarity must have told Quinones once in a Spenser class that Spenser and Chaucer have everything in common, for instance surnames spelled with seven letters ending in the last syllable of "You're darn right, sir"; and it's no trouble to reaffirm this most preposterous of literary couplings if one hasn't the flicker of a response to Chaucer's elasticity of diction, pace, tone, temperament, his quicksilver and impromptu manner. Quinones regards literature as a collection of truths to be extracted like wisdom teeth from the texts of the masters—say, Shakespeare's third, final, and serene period (the plateau of reconciliation), from the height of which the Bard pauses for a last paranoid glare at the age-old question: Is uxoricidal jealousy on the whole ill-advised, especially if the lady hasn't so much as looked cross-eyed at the milkman? Quinones sees it differently, because in another classroom long ago he was told about myth and allegory:

> If the essential stages of male growth are suggested, so are those of womanhood, from Perdita's innocent natural grace to her mother's return as a middle-aged woman. Here, too, the reader is moved by an irresistible urge to respond to the mythic suggestivity of the piece. . . .

How did he fill all these pages? He has read many books and taken many notes (out of an "inner psychic need" no doubt, as he says of Othello in another connection), and much of his own distended volume is synopsis and paraphrase (excelsior and styrofoam). His thesis is vague enough to allow him to drift off in almost any direction till he jerks himself upright with an admonitory pretense of having been on course all the time, and who's to say no, since what's the course? He seems never to have questioned a literary judgment uttered by a full professor: all the classroom chestnuts are here, rolling off the page in a steady mindless rattle. He has no ideas of his own, and not more than two or three of anybody else's, such as the one that dithers on about how masterpieces get written by the *Zeitgeist:* "it almost seems inevitable that the century that began with Erasmus' *Praise of Folly* should terminate with *Hamlet*." Not only can't he write acceptable English sentences; his sentences are often so bad as to disorient the wincing reader, who comes to expect any syntactical or verbal aberration whatever. According to the printed text, for instance, Macbeth is "Bellona's bridgegroom [sic]," and by this time—the book having obviously been approved for publication without the intervention of editors, it may also have materialized in cold print without the intervention of typists or compositors—grooming bridges seems as likely a hobby for Macbeth as Maypole dancing for Milton. "One of the byproducts of sixteenth-century . . . closed comedy," begins another skullbreaker, ". . . is the quest for equanimity in cuckoldry": the cuckold learning not to fret because, in Quinones's explanation as printed, "It is his destiny, not his dessert, to be so used"; and why shouldn't strawberry parfait with horns on it find a place among the howlers? But the book is less a personal than a collective disaster, perpetrated by the scholar's scholars and critic's critics who wrote admiring blurbs for it, by the experts who recommended that the Harvard University Press publish it, by the professional meetings at which such stuff is declaimed and applauded, by the whole shady enterprise of American literary scholarship.

IV
Books in Bunches: The Fox and the Grapes

Old Pros with News from Nowhere[1]

Do monsters ever take a break for toast and tea? One of fiction's consummate monsters is the nurse, midwife, and layer-out-of-corpses in *Martin Chuzzlewit*, Mrs. Gamp, for whom Dickens invented a dialect and a professional manner so uninterruptedly expressive as to seal her off like a true monster from every outward influence; yet, once she settles herself in the sickroom for a long night, the impression she makes isn't unique or monstrous, rather it's typical and domestic, as if in her need and relish for comfort she were just like the rest of us:

> She now proceeded to unpack her bundle; lighted a candle with the aid of a fire-box on the drawers; filled a small kettle, as a preliminary to refreshing herself with a cup of tea in the course of the night; laid what she called "a little bit of fire," for the same philanthropic purpose; and also set forth a small tea-board, that nothing might be wanting for her comfortable enjoyment. These preparations occupied so long, that when they were brought to a conclusion it was high time to think about supper, so she rang the bell and ordered it.

That zone of quiet doesn't interest some of our best-known writers nowadays, who in their so-called comic novels invent monsters merely as laboriously disagreeable as themselves:

---

[1] This piece is the Fiction Chronicle in the Autumn 1973 issue of *The Hudson Review* (with a splice from my earlier discussion of Nathalie Sarraute in the Spring 1969 issue). Philip Roth, *The Great American Novel* (Holt, Rinehart and Winston, 1973). Kurt Vonnegut, Jr., *Breakfast of Champions* (Delacorte, 1973). Alan Lechuk, *American Mischief* (Farrar, Straus and Giroux, 1973). Edwin Shrake, *Strange Peaches* (Harper's Magazine Press, 1972). John Berryman, *Recovery* (Farrar, Straus and Giroux, 1973). Brian Moore, *Catholics* (Holt, Rinehart and Winston, 1973). Nathalie Sarraute, *Tropisms* (Braziller, 1963). Nathalie Sarraute, *Portrait of a Man Unknown* (Braziller, 1958). Nathalie Sarraute, *Martereau* (Braziller, 1959). Nathalie Sarraute, *The Planetarium* (Braziller, 1960). Nathalie Sarraute, *The Golden Fruits* (Braziller, 1964). Nathalie Sarraute, *The Age of Suspicion* (Braziller, 1963). Nathalie Sarraute, *Between Life and Death* (Braziller, 1969). Nathalie Sarraute, *Do You Hear Them?* (Braziller, 1973). Edmund White, *Forgetting Elena* (Random House, 1973). Ian Mowatt, *Just Sheaffer or Storms in the Troubled Heir* (Harcourt, Brace, Jovanovich, 1973). Chinua Achebe, *Girls at War and Other Stories* (Doubleday, 1973). Doris Lessing, *The Summer Before the Dark* (Knopf, 1973). Johanna Davis, *Life Signs* (Atheneum, 1973). Judith Rascoe, *Yours, and Mine* (Atlantic Monthly Press, 1973). John Cheever, *The World of Apples* (Knopf, 1973). Bernard Malamud, *Rembrandt's Hat* (Farrar, Straus and Giroux, 1973). Vladimir Nabokov, *A Russian Beauty and Other Stories* (McGraw-Hill, 1973).

> I have conquered insomnia many a night reciting . . . [from the Prologue of *The Canterbury Tales*] to myself, aloud if I happened to be alone, under my breath (as was the better part of wisdom) if some slit was snoring beside me. Only imagine one of them bimbos overhearing Smitty whaning-that-Aprille in the middle of the night! Waking to find herself in the dark with a guy who sounds five hundred years old! Especially if she happened to think of herself as "particular"! Why, say to one of those slits—in the original accent—"The droghte of Marche hath perced to the rote," and she'd kick you right in the keester. "There are some things a girl won't do, Mr. Word Smith, not even for dough! Good*bye*!" On the other hand, to do women justice, there is one I remember, a compassionate femme with knockers to match, who if you said to her, "So priketh hem nature in hir corages," she'd tell you, "Sure I blow guys in garages. They're human too, you know."
>
> But this is not a book about tough cunts. Nat Hawthorne wrote that one long ago. . . .

Word Smith—yes, that's his name, the initials coincident (as he informs us) with Shakespeare's—stands out there swinging those pudgy allusions from the word go: "Call me Smitty" is the first sentence of *The Great American Novel*. As for the opening of *Breakfast of Champions:* "This is a tale of a meeting of two lonesome, skinny, fairly old white men on a planet which was dying fast"; so fast, indeed, that nobody has time for Mrs. Gamp's or the human race's petty contentments, though there's always time for lots of laughs on the scratchy soundtrack:

> When Kilgore Trout accepted the Nobel Prize for Medicine in 1979, he declared: . . .
>
> "There were two monsters sharing this planet with us when I was a boy . . . and I celebrate their extinction today. They were determined to kill us, or at least to make our lives meaningless. They came close to success. They were cruel adversaries, which my little friends the beavers were not. Lions? No. Tigers? No. Lions and tigers snoozed most of the time. The monsters I will name never snoozed. They inhabited our heads. They were the arbitrary lusts for gold, and, God help us, for a glimpse of a little girl's underpants. . . ."

Breakfast of Champions is very bitter about something or other, probably politics, the second law of thermodynamics, the Second Coming, or ecology: Kilgore Trout tells his parakeet, Bill, that "humanity deserved to die horribly, since it had behaved so cruelly and wastefully on a planet so sweet":

> After Trout became famous, of course, one of the biggest mysteries about him was whether he was kidding or not. He told one persistent questioner that he always crossed his fingers when he was kidding.

"And please note," he went on, "that when I gave you that priceless piece of information, my fingers were crossed."

And so on.

"And so on," a three-word paragraph of apparently limitless significance to Vonnegut (as "So it goes" was in an earlier Vonnegut best-seller), averages an appearance every dozen pages in this 300-page novel, which scatters among the author's kiddie-style illustrations of flags and beavers a number of the most unresourceful verbal tics since "frankly," "hopefully," and "you know." Here is what the here-is-what tic looks like: "Here is what Dwayne said to the policemen as they cuffed his hands behind his back: 'Thank God you're here!'"; "Here is what the pennant said . . . "; "Here was the explanation . . . "; "Here was the F.B.I. evaluation . . . "; "Here is what the badges said . . . "; "He snarled at his recollection of it afterwards. Here is what he snarled: 'Dumb fucking bird.'" Here are samples of the ironically (not to mention undeniably) simple-minded definition: "A Nigger was a human being who was black"; "Thanksgiving Day was a holiday when everybody in the country was expected to express gratitude to the Creator of the Universe, mainly for food"; "the clitoris, a tiny meat cylinder which was right above the hole in women where men were supposed to stick their much larger cylinders"; "He was a graduate of West Point, a military academy which turned young men into homicidal maniacs for use in war." And here quite at home is the mindless repetition:

> Trout marveled at what a big animal the idiot was. The idiot's happiness was fascinating, too, as he stoked himself with calories which would get him through yet another day.
> Trout said this to himself: "Stoking up for another day."

"Trout did another thing which some people might have considered eccentric: he called mirrors *leaks*"; whereupon, when somebody says "I'm going to take a leak," Trout is empowered to retort: "Back where I come from, that means you're going to steal a mirror." About halfway through the book Vonnegut begins recording for posterity, with no immediate dramatic provocation, the length and circumference of the engorged penis ("like a plugged-up garden hose") of each of his male characters. There is even, surprisingly, a gratuitous libel on chimpanzees: "Trout couldn't tell one politician from another one. They were all formlessly enthusiastic chimpanzees to him. He wrote a story one time about an optimistic chimpanzee who became President of the United States." Vonnegut has lost his bearings: chimpanzees are (like beavers) *lower* animals, therefore morally and ecologically *sound*, would therefore make *great* Presidents, would do *good*. Here is the good they would do . . .

Poor Roth has lost not only his bearings but his marbles, mixing alliterative dictionary lists, baseball, skits on anti-Communism, funny names (Word Smith, Gil Gamesh, Sy Clops, Base Baal, Spit Baal, Capt. Smerdyakov, Maj. Stavrogin, Col. Raskolnikov, "the International Lenin School for Subversion, Hatred, Infiltration, and Terror, known popularly as SHIT"), literary jokes ("Mister Fair-smith cried out twice, a cry that was no more than a breath: 'The horror! The horror!'"), and a bellyful of sex nausea into *The Great American Novel:*

> "Aw, lay off, Hot," said Big John. "It warn't no old lady. If you ask me, it was a ringer named Gamesh."
>
> But Nickname, wiping the warpaint of his own blood and tears across his cheek with the back of his mitt, blubbered, "But it *was* a old lady, Jawn, that's the worst of it. *That's* how come I dropped the ball! It weren't them spikes that scared me, Hot. Look, I took 'em full in the letters."
>
> "Then *what?*" screamed Hot. "Was you bein' *polite* to her that you lost the ball?"
>
> "No! No! It's, it's when she raised up her leg—that's how come I lost it! I damn near went unconscious."
>
> "*Why?*" demanded Hothead.
>
> "Aw jeez, Hot, I ain't never smelled nothin' like that at second base before. Or in a cathouse even. It stunk like somethin' that's been left out somewhere and turned green. I ain't lyin' to you, Hot—I thought maybe it was a shrimp boat dockin' at the bag. Only worse! Then my whole life flashed before my eyes, and I thought, by Jesus, I'm gonna *die* from whatever it is."
>
> "That keen, huh?" said Big John.
>
> "Keen? I'druther be drownin' in a swamp!"
>
> "Well," said Big John, consoling the catcher as he and Nickname each took the dumbstruck Hothead by an arm and helped him back to the Mundy dugout, "old or young, they all of them knows how to get the use out of that thing, don't they? Cheer up now, ol' Hothead, you ain't the first feller to get done in by the black hole of Calcutta—or the last either."

So much for the national sport.[2]

Roth was doubtless pleased to learn, having credited Smitty with a nocturnal passion for Chaucer, that Alan Lelchuk (or one of his narrators) regards Chaucer as a talented precursor of Roth's: "there's enough real obscenity . . . [in Chaucer,] scatological humor and sexual farce to make him a very contemporary figure, a kind of Philip Roth of the fourteenth century. . . ." Such dense and flashy intellectual pearls drop often from Lelchuk's pages—"those two smart Jews, Proust and Freud"; "the shrewd psychopath" Dostoevsky; "Tolstoy, Goethe, and other sentimentalists"— though the reader must bear in mind that *American Mischief,* told entirely through the consciousnesses of two highly unreliable narrators, teems with irony, ambiguity,

---

[2] Have Roth and Vonnegut "never seen anything worth seeing nor loved anything worth loving"? Santayana seems to have had the two of them in mind: "The picture of life as an eternal war for illusory ends was drawn at first by satirists, unhappily with too much justification in the facts. Some grosser minds, too undisciplined to have ever pursued a good either truly attainable or truly satisfactory, then proceeded to mistake that satire on human folly for a sober account of the whole universe; and finally others were not ashamed to represent it as the ideal itself—so soon is the dyer's hand subdued to what it works in. . . ."

paradox, and bad writing. The first narrator is a college dean who not only services six mistresses but serves as their psychotherapist without portfolio; a lay analyst so to speak: "Scarred by the lack of a father's closeness and by the confusions of her past, poor Gwen craved intelligent but decisive authority in a man"; "the source of her crazed sexuality . . . [was] the fact that with two small bumps for breasts, she had to compensate somehow (to win her father and the rest of us men)";

> One day, . . . leafing through a childhood scrapbook of Kate's, I came across an interesting photograph. It showed Kate's father, a handsome jut-jawed man in his thirties, holding his little daughter upon his lap, while Mother sat next to him. What struck me immediately was that his hand seemed to be placed beneath the flimsy skirt of the five-year-old girl, upon her haunches. I questioned Kate and found out, after some embarrassed hedging and forgetting, that one of Daddy's fondest terms of affection was "my little fanny love," a tribute to his special feeling for that part of her anatomy. Gently I continued my probing and precipitated in Kate the memory of frequent "mock spankings" that her father administered to her. . . .

American Mischief aspires to be the thinking man's *Jonathan Lovestory Segal*, but turns into another kiddie-book of monsters. Gently probing all the way, it hits bottom with the assassination of "Norman Mailer" by means of a bullet up his ass. The assonant assassin is a meteorological menace named Lenny Pincus, the second of Lelchuk's narrators, who draws us into the very vortex of the Weather Underground: "Yes," muses Lenny, "there was something special about abandoning morals or transcending them." He and his confederates do various messy things inside museums and libraries. They also set up a concentration camp for New York intellectuals, who unlike "Mailer" aren't given names but only single initials: "A." has a "boyish" unruly forelock and a propensity for going down on nubile seamen; "E." is a professor at Columbia, an Arnold and Forster specialist, who as a phase of his re-education is forced to watch fellatio being performed on Lenny (by a *girl*, thank God!). According to a recent news account Mailer (not "Mailer"), apprised of his fictional death, is said to have promised that when he was through with Lelchuk (not "Lelchuk") nothing would be left "except a few fillings." The New York intellectual called "A." died (really) a few months ago; no ruminative think-piece from "E." so far on the relation between traditional culture and shlock-shock-sock pseudo-nonfic novels.

Strange Peaches also raids the headlines for its pasteboard monsters, among them a 93-year-old Texas oil billionaire who can break out anywhere—shopping at a supermarket, for instance—into a piping rendition of one of his own home-made pieces of backwoods music. The place is Dallas, the year is 1963; and, if Shrake wanted to prove that maybe Stendhal or Tolstoy could deal with such iron necessity in a novel but that nobody else could, he has succeeded. The Texas establishment flaunts its king-size mediocrity; Jack Ruby struts and frets on and off stage; the protagonist—star of the top TV cowboy series—lives on bennies, martinis, Scotch, and Almond Joy candy bars, threatening to make the authentic movie about Texas; Shrake's mind and style aren't up to much beyond human-interest journalism and hard-boiled dialogue; The Event looms closer and closer; and when at last it's here Shrake doesn't find anything new or sensational to say about it. Yet because he isn't trying to exploit it, because—on the assumption that there's something to understand—he's still trying to understand and assimilate it, the book has a small, touching note of bewilderment and sadness.

John Berryman's unfinished posthumous novel makes do without monsters, but its subject is as impossible as Shrake's: the hospital treatment of alcoholics. The trouble with sick people is that they nurse the indispensable delusion that there is a human condition called health. If *Recovery* is a truthful account (and it reads like one, crammed with busy, noisy, daily, infinitely hopeless "challenges," "encounters," "confrontations"), alcoholics are commanded to believe that, if they keep examining their own motives and everybody else's with perfect honesty twenty-four hours a day, they will find the way back to health:

> Alan and Hutch made common cause. Each had been accused of being unable to level. "Okay," Severance said to the big man on the way down to lunch after Group, "maybe we can help each other. Let's talk after lecture this afternoon." They agreed on Hutch's room, and picking up a cup of coffee at two-fifteen he went carefully down the hall and knocked on the half-open door, heard a voice, and walked in.
>
> Hutch was standing on the near side of the bed, with a book in his hand, looking as if he had been about to go somewhere. The bed-table had a book and a magazine on it. The bed was neat and empty. The long windowsill, where patients kept things, was empty. No clothes were visible. The top of the bureau was empty. Severance felt odd before he realized why he felt odd: the room was *all right*. That is to say, all wrong. It looked as if nobody lived there.
>
> "Hutch," he said involuntarily, "why is your room so damned neat?"
>
> "What's neat about it?" very defensively.
>
> "Well, look at it."
>
> Hutch looked around uneasily. "What's wrong with that? I'm just neat, that's all."
>
> "You are? You told me the other night your workshop was a shambles."
>
> "My office is open to inspection at any moment." He sounded angry. . . .

There is no end to this sort of thing except hatred and collapse, followed by a new round of attack-and-defense in the guise of straight-from-the-shoulder, comradely exchanges: "leveling"; and Berryman, who seems to have been a decent man and an accurate observer, doggedly registered the recurrences even while he tried to suggest that recurrence isn't fate but only will or accident. Though Berryman's notes indicate that his hero would have been back out into the world at the close, feeling "lucky," "happy," "fine," the title is an embarrassment and the book full of unacknowledgeable despair.

Of course *Recovery* isn't a novel except by courtesy; it has the interest and pathos of a personal document. *Catholics,* on the other hand, is all fabrication, from the first two sentences: "The fog lifted. The island was there." Chapter 2 begins: "The helicopter drifted over the crossroads, the pub, the yard, then, tilting slightly forward, moved downwind to land in a field on the edge of the bog. The rotor blades still turned at take-off speed as Kinsella hurried towards the machine in the afternoon's continuing drizzle, ducking under the great propellers as the pilot slid the door aside and held out a hand to take him up." And Chapter 3:

> Kinsella woke at seven. In the rectangle of window above his bed, the sky was already light. Gulls rode that sky, kites held by invisible string. When, dressed and shaven, he opened the guest house door and stepped outside, he met the rush of breakers on shore, a long retreating roar of water. Obbligato of gull cries overhead, their harsh, despairing scream seeming to mourn a death. Winds whipped like penny tops, spinning the long grasses this way and that. The sky, immense, hurried, shifted its scenery of ragged clouds. From the cove below, four curraghs were putting out to sea....

Such efficient descriptive prose it is, almost as efficient as the movie shots into which it will be converted frame by frame from this slick script, which doesn't scruple to tip off the casting director besides: "With his curling red hair, freckled skin, snub nose and white fisherman's sweater he looked like Dylan Thomas"; "Father Matthew, six feet five inches tall, the biggest man on Muck, ... physically and in temperament, ... resembled General de Gaulle." *Catholics*—my God it's money in the bank, Brian Moore must have thought while dreaming it up—is about a time very soon when Rome has become Amsterdam and Amsterdam the ecumenical capital of the world ("the *apertura* with Buddhism"), and the only Latin Mass and private confession in the world are being given by the monks of an island abbey off the coast of Ireland. Tourists, alerted by a BBC program, flock in by supersonic jet, and a young American priest in the new denim uniform is despatched from Rome to put down the heretics. Daniel Berrigan plays the American priest; the Archangel Gabriel plays the Abbot of Muck, his weathered old mug aglint with wisdom, doubt, and anguish: *"Aggiornamento,* was that when uncertainty had begun? ... And, long ago, that righteous prig at Wittenberg nailing his defiance to the church door." And long long ago that silly girl who ate of the forbidden fruit. And Lucifer, damn him.

Nothing would appear to be more of a fabrication than the *nouveau roman,* of which Nathalie Sarraute continues to turn out her nevertheless utterly personal, crabbed, cranky, grimly literary (at any rate not cinematic!) instances. Among "the most curious features of our literary epoch," says Sartre in his introduction to one of Sarraute's books, is "the appearance . . . of penetrating and entirely negative works that may be called anti-novels. . . . They are works of the imagination with fictitious characters, whose story they tell. But . . . their aim is to make use of the novel in order to challenge the novel, to destroy it before our very eyes while seeming to construct it." Not that Sartre thinks they show any "weakness of the novel as a genre; all they show is that we live in a period of reflection and that the novel is reflecting on its own problems."

Sarraute, though, thinks they show nothing less than the death of the traditional novel. "Character" and "psychology," names and clothes, kinships and commodities, themes and plots—all those Balzacian engines—are played out. "Since the happy days of Eugénie Grandet when, at the height of his power, the character occupied the place of honor between reader and novelist, . . . he has continued to lose, one after the other, his attributes and prerogatives . . . from the silver buckles on his breeches to the veined wart on the end of his nose." (Balzac is the indispensable bull in the china shop of French literary decorum. If he hadn't existed, Sarraute would have been obliged to import him from Smollett's or Dickens's England.) "The character as conceived in the old-style novel. . . does not succeed in containing the psychological reality of today. . . . So that, as a result of an evolution similar to that in painting, . . . the psychological element, like the pictorial element, is beginning to free itself imperceptibly from the object of which it was an integral part."

Tropisms, though just published here, was Sarraute's first book. It was also her source book, providing "all the raw material that I have continued to develop in my later works." Narrative, warts, personalized psychology give way—so the title suggests—to certain organic tendencies: barely perceivable minutiae of motive, "tropisms" almost botanical in their dissociation from will and consciousness, "certain inner 'movements' . . . in the form of un-definable, extremely rapid sensations. . . . Since, while we are performing them, no words express them, not even those of the interior monologue . . . [the novelist could not] communicate them to the reader otherwise than by means of equivalent images that would make him experience analogous sensations. It was also necessary to make them break up and spread out in the consciousness of the reader the way a slow-motion film does. Time was no longer the time of real life, but of a hugely amplified present."

"That too is possible" (Stravinsky reports Rimsky-Korsakov's comment on somebody else's new symphony). But *Tropisms* itself, far more modest than its author's claims for it, is a pamphlet-sized collection of vignettes most of which manage to be at the same time tiny, diffuse, and banal. In one of them, for example, a professor, "like the gentleman in the advertisements who . . . smilingly recommends Saponite," enjoys "prying, with the dignity of professional gestures, with relentless, expert hands, into the secret places of Proust or Rimbaud . . . "; while,

> Avoiding the shops filled with pretty things, the women trotting briskly along, the café waiters, the medical students, the traffic policemen, the clerks from notary offices, Rimbaud or Proust, having been torn from life, cast out from life and deprived of support, were probably wandering aimlessly through the streets, or dozing away, their hands resting on their chests, in some dusty public square.

Or consider the city people, who inhabit "apartments giving on to dark courtyards, perfectly decent, however, and comfortably equipped," people who "never tried to recall the place in the country where once they had played, . . . never tried to recapture the color and the smell of the little town they had grown up in," and so forth. This bucolic mawkishness is the obverse of the author's hatred for the petty bourgeoisie, especially its women:

> With their handbags under their arms, their gauntlet gloves, their little regulation "bibis" at just the right angle on their heads, their long, stiff lashes set in bulging lids, their hard eyes, they trotted along in front of the shop windows, stopped all of a sudden, ferreted about with an avid, knowing look.

"Sensible men" condescend to the illustrious dead, while living poets roam the streets unhonored; Wordsworthian country pleasures haven't yet perished in Sarraute's not quite steely bosom; women on the lookout for bargains make an unattractive spectacle. Only once or twice in the book does the method achieve something like a Joycean epiphany; disclosing, for instance, the consciousness of a little boy taken for a walk by his mild, fussy grandfather, who likes to talk

> about his advanced age and his death. "What will you say when you won't have any more grandfather, he'll be gone, your grandfather will, because he's old, you know, very old, it will soon be time for him to die. Do you know what people do when they die? Your grandfather too had a mamma once. But where is she now? Yes! Yes! Where is she now, darling? She's gone, he hasn't any more mamma, she's been dead a long time, his mamma has, she's gone, there's no more mamma, she's dead."
> The air was still and gray, odorless, and the houses rose up on either side of the street, the flat masses of the houses, closed and dreary, surrounded them as they proceeded slowly along the pavement, hand in hand. And the child felt that something was weighing upon him, benumbing him. A soft choking mass that somebody relentlessly made him take, by exerting upon him a gentle, firm pressure, by pinching his nose a bit to make him swallow it, without his being able to resist—penetrated him, while he trotted docilely along, like a good little boy, obediently holding out his little hand, nodding his head very reasonably, while it was explained to him that he should always proceed cautiously and look well, first to the right, then to the left, and be careful, very careful, for fear of an accident, when crossing between the lines.

That too is possible; it is even very good; but it doesn't justify manifestoes.

Even at its best, Sarraute's method justifies attention but not manifestoes. Her least interesting books are *Tropisms* and *The Age of Suspicion* (which is the expectable collection of tendentious essays by a practitioner of the *nouveau roman*). The silliest is *The Golden Fruits,* a catty and trivial exposé of French literary society, which on the evidence of the book combines the least attractive features of an academic cocktail party and a public hanging.

Portrait of a Man Unknown, however, deserves attention. It's Sarraute's first full-scale application of her method; and it makes clear her self-admitted affinities with the Dostoevsky of *Notes from Underground*. Yet the differences in intention (not to speak of differences in power of realization) are much greater than she might be willing to acknowledge. Dostoevsky's underground man wanders forever in the labyrinths of motive, which have been opened by the nineteenth-century denial of will and action: the horror is metaphysical, it is in the endlessness of his quest, not in the malice he dredges up along the way. Sarraute, on the other hand, limits herself to observing the sporadic jets of spleen and hatred that she considers "the secret source" (doesn't she wish to say, rather, the most immediate manifestation?) "of our existence"; as when the rich and miserly old bourgeois thinks he has surprised his daughter in the act of stealing a bit of household soap:

> He began to hurry, quick, no time to look for his slippers, and barefooted and in his nightshirt he raced through the hall to the kitchen and climbed on a chair to look: there it was, on the shelf above the sink—the bar of soap was there, the edge fresh cut, the very edge, sharp and well defined, of reality itself. . . .
> By now he had reached the very limit. He had plumbed the very depths. There was no need to look any further. After this paroxysm he felt a sort of relief. The clutched hand about his throat and chest had relaxed, he was breathing more freely as he returned to bed, carrying it with him—this concrete, hard fact—like a bone to be gnawed upon, undisturbed, in his kennel. . . . He had been right in his impression that the soap had been vanishing pretty fast of late. . . . Like the butter last year, and the shoe polish . . .

—because people need each other, but not for love: "contact" is what they seek (for which—crablike, insectlike—they make use of their "tentacles," "delicate little suckers," "sticky juice"); but, people being what they are, contact prompts every one of them to secrete quantities of hatred and malice, puffs up his "poison sac" (another of Sarraute's recurrent images) until it bursts and flows.

This is a special but not altogether implausible view of things. The episodes and relationships that illustrate it are often tedious enough to undermine the reader's patience; but evidently Sarraute will stop at nothing toward her aim of defining paranoia as the characteristic mode of consciousness. *Martereau* supplies a fresh set of episodes, and (except for an additionally irritating element of detective-story mystification) works in much the same way.

Martereau also has a few touches of what might be called the comedy of paranoia; for instance, in the game of one-upmanship played between an aging boorish man and his stubborn shrew of a wife:

> This time she's held her own for a long time. The matter at stake is worth it: that awful suburban house that he persists in wanting to buy, and then,

above all, to punish him severely for his outburst of fury, his rudeness, the entire house had resounded with his shouting.

With him, once the usual first phase is over—threatening silence, angry looks, sour remarks addressed to us, to his daughter and to me, and which, we all know, are aimed at her—his strength diminishes visibly. It's been evident for some time now, that he would like to patch it up: during the last few days, he has been making timid, touching efforts to edge in sidewise on the conversations she has with us at every meal, growing proportionately more sprightly and full of life as his level lowers.

Man, the autonomous and parasitic animal, exists submerged in his feelings, moods, euphoria and depression, self-love and self-loathing, which exercise themselves pretending to be reasonable (and therefore derivable from relations with persons and things), voluntary (and therefore independent of such relations), flowing out of unconscious sources (and therefore anterior to will and reason), and which outwit all explanations by the power of their presence and the unpredictability of their direction. Sarraute's best book is *The Planetarium,* chiefly because its great opening episode is the apotheosis of this sort of comedy: among all of the author's cranky and interminable disembodied voices, the dazzling virtuoso aria. The episode is Dostoevskian because, for once, Sarraute exposes the metaphysical horror at the heart of grievance, resentment, malice, apprehension, the sense of the heavens opening out into the void for the little old lady pacing her redecorated apartment, driven half-mad by the irreparable indifference of what is outside the self:

So, believe it or not, I went . . . at eleven o'clock at night . . . I know her. In any case, I was done for, she would have waked me at six in the morning . . . she would have spent the entire night walking up and down in front of her door like a caged animal . . . I saw right away, as soon as I got there, that she was in a bad way. She looked fairly haggard. And the entire place was in what, for her, was terrible disorder; a can of furniture polish on the table, bottles and rags of every description on the floor . . . She let me in, a rag in her hand: Come and see, it's incredible what they've gone and done, your friend Renouvier is no good . . . Look at the door . . . I saw an awful new door such as you see everywhere, a pretentious, interior decorator's sort of door, which was there nobody knew why . . . A mad idea she had had all of a sudden . . . But I didn't say anything, it was too late, there was no longer any question of that. . . the fingerprint plaque had been removed and it had left holes in the wood, tiny marks that had been stopped up with putty and which she was rubbing, painting with all her might. . . Almost weeping she begged me . . . Look . . . tell me the truth, I can't judge any more, I can't see anything but that . . . The nail marks were undoubtedly visible . . . If she had said nothing, I shouldn't have noticed anything, but now that she had told me . . . It was, indeed, too bad, but there was no doubt about it, I did see them. Some devil must have prompted me, I couldn't help saying to

> her: Oh, if you don't think about it, you can hardly see anything, but now that you've told me, I do see the filled-in spots . . . But so tiny . . . you have to know they're there . . . [all ellipses in this and the following extracts from Sarraute are Sarraute's]

So much energy! though the rest of *The Planetarium* is the mixture as before, expertly put together, really another novel about the stupid lives of very disagreeable people. Sarraute has devoted her career to dramatizing the psychopathology of everyday life, and everyday life—crazy or not—turns out to be, with certain volcanic exceptions, as lavishly dull as other novelists have already led us to suspect.

Finally, the show is almost over: motives continue to range freely between malice and paranoia, but the manner is finally as assured as a funeral director's, and the familiar substance becomes thinner and thinner. *Between Life and Death* is the last volume of her trilogy (the first two: *The Planetarium* and *The Golden Fruits*) about French literary life, which she continues to represent as mere murder:

> "We, in any case . . ." and before he can move away, that sudden pounce . . . "we, in any case, we will at least have had that . . . "in one second the enormous rings have curled up, they are clasped around him . . . "we shall have had at least that, to have lived at the same time he did . . ." and the cracking of his crushed bones.

Artists have to face up also to the virulently contemptuous bourgeoisie: "ah, these poets"; and "How much did they take to publish that?" Artists are touchy: "they must all have heard the rending sound his skin made as it came off like the hide of a rabbit being flayed." Sarraute tries to vindicate the sensitive plant by showing it in the very act of producing leaves and flowers:

> It's first one image then another . . . it's snatches of conversation, or perhaps merely an intonation, an accent through which runs a rapid movement, that are as though seized, shaken by a brief convulsion.
>
> This movement must be caught, we must isolate it, try . . . wouldn't it be possible in order for it to recur more clearly and evolve, to create more favorable conditions? . . . to insert it elsewhere, among other, better assembled images, other words or intonations, the way we transplant a wild shoot in improved earth, enriched with loam, fortified with fertilizer, in an enclosed spot, a hothouse in which the appropriate temperature is constantly maintained? . . . .

But the reader keeps hoping for a better product and not so much bad feeling at the root of it.

With *Do You Hear Them?* the reader comes to the end of his hope, for Sarraute's latest novel is all bad feeling and no acceptable product at all:

> —Scold? . . . Ah, a lot they would care. That would be something. It's been a long time since I had the right to say a word. They are the ones who lay down the law. Somebody said that at present parents treat their offspring like distinguished guests . . . with infinite consideration . . . You walk on tiptoe, you shrink in size, you feel rewarded when they deign to show forbearance . . . But then you must have deserved it. Nothing is overlooked . . . not so much as that . . . He makes a clacking sound with his thumbnail against his teeth . . . and believe me, there are no limits. The more you give in to them, the more exigent they become. . . .

—not an unduly protracted joke, but a whole book of (somebody's) malice and paranoia on the sins of children, those murderers of art, authority, and the past, jeering monster-children who intend to drive their elders mad:

> —That laughter . . . do you hear them? Those little titters . . . sharp as needles . . . But wake up, don't look so vacant . . . Those titters like the drops of water that are made to drip on the heads of torture victims . . . they drip on us, to make us suffer, to destroy us . . . Don't you really hear them? What are you made of, anyway? No, of course, you can't believe me. You can't believe such deceit as that . . . The other sits up, staring wide-eyed at him . . . But how could you not notice when . . . at the moment when you had the imprudence . . . when you were mad enough . . .—I? Mad? Ah, that's a good one . . .—Yes, mad . . . leaning over, seizing the animal with both hands, brandishing it in his face . . . Yes, I'll say so, mad. Fit to be tied . . . to dare, in front of them, to go and take it, set it there, contemplate it . . . they rose, they pushed it away, they went upstairs, and now they're defiling, destroying . . . everything . . . everything that makes life worth living . . . look how they make me talk . . . what grandiloquence, what lack of reserve . . . see what they're doing to me . . . they're slowly finishing me off. . . .

No doubt *Do You Hear Them?* was meant as a dramatization of one possible psychotic attitude.

Edmund White, mere male, tries to domesticate Sarraute by serving this vegetarian imitation of her vampire intentions:

> Suddenly Herbert slams his book down on the table between us and says, "I think we have a little work to do today, don't you?" He says the first few words too loudly and immediately lowers his voice. He's staring at me with determination, or is it anger, as though he's let things out of hand and must now, belatedly, buckle down. No, maybe he's received orders from above and is so embarrassed about transmitting them to me that he's hiding his embarrassment behind gruffness. . . .
>
> He stands and I do the same, though, somewhat clownishly, I pause for an instant, pretending laziness or reluctance, before levering myself

out of the chair in a burst by grabbing the armrests with my hands and pushing down; a slight joke, registered by my body alone and not by anything so controversial as a smile. Even so, I mustn't lend so much character to my actions until I discover what sort of person I'm generally considered to be.

Such mystifications derive from the premise that the hero of *Forgetting Elena* has amnesia but for reasons unrevealed to us can't just say so and find out who the hell he is rather than finicking on and on: I didn't know whether to wink or blink. I decided to blink, and, blinking, feared I ought to have winked. I noticed that X's face assumed—or did it fall naturally into?—an expression supercilious if not in fact fawning.

Just Sheaffer or Storms in the Troubled Heir is one of those uproarious British romps that, if they happen to be put together in the guise of plays, hold unwary American visitors to London theaters transfixed in wild surmise at British bum-humor (such names as "Ramsbottom," "Winterbottom," "Ramupsavich"), watercloset-humor, and (compound imperial tasties for the jaded palate) Queen's-bum-and-watercloset-humor:

> ". . . good place for a ponder, the old bowl. You don't happen to know if the Queen gets her toilet paper free?"
> "What?"
> "The Queen," repeated Sheaffer. "Does she pay for her own toilet tissue?"
> "Never thought about it," said Father Scraw, cackling into the receiver.
> "Well," continued Sheaffer, "you know that businesses make goods by appointment to the Queen—purveyors of this, that, and the next thing. Well, maybe there's a purveyor of toilet paper."
> "Could be," said Father Scraw. "Wonder what kind she uses."
> "Something soft for the royal bum," said Sheaffer. . . .

Sheaffer, flushed with success, whooshes away down the drain while, out in the Queen's former colonies, rather less bubbly chaps are trying to find ways of accommodating Asian or African particularities to what's left of English fiction. Chinua Achebe is a Nigerian: most of his stories are correct and unsurprising in style, treatment, and subject—chips off Waugh's *Black Mischief* ("The Voter"); cross-cultural conflict ("Dead Man's Path"); incomplete adaptations to English culture and religion ("Vengeful Creditor," "Marriage Is a Private Affair"); the Nigerian civil war ("Civil Peace," "Sugar Baby," "Girls at War"); growing up with an alien language ("Chike's School Days," a pleasant story about a little boy who collects English words as if they were seashells). The only pieces freshly imagined are the retellings and reinventions of local legend, especially "The Madman":

> The madman watched him for quite a while. Each time he bent down to carry water in cupped hands from the shallow stream to his head and body

the madman smiled at his parted behind. And then remembered. This was the same hefty man who brought three others like him and whipped me out of my hut in the Afo market. He nodded to himself. And he remembered again: this was the same vagabond who descended on me from the lorry in the middle of my highway. He nodded once more. And then he remembered yet again: this was the same fellow who set his children to throw stones at me and make remarks about their mother's buttocks, not mine. Then he laughed.

Nwibe turned sharply round and saw the naked man laughing, the deep grove of the stream amplifying his laughter. Then he stopped as suddenly as he had begun; the merriment vanished from his face.

"I have caught you naked," he said.

Nwibe ran a hand swiftly down his face to clear his eyes of water.

"I say I have caught you naked, with your thing dangling about."

Naked-shameless mirroring naked-shamed, madman mirroring not-yet-tempted, till, tempted, the pursued turns pursuer and goes mad in the pursuit.

The three other books by women are all of them manifestations of feminine sensibility (Sarraute, bless her dripping fangs, is too obstinately eccentric to disclose any secondary sex characteristics). The best book of the three, and her own worst, is Doris Lessing's *The Summer Before the Dark*. Its subject is the disintegration of a middle-aged middle-class housewife, during her first summer past the point of usefulness to her once-dependent husband and children. She has a summer of adventures: as an interpreter with an international agency; in an affair with a young American, whom, reverting to her accustomed role, she must tend in his illness; anonymously back in London, very ill herself, then sharing a hippie pad with a girl who becomes her confidante, mentor, daughter, surrogate, till (unconvincingly) the housewife decides to pick up and go home. The first half of the book carries on under a burden of desiccated post-mortem ironies:

> in their joint bedroom, were two books, side by side, one by Bertrand Russell called *The Conquest of Happiness,* and one by Van der Velde, *Ideal Marriage*. From Kate to Michael—Russell; and-from Michael to Kate—Van der Velde. Both inscriptions read: "For The First Phase. With all my love." This commemorated the fact that a phase had ended when their delicious love affair had to end, and they married. They had known that things must change, that the deliciousness must abate, and their long discussions about it all were summed up by these friendly books, From Kate to Michael, From Michael to Kate, *For The First Phase*. Now, picking up these books and opening them on the inscription page, both might have been caught out in a humorous grimace, *had* been caught out by each other, which led to frank and certainly healthy laughter. (Laughter is by definition healthy.) The point was why the humorous grimace at all? . . .

The second half is less offensive because in this half the stink of the sickness is out in the open and all around us, as, for instance, when Kate Brown demonstrates that "it's all a con":

> High in the air men walked on planks, dangled buckets, wielded trowels, manipulated cranes. Men were working, too, at ground level, preparing what was to be hoisted aloft. Kate realised that she was standing still, staring; had been for some minutes. The men took no notice of her.
> The fact that they didn't suddenly made her angry. She walked away out of sight, and there, took off her jacket—Maureen's—showing her fitting dark dress. She tied her hair dramatically with a scarf. Then she strolled back in front of the workmen, hips conscious of themselves. A storm of whistles, calls, invitations. Out of sight the other way, she made her small transformation and walked back again: the men glanced at her, did not see her. She was trembling with rage: it was a rage, it seemed to her, that she had been suppressing for a lifetime. And it was a front for worse, a misery that she did not want to answer, for it was saying again and again: This is what you have been doing for years and years and years.
> She made the transit again, as a sex object, and saw that a girl dressed like a Dutch doll stood on a corner opposite, watching. Full yellow skirts, a tight red jacket, hair in yellow curls, a bright pink patch on either cheek, wide blue eyes.
> Kate arrived beside Maureen and said, "And that's what it is all worth."

The narrator seems to be not just describing, here and elsewhere, a nervous breakdown but actually having one.

Life Signs transposes the etiology of that epidemic ailment housewife's staggers to a Greenwich Village apartment and a psychiatrist's office uptown. Pregnant Camilla, beautiful bright coed metamorphosed into jittery young wife-and-mother, begins to wake up screaming. Visits to a psychiatrist do no good, an idyllic session with a breast-fetishist does no good, smart-alec yackety-yack does no good, till smart Alec discovers what is the (most recent) cause of all the misery in the world—the psychiatrist's psilly pills! and sweeps his little family majestically out of the lair of the crazy shrink:

> Manos, exasperated, shook Alec's hand. "It isn't just the pills," he argued. "She badly needs her sleep patterns regulated, she should be removed from the family situation . . ."
> "There we have it, begging your pardon, in a nutshell," said Alec, plucking Jacob off the lavender wall-to-wall onto which (Camilla, already elated, made room for bonus delight) he had emptied the major portion of his juice bottle. "See, it's not a family situation, Dr. Manos," continued Alec, wincing with the sudden blast of April sunlight outside the door. "It's a family."

That cocky definitive riposte and blast of sunlight warm the soapy cockles; but *Life Signs* ends, after the Alec-assisted birth of Emma, with an unmistakable air of whistling in the dark: "It was one whole week before she began to sleepwalk. Just as well, she and Alec agreed, since she had to be up anyway, to feed Emma. It was nothing worth worrying about, in any case. Nothing was." Alec had better get smart again soon—like by Wednesday next.

Judith Rascoe's collection of stories emphasizes how fragile women are: "a daughter, who was moody and talkative, already damaged by the broken marriage." Also how large and brutally experienced any self-respecting horse has the obligation to be: "After the divorce I often saw Louis at parties accompanied by the lady of the porcelain horse, who was small and brutally inexperienced. She glanced at other people through brilliant blue contact lenses with no curiosity whatsoever." Marriage is a series of random catastrophes, life is the brilliant blue anteroom at Forest Lawn, men are chumps:

> My friends . . . tried to find me somebody else. Charley and Betsy called me to come to dinner. Betsy served roast beef and Charley served his old school friends, most of whom were a good deal like Charley. They were all slight of build, even-tempered and scared of women, and most of them scientists of one sort or another. . . .

"Yours, and Mine" (note the comma, signifying separation) is sheer rampant girlish guck, a one-woman exhibition of *Angst* in beautiful Santa Barbara, and appropriately concludes with a thunderous symbolic allusion to the Santa Barbara oil spill:

> A magazine had pictures of it, and I cut one out. It shows a man standing in the water and holding up a dying bird. You can't tell its species. It had seen a fish glinting through a wave, I suppose, but when it dived to seize it, oil flowed over the surface of the water and clung to its feathers, and it couldn't fly away. The oil companies have promised to rescue as many of these birds as they can.

In fact the bird was later identified as a red-eyed bluetit, more or less female.

Rascoe writes what critics used to call, before they were intimidated by angry rebuttals from *New Yorker* editors who insisted that there was no such thing, a *New Yorker* short story: which, if there *were* such a thing, would rely on a manner deliberately sleek and casual to imply dizzying unplumbed depths; a predilection for childlike whimsy, wry irony, nostalgia, life's bitter mystery; an occasional offhand boulder-sized symbol to make a dot-sized point—

> [cactus hedges] are what all plants must be at the core. They get hideously scarred and go on living, unable to cast off the scarred portions, growing slowly and stubbornly, looking as if they have the right by their very ugliness to dispute every inch of ground with man and animal. Oh, I should

like to remember the exact color of the meadow covered with tall grass, but I remember the cactus more clearly . . . .

—Rascoe's apprentice best. Donald Barthelme, the quirkily "modern" *New Yorker* master, does better; and John Cheever, old pro, is the smoothest of all, managing in most of his stories to veil past, present, and future in a fine gray spittle of arbitrary disillusion:

> "Will you never learn, Leander, that lamb must be carved against the grain?" she would ask. . . . After five or six wounding remarks my father would wave the carving knife in the air and shout: "Will you kindly mind your own business, will you kindly shut up?" She would sigh once more and put her hand to her heart. Surely this was her last breath. Then, studying the air above the table she would say: "Feel that refreshing breeze."
>
> There was, of course, seldom a breeze. It could be airless, midwinter, rainy, anything. The remark was one for all seasons. Was it a commendable metaphor for hope, for the serenity of love (which I think she had never experienced), was it nostalgia for some summer evening when, loving and understanding, we sat contentedly on the lawn above the river? Was it no better or no worse than the sort of smile thrown at the evening star by a man who is in utter despair? Was it a prophecy of that generation to come who would be so drilled in evasiveness that they would be denied forever the splendors of a passionate confrontation?

(That last rhetorical question is nonsense—What "generation to come" is he talking about? the Lost Generation? post-World-War-II?—but part of the charm of such writing is that its disillusion depends on a strict abstention from thinking.) Today, in the American tourists' Rome, the narrator hears a different voice, "the voice of an American woman. She is screaming. 'You're a goddamned fucked-up no-good insane piece of shit. . .' . . . Why would I sooner describe church bells and flocks of swallows? Is this puerile, a sort of greeting-card mentality, a whimsical and effeminate refusal to look at facts? . ." (The answer to *this* question seems obvious—such writing aims at intimating that, though life is almost nothing but questions, the few answers are all obvious: beauty, truth, church bells, money. . . .)

Cheever has a thing about pornography, and nearly loses his temper attacking it directly in two of the stories. Moreover, in the title story of *The World of Apples* he seems to be offering his careful and oblique rejoinder to the threat. A Frost-like American poet in his eighties, resident in Italy, finds himself suddenly and against his will a dirty-minded old man; makes a pilgrimage to "the sacred angel of Monte Giordano," to whom he gives his most cherished literary medal and, kneeling, prays "loudly: 'God bless Walt Whitman. God bless Hart Crane. God bless Dylan Thomas. God bless William Faulkner, Scott Fitzgerald, and especially Ernest Hemingway'"; bathes naked under a waterfall as he remembers having seen his father do many years ago; and is restored—"in the morning he began a long poem on the inalienable dignity of light and air that, while it would not get him the Nobel Prize, would grace the last months of his life." End of book, and just as well too, since that poem would be as easy to predict as it was to propose.

Of course the *New Yorker* story isn't a story in the traditional meaning of the word, it's a pretext for the writer's sensibility (which is likely to seem feminine because displays of sensibility have been considered a woman's prerogative). One of the pleasures of reading Malamud's new collection is that his stories make so archaic an effort to establish themselves as distinct structures: they can even be *remembered*.

The best of them are the two shortest, hardly more than vignettes, rigorously bleak. "The Letter" is an unsealed blank envelope with four blank sheets of paper inside; Teddy, one of the inmates at the state hospital, asks Newman to mail it for him whenever Newman is on the way out after visiting his father, and on the last occasion Teddy's father, also an inmate, adds his own plea:

> "Mail it anyway for the poor kid," said Ralph. His tall body trembled. He was an angular man with deep-set bluish eyes and craggy features that looked as though they had been hacked out of a tree.
> "I told your son I would if he wrote something on the paper," Newman said.
> "What do you want it to say?"
> "Anything he wants it to. Isn't there somebody he wants to communicate with? If he doesn't want to write it he could tell me what to say and I'll write it out."
> "Tough turd," said Teddy.
> "He wants to communicate to me," said Ralph.
> "It's not a bad idea," Newman said. "Why doesn't he write a few words to you? Or you could write a few words to him."
> "A Bronx cheer on you."
> "It's my letter," Teddy said.

"My Son the Murderer" launches itself from the son's gloom about the imminence of his being drafted for Vietnam, but becomes a touching image of the father's love and fear:

> Harry, I'm frightened. Tell me what's the matter. My son, have mercy on me.
> I'm frightened of the world, Harry thought. It fills me with fright.
> He said nothing.
> A blast of wind lifted his father's hat and carried it away over the beach. It looked as though it were going to be blown into the surf, but then the wind blew it toward the boardwalk, rolling like a wheel along the wet sand. Leo chased after his hat. He chased it one way, then another, then toward the water. By now he was crying. Breathless, he wiped his eyes with icy fingers and returned to his son at the edge of the water.

> He is a lonely man. This is the type he is. He will always be lonely.
> My son who made himself into a lonely man.
> Harry, what can I say to you? All I can say to you is who says life is easy? Since when? It wasn't easy for me and it isn't for you. It's life, that's the way it is—what more can I say? But if a person don't want to live what can he do if he's dead? Nothing is nothing, it's better to live.
> Come home Harry, he said. It's cold here. You'll catch a cold with your feet in the water.
> Harry stood motionless in the water and after a while his father left. As he was leaving, the wind plucked his hat off his head and sent it rolling along the shore.
> My father listens in the hallway. He follows me in the street.
> We meet at the edge of the water.
> He runs after his hat.
> My son stands with his feet in the ocean.

"Man in the Drawer" is an ambitious story about an American's encounter in Moscow with a Russian writer who can't get published; but the moral issue is too clear, the synopses of the writer's pieces make them seem dull; the story is inert. In "Notes for a Lady at a Dinner Party" Malamud returns, in an uncomfortable dinner jacket, to the academic scene. The other stories are competent journeyman's work, sometimes better than that, the kind of thing however that Malamud has already done well in his earlier books: "The Silver Crown," Jewish customs with a sinister whiff of magic; "Talking Horse," an amusing beast-fable that goes on too long and is too philosophical. But Malamud repays attention, if only for the sake of the discovery that even honest writers can repeat themselves or write mechanically.

Nabokov's collection of early stories (dated 1927-1940) shows that he was an earnest reader of at least Chekhov and Mann, not necessarily to his advantage. "The Potato Elf," about a circus dwarf, is just as false, and false in the same ways, as Mann's "Little Herr Friedemann": patronizing, sentimental, calculable in the humiliations that the author, fancying himself a well of compassion or of objective truth, heaps on his homunculus. "Lips to Lips" and "An Affair of Honor" are more Chekhovian-ironic, but like "The Potato Elf" they take rather too much satisfaction in the humiliations suffered by the protagonists, who differ from any of Chekhov's by being all but absolute sad sacks. Nabokov seems to prefer stationary targets: in "The Leonardo" he goes after Nazi-type brutes ("Gigantic, imperiously reeking of sweat and beer with beefy voices and senseless speeches, with fecal matter replacing the human brain . . ."); in "A Dashing Fellow" he fires away at the sexual peccadilloes of a traveling salesman ("We are alone in a third-class compartment—alone and, therefore, bored") and ends with a stupefying moral thud:

> The train was crammed, the heat stifling. We feel out of sorts, but do not quite know if we are hungry or drowsy. But when we have fed and slept, life

will regain its looks, and the American instruments will make music in the merry cafe described by our friend Lange. And then, sometime later, we die.

The title story is near-Chekhov with a mild Nabokovian sneer; there are a couple of long pieces foreshadowing the precious, unctuous, ferocious, and cynical American prestidigitator who arrived in a puff of Mephistophelean smoke with *Lolita;* even a story ("Terra Incognita"), not very interesting in itself, that suggests its author may have been reading Raymond Roussel. "The Visit to the Museum," on the other hand, after a characteristic indulgence in digressive snobbery, settles down as a personally felt and impressively constructed piece in the form of an exile's nightmare; "Breaking the News" is slighter in subject and theme but affecting throughout: in both of them the author, for a change, becomes too personally involved to keep playing his roguish tricks of personality—

> every time I turned and tried to retrace my steps along the passages, I found myself in hitherto unseen places—a greenhouse with hydrangeas and broken window-panes with the darkness of artificial night showing through beyond; or a deserted laboratory with dusty alembics on its tables. Finally I ran into a room of some sort with coatracks monstrously loaded down with black coats and astrakhan furs, from beyond a door came a burst of applause, but when I flung the door open, there was no theater, but only a soft opacity and splendidly counterfeited fog with the perfectly convincing blotches of indistinct streetlights . . . .

Malamud hasn't developed at all from his earliest stories, and admirers of Nabokov will be outraged by the mere naming of their hero in the same sentence; but Nabokov's development tends to resemble a creeping elephantiasis of traits that weren't attractive from the beginning, though in the beginning they at least permitted him to have literary ancestors. Ultimately Nabokov, like Joyce, eliminates art by creating the autonomous author: sensibility orbiting perpetually on itself. Malamud isn't a great writer, but he isn't a monster either, and he never tires (as Nabokov tired early) of breaking the news from somewhere out in the world.

Fiction and Truth[1]

Poets lie, said Plato; but novelists don't always tell the truth either. E. M. Forster made his reputation from novels in which respectable Englishmen and Englishwomen try to work out their fates under circumstances that wouldn't have seemed outlandish to Trollope or Jane Austen. Meanwhile, between his two best-known novels, in 1913-14 ("at the height of his powers," according to the blurb), he wrote *Maurice*. Now at last *Maurice* is in print, posthumously, with evidence of Forster's primary and lifelong commitment to circumstances that neither *Howards End* nor *A Passage to India* found room for, that indeed at the time weren't even mentionable in private conversation except (as Forster indicates in his "Terminal Note," dated 1960) among "carefully picked" friends:

> "Alec, wake up."
> An arm twitched.
> "Time we talked plans."
> He snuggled closer, more awake than he pretended, warm, sinewy, happy. Happiness overwhelmed Maurice too. He moved, felt the answering grip, and forgot what he wanted to say. Light drifted in upon them from the outside world where it was still raining. A strange hotel, a casual refuge protected them from their enemies a little longer.
> "Time to get up, boy. It's morning."
> "Git up then."
> "How can I the way you hold me!"
> "Aren't yer a fidget, I'll learn you to fidget." He wasn't deferential any more. The British Museum had cured that. This was 'oliday, London with

---

[1] This piece is the Fiction Chronicle in the Spring 1972 issue of *The Hudson Review* (with a splice from my earlier discussion of Anthony Powell in the Spring 1964 issue). E. M. Forster, *Maurice* (Norton, 1971). E. M. Forster, *Albergo Empedocle and Other Writings* (Liveright, 1971). Anthony Powell, *A Dance to the Music of Time: First Movement* (Little, Brown, 1963). Anthony Powell, *A Dance to the Music of Time: Second Movement* (Little, Brown, 1964). Anthony Powell, *A Dance to the Music of Time: Third Movement* (Little, Brown, 1971). Anthony Powell, *Books Do Furnish a Room* (Little, Brown, 1971). Joyce Carol Oates, *With Shuddering Fall* (Crest, 1971). Joyce Carol Oates, *A Garden of Earthly Delights* (Crest, 1970). Joyce Carol Oates, *Expensive People* (Crest, 1970). Joyce Carol Oates, *them* (Crest, 1970). Joyce Carol Oates, *Wonderland* (Vanguard, 1971). Philip Roth, *Our Gang* (Random House, 1971). John Updike, *Rabbit Redux* (Knopf, 1971). Ann Cornelisen, *Torregreca* (Atlantic-Little, Brown, 1969). Ann Cornelisen, *Vendetta of Silence* (Atlantic-Little, Brown, 1971). Ronald Blythe, *Akenfield* (Delta, 1970).

Maurice, all troubles over, and he wanted to drowse and waste time, and tease and make love.

The British Museum didn't brace up Alec with a series of lectures on equality and sex hygiene, it was merely the locale in the previous chapter where Maurice Hall talked him out of blackmail ("Mr. Hall—you reckernize it wouldn't very well suit you if certain things came out, I suppose") and over to true love: Forster, however, is scrutinizing those sinewy limbs, not problems of denotation. And if you've begun to suspect that, a dozen years before *Lady Chatterley's Lover,* Forster had already hit on the theme of sex as the solvent of English class distinctions, you'll be delighted by the information that Alec too is a gamekeeper! Lady or lord, soft or sinewy, it's all in the same bag.

The trouble with homosexuals is that they're snobs: "The love that Socrates bore Phaedo now lay within his reach, love passionate but temperate, such as only finer natures can understand . . . ";

> "I'm a bit of an outlaw, I grant, but it serves these people right. As long as they talk of the unspeakable vice of the Greeks they can't expect fair play. It served my mother right when I slipped up to kiss you before dinner. She would have no mercy if she knew, she wouldn't attempt, wouldn't want to attempt to understand that I feel to you as Pippa to her fiancé, only far more nobly, far more deeply, body and soul, no starved medievalism of course, only a—a particular harmony of body and soul that I don't think women have even guessed. But you know."

All the Platonizing doesn't protect Forster's metaphors against frequent oral and colonic irrigations: "Clive knew that ecstasy cannot last, but can carve a channel for something lasting, and he contrived a relation that proved permanent. If Maurice made love it was Clive who preserved it, and caused its rivers to water the garden. He could not bear that one drop should be wasted. . . ."

Maurice, bad as it is, nevertheless is Forster's only truthful book, full of nerves, hysteria, infatuations, bitterness ("England has always been disinclined to accept human nature"), and facts about the England of 1914 that help explain Maurice's choice of the unspeakable vice: "When he arrived in her room after marriage, she did not know what he wanted. Despite an elaborate education, no one had told her about sex. . . . So much could never be mentioned. He never saw her naked, nor she him. . . ." The "great novels" are mirages. *A Passage to India* has some travel-diary observation and momentum, but the crudeness of Forster's sensibility is illustrated by the climactic trope he invents for the coming together of Fielding and Miss Quested: "A friendliness, as of dwarfs shaking hands, was in the air."[2] *Howards End*—"undoubtedly Forster's masterpiece," says Lionel Trilling—is part boy-scout

---

[2] Wayne C. Booth, a snob about dwarfs as Forster is about women, gets awfully excited pointing out that "no one in the book is capable of that simile except the narrator, the one character who sees the full

oath ("Only connect! That was the whole of her sermon. Only connect the prose and the passion, and both will be exalted, and human love will be seen at its height . . . "), part Put-Christ-back-into-Christmas ("How many of these vacillating shoppers and tired shop-assistants realized that it was a divine event . . . ?"), part *East Lynne* ("he was rotten at the core"), part snobbery again ("She was a rubbishy little creature"), part wisdom ("Science explained people, but could not understand them"), and all lies. As for the posthumous collection, *Albergo Empedocle and Other Writings*, it's a miscellany of very old pieces: the long and disagreeable crypto-homosexual fantasy named in the title; some unpretentious essays and reviews about war, India, and literature; Cambridge *juvenilia*, among which (in an amusing takeoff on *Agamemnon*) appears the deathless stage direction—"Exit Aegisthus, leading Chrysothemis weeping and Electra kicking his shins."

In one of the reviews Forster, liberated Edwardian, attacks the Victorian dispensation, which no doubt deserves everything he can think of to throw at it. What's equally obvious is that (with the great exception of Lawrence) English novelists since the Victorians haven't been able to do better than class-writing and coterie-writing, provincialism, Bloomsburyism, irony (of the twentieth-century, facing-both-ways variety: if you like it, I mean it; if you don't, I'm camping it up), nothing much going on but much gesticulation and manner, tricks. In the rare instances—Anthony Powell is one—where a large *oeuvre* is produced, it has none of the substantiality and assurance of even the minor Victorians.

For many years Powell has been quietly assembling an Anglo-American cult with the ten books that now constitute the three thick volumes (plus one-third of the next) of A *Dance to the Music of Time*. Since the plan of this "novel" is indefinitely expansible while its protagonist (and author) remains at the ready to pry with pathologically unflagging tidiness into the tepid lives of two or three dozen upper-class English families, it won't fail to turn up in the *Guinness Book of World Records* as the longest novel ever written (it is already twice as long as *War and Peace*).

Powell's early novels resemble those of his friend, Evelyn Waugh, without Waugh's comic inventiveness or frivolously sadistic twists of plot. They have the standard Oxbridge anti-American and anti-Semitic revulsions (from *Afternoon Men*: "He was dark and had bags under the eyes and rather a thick nose, but the general effect was not bad and he hardly looked like a Jew at all"); they tell about 'twentyish emancipation, silly parties at which drunks behave stupidly, ambitious young men on the make for the daughters of fox-hunting families, all with an air of slightness and couldn't-care-less. *From a View to a Death,* published over thirty years ago, has an amusing post-Dickensian eccentric of a Major, whose hobby, one might say, is tranvestism; but not much else except that air of contrived insouciance.

Now the subject-matter of A *Dance to the Music of Time* is no more serious; only, Powell seems to assume that if you do the same slight material over and over again, left and right, backward and forward, upstairs and down, you will achieve weight and

---

value of being sensible, honest and subtle, and yet sees that men and women may exemplify these virtues and still be only amiable dwarfs." *The Rhetoric of Fiction* (University of Chicago Press, 1961), p. 189.

substance: an apotheosis, no doubt, of the frightfully literate mysteries of English social twaddle, which carries snobbery to unexampled heights of tedium. His devotees will argue that what counts is Powell's intelligence, which they say plays over these pointless lives with Chaucerian (or Proustian) irony and compassion. One trick of his intelligence is to devise an action in which otherwise unassociated characters keep stumbling over one another in the most remote circumstances, so that somebody's unexpected reappearance may be said, complacently, to help "prove somehow rather consolingly, that life continued its mysterious, patterned way": not even Hardy's stacked deck of malign chance, but just a pretext for bringing the same people together again for another bout of gossip, reminiscence, news—"a little grayer," "scarcely changed," "a little fuller," and as damned dull as ever. His intelligence doesn't boggle, either, at frequent doses of that cheapest rhetorical pretense of subtlety, the adverbial mystifier: "curiously overpowering," "curiously unrelenting," "curiously harsh," "in an obscure way depressing," "I was for some reason reminded," "oddly interesting." Nor at bogus insights about life, death, marriage, money, men, women, and children.

Powell's method of getting on with the story must be the most ponderously inefficient of all time. To begin with, each character is introduced as he first appears to the narrator, who immediately speculates for three or four pages on the probable nature of a character who is blond, has small ears, and wears a black overcoat. The overcoat then says a few desultory words, whereupon the narrator takes several pages of pains to modify his original opinion in the light of this additional evidence. Whenever the overcoat turns up later in the same book, the narrator cleverly seizes on new bits of evidence which, again, satisfy or disappoint or modify, but in any case are incorporated into, his bulky expectations. The procedure lapses into real lunacy in all the books after the first, since each character described in Book I is recapitulated in virtually the same terms and at the same length in Books II, III and so on, before new desultory information is produced and incorporated: this spreading tumor of speculation being intended, one supposes, to serve for as true an image of the character as the mind of man affords. It need hardly be noted that there is astonishingly little dialogue—how could there be? Powell is too busy reminding us who Lady Warminster or Erridge or Quiggin is, to let them have a go at defining themselves by speaking out, even if he could think of something interesting for them to say. Powell is suffering from an elephantiasis of the will, making immense harrumphing preparations for something that never happens: "a pedestal without a statue," as Tchaikovsky remarked of some of Brahms's music.[3]

Book III (*The Acceptance World*) breaks free enough of the straitjacket of Powell's procedure to present genuine events, crises, even lively dialogue: it opens with Uncle

---

[3] The honorific musical analogy for his novel, which Powell solicits and which his admirers are only too happy to afirm, will not work. The periodic repetition of a statement or description in a novel is not analogous, not indeed comparable, to the periodic repetition of a theme in a piece of music. (Even the use of a refrain in verse presupposes, or suggests, a musical setting: the possibility of song validates the recurrence of the words.) Prose statement functions in a nexus of facts, premises, conclusions, principles: a nexus in which repetition appears as a blocking, a kind of mental stuttering or incapacity.

Giles, Powell's meanest and most vivid eccentric, at the top of his form; introduces Giles's friend, the ominously placid prophetess, Mrs. Erdleigh; moves through a séance at which the voice of Karl Marx speaks, rather querulously; warmly memorializes the narrator's hopeless affair with a girl he can't begin to try to understand. But Books I, II, IV, and V are maddening catalogs of trivia, and Book VI is a symbolified piece of solemn quackery about England on the eve of both wars. Even though Arthur Mizener seems to disagree,[4] Powell is not the greatest living novelist.

He is very likely the most copious, though copiousness isn't of itself necessarily a virtue. On the publication of the latest volume of *The Decline and Fall of the Roman Empire,* the Duke of Gloucester remarked to its author: "Another damned, thick, square book! Always scribble, scribble, scribble! Eh! Mr. Gibbon?" *A Dance to the Music of Time: Third Movement* (consisting of three sections—*The Valley of Bones, The Soldier's Art, The Military Philosophers*) and *Books Do Furnish a Room* have now appeared, Installments Seven through Ten of what has developed beyond fiction into the most interminable soap-opera since Australopithecus; and the Duke of Gloucester of blessed memory, if he were still among us, would no doubt be competent to take proper notice of the event. Unarmed with the Duke's prerogative of forthrightness, the reviewer is tempted to try something witty and indirect, like parody, for example, of Powell's clairvoyant-narrator trick: "There was about him something melancholy, perhaps even tragic, that was hard to define"; "She had a quiet, rather sad manner, suggesting one of those reserved, well behaved, fairly peevish women, usually of determined character, often to be found as wives, or ex-wives, of notably dissipated men"; "As the gas flared up again, its hiss for some inexplicable reason suggested an explanation of why Pamela had married Widmerpool." Or of Powell's everybody-somehow-reminds-me-of-everybody-else trick: "There was something of Kedward about him; something, too, which I could not define, of my brother-in-law, Chips Lovell"; "When I first met Umfraville I had noticed some resemblance to Buster Foxe, now revealed as that similarity companionship in early life confers on people"; "He had a voice of horrible refinement, which must have taken years to perfect, and somewhat recalled that of Howard Craggs, the left-wing publisher." Or of Powell's Peter-Pithy-used-to-pontificate trick: "Was he, in principle, regardless of personal idiosyncrasy, what Sir Gavin Walpole-Wilson used to call 'a man of taste'?"; "In short, Frederica's most notable characteristic was what Molly Jeavons called her 'dreadful correctness'"; "Thought I'd try Kenya, the great open spaces where men are men, as Charles Stringham used to say." Or of Powell's sudden-rash-of-associationism trick—

> [Lord Aberavon's] name was merely memorable to myself as deceased owner of Mr Deacon's *Boyhood of Cyrus,* the picture in the Walpole-Wilsons' hall,

---

[4] "The effect of *The Music of Time* is a very remarkable one for the mid-twentieth century. It is as if we had come suddenly on an enormously intelligent but completely undogmatic mind with a vision of experience that is deeply penetrating and yet wholly recognizable, beautifully subtle in ordination and yet quite unostentatious in technique, and in every respect undistorted by doctrine." Arthur Mizener, *The Sense of Life in the Modern Novel* (Houghton Mifflin, 1964), p. 102

which always made me think of Barbara Goring when I had been in love with her in pre-historic times. Lord Aberavon had been Barbara Goring's grandfather; Eleanor Walpole-Wilson's grandfather too. I wondered what had happened to Barbara, whether her husband, Johnny Pardoe (who also owned a house in the country of which Gwatkin spoke), had been recalled to the army. Eleanor, lifelong friend of my sister-in-law, Norah Tolland, was now, like Norah herself, driving cars for some women's service. . . .

Cobwebs and dishwater, condescension, malice, inertness, tics, false specification, simpering imprecision, endlessly unsorted gossip, on and on and on, not preliminaries or bridge-passages but the staple, the thing itself, the world as a closetful of baseless opinions (even in dialogue Powell's characters are empty coats dangling on the coathangers of his opinions about them); because none of these quotations, sad to admit, is parody at all, they justly represent Powell's range and are from one or another of the four new novels, of which the only startling sentence occurs in *The Valley of Bones*, page 197: "For a moment the name conveyed nothing." It's the only such moment in the so far two and a half thousand pages of Powell's otherwise unstoppable or immovable name-spinning machine.

"When the time," said *Time* about *The Music of Time*, "comes for the historian to get the sense of what life was like for the British between and during the two big wars . . . he can wrap up the whole era with Anthony Powell's incalculably brilliant series. . . ." Shortly, if not sooner, some hack who indefinably resembles the Droeshout engraving of Shakespeare, with under the earlobes a touch of my brother-in-law Legs Diamond, will write something comparable about an American novelist who bids fair to break all the track records long before she's forty. Joyce Carol Oates was born in 1938: she has already published volumes of verse, volumes of short stories, and five novels; among her many prizes, she won the National Book Award for her fourth novel, *them;* when the time comes for the historian to get the sense of what life was like in the U.S. between FDR and Nixon, he can empty out the whole sack of Oates and scratch around in the true grain of America, incalculably caustic, homicidal (nay bloody and violent), scurfy, cruddy, gritty, nutty, running the national gamut from Dustin Hoffman to King Kong.

Typical activities in Oates novels are arson, rape, riot, mental breakdown, murder (plain and fancy, with excursions into patricide. matricide, uxoricide, mass filicide), suicide. None of these is more than sketchily motivated, because experience and feeling are by their nature mysteries, dissociated and inexplicable ("All of my writing," says Oates, "is about the mystery of human emotions"), though it's not clear why inexplicable mysteries are always nasty rather than nice. Typical and predictable equations: man = irrational brute force; woman = irrational treacherousness; love = hate; passion = murder. The typical Oates plot begins at the bottom of the Depression (the extended time-scheme seems to have epic intentions, but its chief effect is a sluggish opening tempo); meanders for a hundred pages or so through a naturalistic account of uninterrupted misery over the long years (an account founded on the axiom that the poor, having read the sociology texts, spend decades at a stretch without a moment's peace or pleasure); and abruptly bursts into a carnival of arson, rape, riot, murder, *etc.* If Oates begins with a whimper, she ends with a bang: *With Shuddering Fall* ends with a probable suicide, vigilante brutality, and the heroine's commitment to a mental hospital (in a "happy" epilogue, she returns home); *A Garden of Earthly Delights*—the title is ironic—ends with attempted matricide, accidental quasi-patricide,[5] suicide, and the heroine's commitment to a mental hospital; *Expensive People* ends with matricide; *them* tunes up with a brisk little inaugural murder, proceeds to a mental breakdown and an attempted murder, and ends with an urban riot and a cop-killing (by the hero of course). In *Wonderland*, which begins on an unexpected upbeat with a family massacre, Oates makes an effort to splice her horrors (necrophiliac heterosexual cannibalism for one: a male doctor reports having taken home a female cadaver's uterus, broiled it, and eaten it) in at regular intervals among the dreary daily round of things: the dissociation and craziness are more evenly distributed; but the effect is rearrangement and aggravation rather than difference.

The novels are quite American in numerous extra-literary ways, influenced for instance by movie images and conventions out of the Hollywood Age of Gilt: the character Max in the first novel is the gross, sweating, middle-aged fat man with a veddy cultivated line of gab but (or therefore) some kind of sex pervert, played by Sydney Greenstreet[6]; a scene in *them* (when Jules first breaks in on Nadine at her home) is, with wild incongruity, in the manner of a Cary Grant-Irene Dunne roguish romantic comedy of the 'thirties; the episodes of rural poverty have the varnished surface of Hollywood social realism; *A Garden of Earthly Delights* presents the triangle of passionate woman, footloose lover, and patient wealthy husband that wrung many a handkerchief in the old Bijou; pregnancy is automatic with the first dime in the meter. Out of the same period (if you'll excuse the expression) comes the women's-magazine diction that Oates seems to be trying to recollect and preserve: "in the hot icy [!] gleam of his eyes that held her rigid," the heroine sees "the uneasiness of the predatory beast that suspects he can never achieve satiation," but she'll be glad to give him a whirl. "'She isn't like you, Clara,' Revere said once. 'She isn't a happy woman.'" "Her hands fell onto her stomach and she thought fiercely that she would betray anybody for this baby; she would even kill if she had to. She would do anything. She would kill Lowry himself if she had to." Shades of Stella Dallas. The quality of the writing, in the first two novels especially, is often low and sometimes beneath contempt; Oates teaches herself to write better, at least more carefully and more professionally, in the later novels; but she never gives up her original preoccupations and her mimicry of heart-clutching femaleness.

---

[5] This calls for a gloss. The boy aims at his mother ("No, you're not going to shoot me! You think you can shoot me? Me? You think you can kill your own mother? People can't do things like that, they can't pull the trigger! You can't pull the trigger! You're weak. . ."), but "at the last instant" he "jerked the gun to one side and when he pulled the trigger it was the old man he hit." The "old man" is, as far as the world knows and even as far as the boy himself has been told, the boy's father; but . . .

[6] As I pointed out earlier (on p. 151), another fictional character played by Greenstreet was Edmund Wilson, because Greenstreet had a weighty manner that could be made to seem epicene or sinister or jovial or like Wilson uncontradictably authoritative.

The only one of the novels that is more than clinically interesting is *Expensive People,* which is also the only one that attempts comedy and satire. Its literary satire manages nothing better than mock-reviews written by the author in what she takes to be the style of one weekly pundit or another: "It is sheer cant (though speculative) that the product of a mad, feverish mind must be in itself mad and feverish . . ."; or she indulges in juvenile hijinks with names—"Johns Behemoth Boys' School," "Vastvalley Country Club," "Dr. Saskatoon." The suburban comedy, however, has moments of shrewdness; the narrator's mother is the only realized character in Oates's novels, a bright, likable, seductive, and impossible woman; and there's a wonderful cameo chapter about "my dog Spark" ("When I was very little Father and Nada gave me a nice Christmas present: a little dog named Spark"), an immortal creature that keeps getting run over by laundry trucks and being brought back a few days later, "safe and sound from the doctor," looking nearly the same as ever. But most of the book wastes its time in the company of the narrator, who turns sniper and eventually shoots his mother dead.

The puzzle in these five novels (when they aren't beneath contempt) is less their crazy violence than the author's indifference to what provokes it, or rather her indifference to the possibility that human feeling may have any natural rhythm or logic or direction or duration at all. It's not that she seems to be trying cynically for sensational effects: the effects aren't sensational, they don't seem cynically contrived; but they are in fact revolting—mainly because she hasn't paid attention, because it's sinful for a writer to remain so perversely innocent (Stella Dallas or Lady Macbeth) while developing considerable skill and expending formidable energy in the practice of the literary genre that evolved to deal with the rhythm, logic, direction, duration—the complete architecture—of human feeling. In an Oates novel, something disgusting and destructive will happen on the next page or in the next chapter, and the reader can't even conclude that it came from somewhere or will issue in something else: the only inference is that life is causelessly vile, and for such an inference the immense machinery of fiction is futile; characters emerging and time passing are unnecessary; an aphorism will do. One grasps at straws: maybe the author is perfectly normal, except for thinking that these are the sorts of things that happen in books.

Dreadful things happen in love in the ripeness of time, maybe we can't hear the lesson too often. But in an Oates novel, since life is lunacy and love is hate and passion is murder, very soon rather than late one or both of the lovers will lapse for long enough—say, the woman doesn't have an orgasm and feels despondent—to demonstrate these equivalences as a *whim*:

> She continued walking alongside him, but on the far side of the sidewalk. Then, out of her pocket, she took an object—Jules looked and saw at first a small black purse. Then he looked and saw a gun. She held this out toward him as if waving him away.
>
> "What are you doing? My God!" Jules said, more in alarm for her than for himself, fearful of her being seen. "What are you doing? Nadine? Put that back, hide it!"

> She walked alongside him as if forcing him along. With the gun she kept him at a distance, assessing him. But there was no recognition in her face. Her beauty had gone all into hardness, in vacuity.
> "Nadine, you're not going to shoot me, not me," Jules said, astonished. "You love me, I love you—don't you love me?"
> She pulled the trigger. The bullet struck him somewhere in the chest, a terrible blow. Jules reeled, seeing the sunshine shattered in the windshields of an acre of large, gleaming, expensive cars.
> The spirit of the Lord departed from Jules.

This misunderstanding occurs in *them*. In *Wonderland* (which should have been titled *it*), Oates surpasses herself from the very beginning, which is a lengthy naturalistic description, from a boy's point of view, of a Depression Christmas for a small-town family afflicted by the father's recent loss of his business (ironic counterpoint for the boy sitting in the car in which his father is driving him home: "The figure of Santa Claus seems to be flying through the closed-in air of the store windows, with his reindeer and sleigh, bundled with presents, one hand lifted in a merry salute"). The episode culminates in the boy's discovery, as he enters the house, of his butchered family:

> There is a jumble of bodies, arms and blood, drifts of hair like field grass, stiff with blood. His sister Jean lies with something shattered beside her—a lamp, maybe—and there is white glass mixed with the blood. A lampshade is splattered with blood. Jean's face is turned away; no, it had bled away, half of it is soaked in the rug, half of it is gone . . . .

and so on. The murderer is his father, who thereupon pursues him through the dark trying to finish the job. Now such things do happen in the world, as we are reminded later in the novel by Dr. Pedersen's scrapbook (called "The Book of Fates"): we have seen them memorialized in brief newspaper accounts, minus the slaughterhouse details that Oates sees fit to supply, minus also the painstaking examination of all these lives that the average reasonable novelist would have the prudence or decency to supply.

Wonderland isn't a diabolist outrage like *Justine* or *Philosophy in the Bedroom*, not little-green-men fantasy or gallows humor, not even Poësque thrills or melodrama; it just doesn't know any better. The boy, Jesse, having escaped his father (who—surprise!—commits suicide), survives to grow up in one household after another, finally Dr. Pedersen's, which seems intended to be sinister but instead is an intermittently amusing sideshow of antiseptic obesity, presided over by the unctuous doctor (Sydney Greenstreet again, or maybe Robert Morley in a change-of-pace rôle): "Perfection is difficult, Hildie, but ultimately it is not as difficult as imperfection. The demands we make upon ourselves constitute our salvation. It is necessary to be perfect. It is not necessary to live." The supreme horror in the book, the wildest of Oates, is a gluttony episode (like the daydream of a precocious eight-year-old kept too long in bed with a boring illness), in which first Jesse and Mrs. Pedersen, runaways from the doctor, together eat four Chinese dinners in her hotel room ("pressed almond duck, beef with Chinese vegetables, shrimps in lobster sauce, chicken chow mein. He had to wait for the food to be prepared and his mouth began to water. So he bought a few candy bars . . . "); then Jesse alone another "handful of candy bars" and, sitting on the floor in the hall outside her room, four more of the same dinners by himself ("His stomach was an enormous open hole, a raw hole, a wound . . . the Chinese food was so delicate, so thin, there was no substance to it. . . . He should have bought some hamburgers, some good solid American cheeseburgers from the hotel's coffee shop . . . "); then to a diner where he orders "six hamburgers with chili sauce on them, three side dishes of French files, and a Coke. He finished the Coke before the food was ready, so he ordered another. . . ." On the next page Jesse goes off to the University of Michigan, does well there, reduces to normal weight, pushes on through medical school, marries unhappily ("She had married him but she did not know him"), becomes a well-known surgeon, discusses brain transplants, almost has an affair ("He loved her, but he was not in love with her. He did not love her with this fierce, sickening certainty . . . "), is upset by the assassination of President Kennedy, inherits $600,000, opens a clinic, tracks down his daughter (who has joined the itinerant drug-culture), carries her to a nearby boat, and drifts away with her—

> "All of you . . . everyone . . . all my life, everyone . . . always you are going away from me and you don't come back to explain. . . ." [all ellipses the author's] Jesse wept.
> He embraced her. He clutched at her thighs, her emaciated thighs, her legs. He pressed his face against her knees, weeping.
> The boat drifted most of the night. Near dawn it was picked up by a large handsome cruiser, a Royal Mounted Police boat, a dazzling sight with its polished wood and metal and its trim of gold and blue.

The End.

Oates is the current *Wunderkind* among American novelists. The last two novelists who had their own strong claims to that title a few years ago, Philip Roth and John Updike, are also on the scene with new books, though it's sobering to imagine that Roth, who was a gifted, intelligent, and hard-working writer, thinks of *Our Gang* as a book. Savor this pungent satire:

> *Tricky* Look! I've stopped sweating!
> *Legal Coach* See? You've weathered another crisis, Mr. President.
> *Tricky* Wow! That makes six hundred and *one!*

Remember Johns Behemoth Boys' School? Roth has fun with names too: Trick E. Dixon, J. Edgar Heehaw, General Poppapower, Lyin' B. Johnson, John F. Charisma, Robert F. Charisma, the Reverend Billy Cupcake—but who can go on without breaking up? (Not Dwight Macdonald, who "laughed out loud 16 times and giggled internally a statistically unverifiable amount. In short, a masterpiece.") To speculate: Some years ago Roth got tired of being the most promising young underpaid American writer and plugged into Chase Manhattan with *Portnoy's Complaint,* the first kosher pornographic novel. Tittering with triumph, he has now excogitated the first political satire suitable for performance at junior high-school assemblies. Testy readers have been heard to say that political satire requires wit and point. It also benefits by appearing to take a modicum of risk, as when Paul Krassner revealed in *The Realist* exactly what Lyin' B. did to the corpse of John F. Charisma aboard Air Force One on the way back from Dallas; or even when, in the year of *Macbird,* the entire Yale Drama School lay awake nights quivering in delicious expectation of a panty-raid by J. Edgar Heehaw and Bill Bucktooth, Jr. clad in red-white-and-blue non-union suits with the Superman emblem in Day-glo mauve across the crotch.

As for Updike, he continues to do well what he has always done well. His special skill and sympathy have always been for American places and atmospheres, textures, idioms, items, the pathos of the consumer society. Nobody is better at accompanying the American male on the short Sunday tour of the open shelves of an American drugstore:

> Up near Ninth and Weiser they find a drugstore open. Thermos bottles, sunglasses, shaving lotion, Kodak film, plastic baby pants: nothing for his mother. He wants something big, something bright, something to get through to her. Realgirl Liquid Make-Up, Super Plenamins, Non-Smear polish remover, Nudit for the legs. A rack of shampoo-in hair color, a different smiling cunt on every envelope: Snow Queen Blond, Danish Wheat, Killarney Russet, Parisian Spice, Spanish Black Wine. Nelson plucks him by the sleeve of his white shirt and leads to where a Sunbeam Clipmaster and a Roto-Shine Magnetic Electric Shoe Polisher nestle side by side, glossily packaged. "She doesn't wear shoes any more, just slippers," he says, "and she never cut her hair that I can remember. It used to hang down to her waist." But his attention is drawn to a humidifier for $12.95. From the picture on the box, it looks like a fat flying saucer. No matter how immobile she gets, it would be there.... He moves on to a Kantleek Water Bottle and a 2½-inch reading glass and dismisses both as morbid....

(Updike, not Oates, for some part of an image of mid-twentieth-century America.) If only he didn't keep bumping up against morbid items—"He stops at a corner grocery for a candy bar, an Oh Henry, then at the Burger Bliss on Weiser, dazzling in its lake of parking space, for a Lunar Special (double cheeseburger with an American flag stuck into the bun) and a vanilla milkshake, that tastes toward the bottom of chemical sludge"—if only he didn't fall to brooding, as he usually does, about whether any of these mere American things has a high enough number on the priority list of Human Values, both he and his novels (and, for that matter, America) would be better off, he would be likely to achieve far more often moments as full of accurate and contradictory vibrations as the one in which Rabbit, having retired early, is awakened by his wife's arrival in the conjugal bed:

> He hears from a mournful smothered radio noise that Nelson is still awake. He thinks he should get up and say good night, give the kid a blessing, but a weight crushes him while light persists into his bedroom, along with the boy's soft knocking noises, opening and shutting doors, looking for something to do. Since infancy Rabbit sleeps best when others are up. . . .
> Something big slithers into the bed. Janice. The fluorescent dial on the bureau is saying five of eleven, its two hands merged into one finger. She is warm in her nightie. Skin is warmer than cotton. He was dreaming about a parabolic curve, trying to steer on it, though the thing he was trying to steer was fighting him, like a broken sled.

But such confidence is uncommon in Updike (when he doesn't have it, he's liable to thumb through mythological dictionaries or be Byzantinely sentimental about sex), and this time he is burdened with a huge ambition that runs the book right into the ground: nothing less than to show the youth-cult and the Black Revolution in collision and collusion with the blue-collar American male. Nobody could manage it, certainly Updike doesn't; and *Rabbit Redux,* which begins appealingly as a rather impassioned defense of the benighted, aging, cuckolded, embittered, bouncy Rabbit, ends in the Oatesian futility of sniping, arson, violent death, and other features of urban apocalypse.

One way out of the mess is geographical, another is formal: you can leave the country and be American elsewhere; you can drop fiction and try telling the truth for a change. "Ann Cornelisen," says the dustjacket of *Torregreca,* "was born in Cleveland, Ohio in 1926. She was educated at the Girls Latin School of Chicago, the Baldwin School in Bryn Mawr, Pennsylvania, and at Vassar (class of 1948). In 1954, she went to Florence to study archaeology; instead, she became interested in the Save the Children Fund, and went to work on a semi-volunteer basis for that British-sponsored charitable agency. For the next ten years she helped to set up nursery centers in the mountainous, impoverished regions of Southern Italy, an experience that provides the point of departure for *Torregreca.* At the present time she lives in an apartment at the top of an ancient palazzo in Rome, and is at work on a second book," which turned out to be *Vendetta of Silence.*

In *Torregreca* Miss Cornelisen is quite the finest flower of finishing-school morality, busy, useful, humorous, and brave:

> In time I became a specialist, one of the few who can fix a toilet float while confuting the Montessori System or expounding on the simplicities of Bowlby's theories of child development, and too I developed that all important quality—*Serietà*. In Southern Italy even the simplest project involves a crochet of relationships and has no hope of success without that intangible aura of respectability. *Serietà* is more external than a moral code. It is proclaimed by a conservative, almost dowdy way of dressing and a manner,

slightly detached, very calm, that suggests incorruptibility. I worked on my *serietà* until men lounging in piazzas no longer considered me a loose woman even though I drove a car, smoked, and enjoyed a coffee or rum punch in a public bar. Indeed I doubt they considered me a woman at all.

At the outset the people seem quaint to her, because so they are by Anglo-Saxon standards: for example Don Gaetano, the postmaster, and Don Domenico, the bank director, coming out on the square every day at noon to breathe the air and enjoy a good leisurely look at everybody but each other, family reasons having for twenty years kept each from acknowledging the other's existence. The quaintness doesn't evaporate, it becomes one quality among many as she moves in to spend the winters and talk and listen and carry on her work. Her curiosity and inwardness about the village and its inhabitants—"men, women, and nuns"—gradually dissolve her resistances (as well as theirs) but not her intelligence: she is as tough and alert about the village as a matriarch about her family. For finally *Torregreca* is a book about family, e.g. this account by a local bride who manages to survive her wedding day, her sister, her husband, and the infernal heat:

> I said I wouldn't get married in Torregreca where everybody'd remember when the baby came too soon, so we had to borrow money to go to Pompeii. It was June of 1950 and hot as hell; that was my first train trip and I'm not apt to forget it. We rode all night—me and Michele, and Tina and Michele's brother. They had to come too, to be the witnesses. Tina complained all the way. "Why couldn't you get married in Torregreca? You should have hired a car so we didn't have to stand on the platform for two hours waiting. You better make this trip fun or *guai à te.*" On and on she went. Michele got mad, said we were *cafoni* and he wouldn't be seen with us. We had to wait hours for the church to open and then I fainted in the middle of the ceremony and they dragged me out into the sacristy. Michele ranted and didn't want to tip the sacristan who'd taken care of me. Then we had to get a room. Michele said he knew a place, and walked us miles and miles in the heat until I thought I'd faint again. He made the deal with the people; all four of us in the same room and the place smelled like a garbage dump. My God, I'll never forget the flies in there, either! Michele took us to a wine shop for something to eat and got drunk, so drunk he picked a fight with the owner of the place and then turned over a cart in the street outside. He said it was all our fault, we were nothing but *cafoni* and he wouldn't stay with us another day. We were going back to Torregreca. We rode all night again, missed the bus at the station and had to wait all day until the five o'clock trip. When we got home, Nunzio gave us a potato and two turnips for our wedding dinner!

So it's shocking to discover that *Vendetta of Silence,* coming back to the same place and people, crams them into a silly plot and turns all these lives into fiction and prettiness: notebooks, letters, flashbacks, newspaper accounts, detective-story suspense, the Oatesian mystery of the human heart—

> A catch deep in her throat made her voice break. When she went on, the silken timbre was muted by some emotion close to controlled despair, if such is possible. "And I had hoped never to see San Basilio again. Never! Never again!"

—all the gimcrackery of novels, plus a smugness in the style which suggests that since *Torregreca* she has forgotten everything:

> In the harsh light of an autumn morning the apricot house glitters on its lone promontory with prim self-importance. It would play castle to its fief, the town across the way, and like other fallen aristocrats, will not admit that the world no longer measures power in these terms. It preens in vain. I am its only serf, only I am subject to its powers, though I have not yet learned that. I watch people who come here, sure that finally someone will share the sense of peace and arrival that floods over me. No one ever does. . . .

No real toad would be caught dead in so imaginary a garden.

Documentaries, however, aren't pure pulsing vitality. *Torregreca* was *written*, it was therefore selected from a mass of materials, the names were changed (to comfort the publisher's attorneys), much editing was done: not only the author-editor's voice but the English language is there all the time to remind us that the Torresi aren't coming to us on PBS without a sponsor. Another recent documentary book, *Akenfield*, makes the riskier choice of appearing to let its characters speak for themselves; and since the "editor," Ronald Blythe, tells us nothing of his method (Are these all taped interviews? Where were they conducted? Who, if anybody, was present besides the speaker and the interviewer? What is cut out or rearranged? What is changed besides the names? Did those interviewed have a chance to hear the tape or read the transcript and approve it or demand modifications, suppressions?), since occasionally we can't help wondering what Blythe is doing almost out of sight around the near corner while his speakers have their say, the effect of the book is less unambiguous than it needed to be. (Luckily, though, Blythe's interstitial comment is arty, quite unlike the talk of the villagers.) That qualification apart, *Akenfield* is an irreplaceable thesaurus of recollections and observations about English rural life during the first two-thirds of the twentieth century. There will always be an England, there always was, and the continuity between all those past and future ghosts is this company that, in their occupations and quietness and solid flesh, would have been country-cousins to Chaucer or the Venerable Bede.

None of these realists would take the past back on a platter. "Fred Mitchell, aged eighty-five, horseman": "You had to nearly perish to bring a family up then. . . . The farmers were sharp with us. . . . I learnt never to answer a word. I dursn't say nothing. Today you can be a man with men, but not then. That is how it was. It will never be like that again. I lived when other men could do what they liked with me. We feared so much." "Leonard Thompson, aged seventy-one, farm-worker," describes the village school: ". . . useless. The farmers came and took boys away from it when they felt like it, the parson raided it for servants. The teacher was a respectable woman who did her best. . . . I looked forward to leaving school so that I could get educated. I knew that education was in books, not in school: there were no books there." The clergyman: "I came to them when they had, for several generations, been literally worked to death. . . . I have sometimes dared to question the incredible perfection attached to certain tasks. . . . The harvest would not have been the less if the furrows wavered a little. But, of course, a straight furrow was all that a man was left with." The young political organizer: "The women never lost their independence during the bad days as the men did. The men were beaten because the farms took every ounce of their physical strength and, as they had no great mental strength because of lack of education, they were left with nothing. Their physical strength was their pride and as soon as it was gone they became timid." "Emily Leggett, aged seventy-nine, horseman's widow": "We took our poorness naturally. We knew within a little what we were going to get and that there would never be any more. So that was that." But it's too easy to stay with a single theme of this book, which is a world without exclusions: "The next morning, along she comes, straight to where I'm about to start. Her arms were stuck out full length and she was all smiles. She got her mouth on my face and, my God, she must have thought it was her breakfast, or something."

It's a book with no end of pride and distinctness. These taciturn, "slow" farmers notice everything, as Leonard Thompson shows describing the burial of the dead (fifty years before!) at Gallipoli:

> We pushed them into the sides of the trench but bits of them kept getting uncovered and sticking out, like people in a badly made bed. Hands were the worst; they would escape from the sand, pointing, begging—even waving! There was one which we all shook when we passed, saying "Good morning," in a posh voice. Everybody did it. The bottom of the trench was springy like a mattress because of all the bodies underneath. At night, when the stench was worse, we tied crêpe round our mouths and noses. This crêpe had been given to us because it was supposed to prevent us being gassed. The flies entered the trenches at night and lined them completely with a density which was like moving cloth. We killed millions by slapping our spades along the trench walls but the next night it would be just as bad. We were all lousy and we couldn't stop shitting because we had caught dysentery. We wept, not because we were frightened but because we were so dirty.

"The war"—the First World War—is a central fact in the lives of those old enough to have been through it, and Emily Leggett remembers her husband dead in the war: ". . . when we married his wages were 13s. a week. He used to give me 12s. and keep a bob for his pocket. We were children together, then lovers, then I married him. He lived in the next door double-dweller. We were both nineteen when we wed.

A beautiful boy he was. It seems a long time now since I saw him. He had six horses to look after and he used to get up at five o'clock every morning to bait [feed] them." But the war took him: "My poor young husband!"

"The old people have gone," says "Sammy Whitelaw, aged fifty-eight, farrier," "and have taken a lot of truth out of the world with them." Yes, but here they are with their ancestors and descendants to the first and last generations. "I have never found time to read," says one of the younger men. "I am a participant." It's helpful to be reminded now and then, while novelists persist in their noisy betrayals of human dignity, that living has a longer history than reading, and truth than fiction.

V

Four Ways of Looking: Books Are Not Life But Then What Is?

Chamber of Horrors

"I WAKED one morning... from a dream, of which, all I could recover was, that I had thought myself in an ancient castle (a very natural dream for a head filled like mine with Gothic story), and that on the uppermost bannister of a great staircase I saw a gigantic hand in armour. In the evening I sat down, and began to write, without knowing in the least what I intended to say or relate."

This account isn't by Coleridge or Blake, or any other visionary poet. It was written at the very hub of the eighteenth century by a self-styled trifler who would have dismissed Blake and Coleridge as moonstruck barbarians, but who himself erected literary and architectural monuments to what he considered barbarism; an ornament of the age of prose, who more than anyone else authorized the word "Gothic" as his age's nostalgic label for that dark time before the Protestant disinfection, when superstition reigned, omens and prodigies trampled the order of nature, and all sorts of powers and passions forbidden to civilization burst freely forth like splendid fatal diseases; a devious, extraordinary, representative man of the Enlightenment who offered this "wild" romantic account of dream-possession and automatic writing as "the origin" of *The Castle of Otranto*.

The life of Horace Walpole spanned most of the eighteenth century and summed up much of it. His position at the strategic center of the century was one which, however shrewdly he profited by it, he received by birth. His father was Sir Robert Walpole, the great and cynical Whig Prime Minister, to whom has been attributed the maxim "Every man has his price," and who for twenty years energetically practiced a policy of peace while England became the leading commercial nation of the world. The son was never an active politician (though he kept a seat in Parliament for a third of his life), but he lived and talked as an equal with the rich and mighty, he observed everything, and he always had something to say.

He isn't among the more attractive figures in English history and literature: a tastemonger whose notion of great poetry was an Ode by his friend Thomas Gray; a social snob who deigned to notice neither Boswell ("about whom one has not the smallest curiosity") nor Johnson ("coarse" and "brutal"), and a literary snob who hadn't the sense to value the books of either; a dilettante who disclaimed labor and ambition; yet he was one of the most prolific writers ever, and much of what he wrote can still be read. He was certainly the most indefatigable letter-writer in English (the Yale edition of his letters has reached thirty-nine volumes, with three more to go as well as "at least six" volumes of index); and he left, to be examined only by posterity, over three million words of memoirs and journals, which together with his letters comprise our major source of information about the doings of the English upper classes and the day-by-day infighting of English politics through more than half of the century. During his lifetime he published, among much miscellaneous prose and verse, a novel, a tragedy, a comedy, essays, a collection of tales, a definitive history of English painting, a "Catalogue of the Royal and Noble Authors of England," a book of unorthodox speculations on the character of Richard III, and a treatise on gardening. He had other interests that kept him busy too. He was the first English art critic, and one of the first English connoisseurs of Continental painting. He was a collector and connoisseur of antiquities—coins, medals, cameos, statuary. He set up and for many years superintended a private press, where he published Gray's *Odes*, the autobiography of Lord Herbert of Cherbury, a number of his own works, and many antiquarian books and tracts. He spent decades "Gothicizing" a country cottage into the battlemented toy castle of Strawberry Hill, which was so popular a showplace as to require him to print tickets for those who wished to inspect it, and which was itself almost as responsible for the Gothic craze in late eighteenth-century England as *The Castle of Otranto*.

Just three years after his novel, Walpole wrote a blank verse tragedy, *The Mysterious Mother*. The verse, which Walpole seems to have regarded as Shakespearean, alternates between rant and metronomic doodling (from "Confusion! phrenzy! blast me, all ye furies!" to "Stranger, did chance or purpose guide thy steps . . . "); the characters are put together out of patchy recollections of Webster and other Jacobean scaremongers. It's a very bad play. It's nevertheless memorable for its subject, which as late as 1927 an Englishwoman writing a biography of Walpole couldn't bring herself to discuss. The subject is incest, but we know about that, having heard of Oedipus; double incest, between mother and son and then—almost—between the son and his daughter by his mother, and Sophocles did not involve Antigone in anything like *this;* still more, the first incest quite deliberately precipitated by the mother, so inflamed with lust for her husband that, when he dies unexpectedly one morning, she enjoys her son the same night as the best available substitute!

The eighteenth century has its own sickness, a kind of spiritual lycanthropy: against its shiny decorum, the tug of a real appetite for horrors. *The Mysterious Mother* was too much for almost anybody except, fifty years later, Byron, who fancied incest as a subject and considered Walpole's play the last great English tragedy. *The Castle of Otranto* is far less direct and far more fun; it was in his novel—this "new species of romance" he congratulated himself for having invented—that Walpole turned the key and opened the door to the secret chamber. What he inaugurated was a literary witches' sabbath, the whole vogue of the Gothic novel, which swept Europe for the rest of the century and, in its attenuated consequences, much longer—Mrs. Radcliffe's polite and "Monk" Lewis's diabolistic Gothicism; Byron's Manfred (like Walpole's hero of the same name, a proud, strong, brooding man with a mysterious guilty conscience) and, through Byron, most of the important Continental poets and novelists of the nineteenth century; Charlotte and Emily Brontë's swooning daydreams; Dickens's nightmares.

Under the rationalist skin a grinning skull, a hankering after chaos and old night. Walpole despised the novelists of his time for their tameness. He found Richardson's novels "deplorably tedious lamentations," Fielding and Smollett boorish, *Tristram Shandy* "insipid." This man of sense and reason scorned a theory of fiction that limited fiction to sense, reason, the common light of day. In his old age he printed at Strawberry Hill six copies of his *Hieroglyphic Tales;* he called them "an attempt to vary the stale and beaten class of stories and novels which, though works of invention, are almost always devoid of imagination." He was nearing seventy, and still an innovator. The tales anticipate Dada, the surrealists, absurdism; their subject matter ranges through incest, cannibalism, excretion and flatulence, necrophily, blasphemy; their tone is unvaryingly cool, amused, judicious; moreover, two of them are miniature masterpieces. "The King and His Three Daughters" concerns a king who insists on marrying off an eldest daughter who never took the trouble to be born. "The Peach in Brandy" is an enormously complicated story about a king who abdicates in favor of his five-year-old daughter, only to have the kingdom perplexed by the subsequent birth to his wife of a stillborn son, whom some wise men regard as the rightful sovereign. The imperturbable crazy train of events culminates in the indigestion of an archbishop, who to ease his pain picks up something in the child-queen's room which "he took for a peach in brandy" and "he gulped it all down at once without saying grace, God forgive him!" The little queen thereupon cries out in consternation: "Mama, mama, the gentleman has eat my little brother!"

There is nothing in Walpole's novel to match that. The tales are conscious fiction, the work of a very personal, quirky, restless imagination. *The Castle of Otranto,* on the other hand, is not so much a novel as a state of mind: it seems to have been written not by a person but by a schizoid Time-Spirit. In its diction and phrasing it is, sentence by sentence, as autumnally Augustan as *Rasselas:*

> The circumstances of his fortune had given an asperity to his temper, which was naturally humane; and his virtues were always ready to operate, when his passions did not obscure his reason.

Yet through these majestic, somewhat hollow periods march the incubi and nightmares which the age has rejected and the style denies: darkness and the howling of the wind; hidden trap doors and subterranean passages; unnatural passions and unacknowledgeable guilt; a portrait that steps out of its frame; a statue that drips blood; a skeleton in a hermit's cowl that prays and warns; groans, claps of thunder, earthquakes; "the clank of more than mortal armour."

The most remarkable Gothic engine in this gooseflesh factory is the materialized presence of the treacherously murdered Alfonso the Good. The first manifestation is the gigantic helmet that falls from the sky, crushes to death Manfred's son, and remains thereafter in the courtyard to threaten and admonish with "its sable plumes." Terrified servants report having seen, in the great chamber of the castle, "the foot and part of the leg" of a giant, who appears to be rising to his feet. Then comes the company of mute knights, of whom a hundred stagger under the weight of the comparably gigantic sword they bear into the courtyard. Out of Walpole's dream emerges the gigantic hand in armor "upon the uppermost bannister of the great stairs." Finally, in a climax that rivals the Second Coming and should bring tears of bliss and envy to the eyes of any epic-minded film producer, the materialization perfects itself, concludes its mission on earth, and is welcomed into heaven by Alfonso's patron saint:

> The moment Theodore appeared, the walls of the castle behind Manfred were thrown down with a mighty force, and the form of Alfonso, dilated to an immense magnitude, appeared in the centre of the ruins.
> "Behold in Theodore the true heir of Alfonso!" said the vision; and having pronounced those words, accompanied by a clap of thunder, it ascended solemnly towards heaven, where the clouds parting asunder, the form of St. Nicholas was seen, and receiving Alfonso's shade, they were soon wrapt from mortal eyes in a blaze of glory.

It is these effects that engage, that may in fact be said to possess, their author. The plot of the novel has been admired, even by recent writers on Walpole (who are disconcerted by the supernaturalistic bravura, and need *something* to admire); but the plot is only carpentry, that ingenious dovetailing of events which critics admire in *Tom Jones* or *Ulysses*. As for the characters, the less said the better. The lovers are out of the popular sentimental fiction that attracted Walpole's sardonic judgment; the self-tormented Manfred is no more imposing in his murky impetuousness than the Byronic hero of whom he is the true ancestor; the "comic" minor characters are modeled with waxworks fidelity on analogous characters in Shakespeare.

It's the outrageous, the uncreditable, the aggressively miraculous—the very claptrap of the chamber of horrors into which Walpole was the first to stumble—that save his fable for its special and minor immortality. *The Castle of Otranto* is not just one of those historical originals which are dimmed and exhausted by their triumphant successors. It survives because the Augustan Walpole, master of ceremonies for the ice age whose breakup he was unintentionally announcing, had a taste for freaks and marvels, disorder and the abyss of unknowing. In France, a few years later, the Marquis de Sade began to indulge a similar taste and to make similar if less innocuous-looking discoveries.

Good and Proper (I)

JANE Austen didn't become a published author till she was thirty-six. But this fact, which hardly suggests precocity, is misleading. Her first three novels were complete in first draft by the time she was twenty-two; and from the age of fourteen she had been turning out squibs, burlesques, parodies (published only in this century) that remain as fresh, malicious, and amusing for us as they were for her delighted family. *Pride and Prejudice*—not to speak of *Sense and Sensibility* and *Northanger Abbey*—settled, almost immediately on reaching a general audience, into its uncontested place among the great English novels; yet in its original form it was, like the cheeky *juvenilia*, written as family entertainment.

On the evidence of what amused them, the Austens were no sober and punctiliously regulated family (nothing like Sir Thomas Bertram's, for instance): "a hard humorous family," E. M. Forster has called them. Though they and their numerous relatives were irreproachable rural gentry, and though Jane's father was a clergyman, they don't seem to have been disposed to limit the prerogatives of wit. Jane might be as impudent as she pleased so long as she was amusing: "Mrs. Hall, of Sherborne," she wrote with characteristic liveliness to her sister, "was brought to bed yesterday of a dead child, some weeks before she expected, owing to a fright. I suppose she happened unawares to look at her husband." She continued to be both impudent and amusing through those pieces, including her first three novels, which comfortably preceded the date when she was obliged to ponder her accountability to the world.

Jane Austen produced her fiction in two distinct and discontinuous periods: a private and a public. At fourteen, within the family, she was already displaying a superlative talent for parody and comic improvisation; by her early twenties, she had written three brilliant novels that waited upwards of fifteen years to achieve print (though two were submitted to publishers). From her middle twenties, except for whatever time she spent revising the still unpublished novels, she seems to have given up writing nearly altogether for about a decade. In 1811, finally, *Sense and Sensibility* was published; and in 1811 *Mansfield Park,* the first of her last three novels, was begun.

The irreverent family entertainer had become a responsible author. *Mansfield Park* was Jane Austen's first novel after this conversion, and she worked on it longer than on any of her others: it took two-and-a-half years of the shortest active career among major novelists. It was also her first novel that, by her own testimony, undertook a wholly serious subject. It would be about "ordination," she remarked to her sister; and for a novelist whose most memorable representation of the English clergy had till then been that meridian of fatuity, Mr. Collins of *Pride and Prejudice,* the choice proved to be as momentous in tone and theme as in subject. The responsible author had a plan, and carried it through. *Mansfield Park* may be described, according to the plan, as a belated and highly conscious profession of faith by a clergyman's daughter.

The plan seems unpromising enough, particularly for a novel by a comic novelist. Jane Austen was seeing *Pride and Prejudice* through the press: it was much on her mind, and she pointed out its "rather too light, and bright, and sparkling" manner, its "playfulness and epigrammatism," from the indulgent and nostalgic distance of her present concern with more consequential matters. Indeed, it's useful to regard *Mansfield Park* as a moral, or moralistic, rewriting of the earlier novel. *Pride and Prejudice* assumes, if not the priority of wit, at any rate its tacit coincidence with judgment, health, amiability, and virtue: Elizabeth Bennet is witty, healthy, amiable, and good; Lady Catherine's daughter (Elizabeth's nominal rival for Darcy) is without conversation, "sickly and cross," and morally null. *Mansfield Park* assumes, or rather it vigorously proposes, that wit may be a superficial and dangerous accomplishment, and that physical health is no guarantee of spiritual purity: Mary Crawford, whose manner and conversation intimately recall not only Elizabeth's but Jane Austen's, is as witty and amiable and energetic as Elizabeth, but she is not good; and Fanny (Mary's rival for Edmund), as solemn as Mr. Collins and as frail as Lady Catherine's daughter, is, in the plan of *Mansfield Park,* judgment and virtue personified. Wit—smiling villainess—will be tested, and found wanting.

Wit comes to appear less an overflow of lively intelligence (as it appeared in *Pride and Prejudice*) than a refinement, perhaps even an inevitable decadence, of manners; and manners are merely an outward show, or possibly a dissimulation, of morals. Manners are personality, and morals are character. In *Pride and Prejudice,* the author was usually content to assume (except for Wickham) an identity between personality and character; in *Mansfield Park,* the terms and their realities are not only separate, but often in conflict:

> Poor Julia . . . was now in a state of complete penance, and as different from the Julia of the barouche-box as could well be imagined. The politeness which she had been brought up to practise as a duty, made it impossible for her to escape; while the want of that higher species of self-command, that just consideration of others, that knowledge of her own heart, that principle of right which had not formed any essential part of her education, made her miserable under it.

What's more, as Julia's dilemma demonstrates, the key to both personality and character is upbringing. Julia has been badly "educated"; Mary too, brought up in the home of Admiral Crawford, "a man of vicious conduct" (says the author):

> ". . . Certainly, my home at my uncle's brought me acquainted with a circle of admirals. Of *Rears,* and *Vices,* I saw enough. Now, do not be suspecting me of a pun, I entreat."

Edmund, after his "eyes are opened," arrives at the obligatory conclusion in his confession to Fanny:

> "Cruel!" said Fanny—"quite cruel! At such a moment to give way to gaiety and to speak with lightness, and to you!—Absolute cruelty."
> "Cruelty, do you call it?—We differ there. No, hers is not a cruel nature. I do not consider her as meaning to wound my feelings. The evil lies yet deeper; in her total ignorance, un-suspiciousness of there being such feelings, in a perversion of mind which made it natural to her to treat the subject as she did. She was speaking only, as she had been used to hear others speak, as she imagined everybody else would speak. Hers are not faults of temper. She would not voluntarily give unnecessary pain to any one, and though I may deceive myself, I cannot but think that for me, for my feelings, she would—Hers are faults of principle, Fanny, of blunted delicacy and a corrupted, vitiated mind. . . ."

That is, Mary can be witty because she is unprincipled: lack of scruples is the mother of wit.

The effect of such a recantation—it amounts virtually to that—is stranger and more unexpected than Jane Austen must have intended. The first impression of a reader familiar with her earlier novels is likely to resemble the judgment of one of her modern critics: "This unnatural censure, to be found only in this novel, of Jane Austen's own standards of judgment, of her independence of outlook and instinctive values, is what the discerning reader finds intolerable. To deny his own light is the worst offence of which an artist can be guilty." The second impression may be a still more disturbing one: that the moral structure of the novel goes about as far as it can go toward eliminating the fundamental illusion which sustains the interest of fiction—the illusion of free will. Julia Bertram has good manners and inadequate morals because she was brought up in a crossfire of purposes by a frighteningly severe father and a grossly subservient aunt; and her sister, Maria, is much the same. Tom Bertram is a frivolous and inconsiderate young man, because he is the undisciplined elder son and heir of a baronet (it takes an almost mortal illness to bring him round, at the end of the novel and with not even a nominal dramatization of the change, to an awareness of his deficiencies). Mary Crawford, who was brought up in a home of rears and vices, exists in the scheme as Edmund's sinister temptation, a poisoned fountain of high spirits and seductiveness. Henry Crawford, raised in the same pernicious environment, uses his accomplished and insinuating manners to dissolve the resistances of women; and, as if seduction were not enough, the author is so anxious to certify Henry's corruptness that, about his enthusiasm for the private theatricals at the Bertrams', she writes with a priggishness worthy of Mr. Collins: "in all the riot of his gratifications, it was yet an untasted pleasure." Upbringing is nearly everything. Not only at Mansfield: Fanny's family in Portsmouth—except for the sailor brother (the discipline of the Navy?) and her sister Susan—are determined by poverty into their own irredeemable acedia.

There are, of course, two major exceptions: Edmund and Fanny. Edmund, the younger Bertram son, is an admirable young man whose principles flourish in the same atmosphere that so radically damages his sisters and his older brother. As for Fanny, in the Bertram household she is—or is intended to appear—a sort of shy intruding angel: natural goodness in its invulnerable modesty, proof against slights, insults, bad examples; a purity of judgment untainted by wit. Fanny's virtue is neither caused nor voluntary, it's merely spontaneous and autonomous: a celestial mistake. It is, however, fortified by her grateful love of Edmund, who alone among the Bertrams shows kindness to her, and who even directs her to the proper books for a young woman's education. And it has a new support and consolation unavailable to Jane Austen's previous heroines: what must, by 1811, be called romantic feeling. Jane Austen contrasts Mary's sophistication with Fanny's interest in a natural setting:

> Her own thoughts and reflections were habitually her best companions; and in observing the appearance of the country, the bearings of the roads, the difference of soil, the state of the harvest, the cottages, the cattle, the children, she found entertainment that could only have been heightened by having Edmund to speak to of what she felt. That was the only point of resemblance between her and the lady who sat by her; in everything but a value for Edmund, Miss Crawford was very unlike her. She had none of Fanny's delicacy of taste, of mind, of feeling; she saw nature, inanimate nature, with little observation; her attention was all for men and women, her talents for the light and lively.

It's true that Fanny's typical ruminations on natural beauty rather suggest the sedateness of her favorite poet, Cowper, than the more tempestuous Romantics:

> ". . . The evergreen!—How beautiful, how welcome, how wonderful the evergreen! . . . One cannot fix one's eyes on the commonest natural production without finding food for a rambling fancy."

Fanny can, though, with the author's obvious approval, occasionally burst into a veritable rhapsody on "nature, inanimate nature":

> "Here's harmony!" said she, "Here's repose! Here's what may leave all painting and all music behind, and what poetry only can attempt to describe. Here's what may tranquillize every care, and lift the heart to rapture! when I look out on such a night as this, I feel as if there could be neither wickedness nor sorrow in the world; and there certainly would be less of both if the sublimity of Nature were more attended to, and people were carried more out of themselves by contemplating such a scene."

And Fanny's favorite room is ornamented with three obvious emblems of the new dispensation: "three transparencies . . . for the three lower panes of one window, where Tintern Abbey held its station between a cave in Italy, and a moonlight lake in Cumberland."

Jane Austen's romanticism dates from the late eighteenth century, but it gradually acclimatizes itself to the nineteenth, at least as far as Wordsworth and his celebration of the natural (i.e. rural) pieties; and it's another weapon that she turns against her own eighteenth-century "playfulness and epigrammatism," her keen and worldly interest in manners. In the plan of *Mansfield Park,* to be under the influence of society and of its worldly imperatives is to be morally imperiled, perhaps beyond salvation. Only those are saved who, like Edmund, begin with principles (how? by being the younger rather than the older brother?), and prepare for what ought to be the most unworldly of vocations; or who, like Fanny, begin with unfallen goodness and safely dissipate their morally unspecifiable impulses in the amplitudes of romantic revery.

If the plan were everything, *Mansfield Park* might just as well be dedicated to the less cheerful innovations of the new century. After its light and bright and sparkling predecessor, it may seem a monument to good behavior, graced with the more unexceptionable heart-stirrings of the new poets, as if Thomas Gray had survived to indite birthday odes to the Prince Regent. But it's also the first novel that Jane Austen wrote in the maturity of her powers; and those remarkable powers could animate the purest and most conventional plan. Fanny and Edmund are her heroine and hero, but they aren't the boundaries of her observation or reflection. *Mansfield Park* is a long novel, her longest, and its length is an index of magnitude. The issues that the plan, and Fanny's angelic intuition, make tidy and simple are often, in their fictional working out, as large and refractory as the natural processes that Fanny is always ready to camouflage with bucolic sentiment.

The issues, insusceptible to sentiment and homily, are issues of feeling. The moral axis of the novel is not Fanny's, between parochial good and evil, or—as in *Pride and Prejudice* (and in William Blake!)—between energy and withering formality, but between love and lack: the never quite explicable mystery of the affections. Fanny can't go wrong—she has Edmund as father, brother, counselor, friend, future lover—but Edmund and everyone else aren't so lucky.

Consider Sir Thomas. He is a good and conscientious man, and presumably deserves good children. Instead, his heir is a wastrel, his two daughters are patterns of trivial vanity; only Edmund is what his father would like him to be. How far is Sir Thomas answerable for his children? The author begins her novel with an account of the three Ward sisters, one of whom was pretty enough to capture the baronet. Sir Thomas "fell in love," he was a man to whom a pretty face promised what his only name for was love; and thirty years later his gravity presides over a torpid wife, her odious sister, and a houseful of intimidated and restive young people. Sir Thomas's principles are unimpeachable; he is a just man, no tyrant, not ill-tempered or rash; yet his presence is so commandingly oppressive that, when he's about to leave on a voyage that will keep him away from home for a year or more, even Fanny's primary feeling is relief. His return, which puts an end to his children's amusements, is the occasion of consternation verging on panic. As for his daughter's betrothal to a very stupid but very wealthy man, he is ready to condone it on the ground that so conventionally magnificent an alliance, "an alliance which he could not [therefore] have relinquished without pain," will hardly discommode a woman not given to strong feeling (Are any women? Think of Lady Bertram!):

> Her feelings probably were not acute; he had never supposed them to be so; but her comforts might not be less on that account, and if she could dispense with seeing her husband a leading, shining character, there would certainly be everything else in her favour. A well-disposed young woman, who did not marry for love, was in general but the more attached to her own family, and the nearness of Sotherton to Mansfield must naturally hold out the greatest temptation, and would, in all probability, be a continual supply of the most amiable and innocent enjoyments. Such and such-like were the reasonings of Sir Thomas—happy to escape the embarrassing evils of a rupture, the wonder, the reflections, the reproach that must attend it, happy to secure a marriage which would bring him such an addition of respectability and influence, and very happy to think anything of his daughter's disposition that was most favourable for the purpose.

Duped by a feeling, thirty years earlier, for which his name was as exact as his genteel vocabulary permitted, enslaved to a word he can only undervalue, incapacitated by his own disaster and the mercenary aspirations of his class from scrutinizing the consequences of such a decision, he condemns to her unlimited private misery the daughter whom he taught the impossibility of love and the necessity of its impolite namesake. When Maria runs off with Henry Crawford, she repudiates her father and follows his example: she too has fallen in love. Not that, at this depth of doomed impulse, she's only a puppet. It's her lack of love, and her need of it, that force her to choose wrongly. Environment isn't fate; it is, though, example. Everyone chooses, but not everyone gets the chance to choose rightly. Sir Thomas, wishing to be kind (wishing to love), but unwilling to make the effort of definition, serves the system that precipitates Tom into folly, Julia into a panicky elopement, and Maria into a wretched marriage and a still more wretched adultery. He is an ogre to his own children, and—in his obdurate disregard for feeling—weaker and more destructive than they. Of course Sir Thomas is a man of principles, and, as Fanny knows, principles are the foundation of everything good. But the novel itself knows better. The fault is not wit, or Henry, or Mary, or the "vicious" Admiral; the fault is Sir Thomas and his unexamined principles.

Or consider the two interlocking triangles: Mary-Edmund-Fanny and Fanny-Henry-Maria. About Mary's feeling for Edmund, Fanny muses resentfully that "she might love, but she did not deserve Edmund by any other sentiment." By "sentiment" Fanny means something like "socially sanctioned and acknowledgeable feeling." In the final meeting between Edmund and Mary, which Edmund, shocked, recollects for Fanny, Mary seems to be offering a feeling, indeed an experience, socially quite unsanctioned:

> ". . . She tried to speak carelessly; but she was not so careless as she wanted to appear. I only said in reply, that from my heart I wished her well, and

earnestly hoped that she might soon learn to think more justly, and not owe the most valuable knowledge we could any of us acquire—the knowledge of ourselves and of our duty, to the lessons of affliction—and immediately left the room. I had gone a few steps, Fanny, when I heard the door open behind me. 'Mr. Bertram,' said she. I looked back. 'Mr. Bertram,' said she, with a smile—but it was a smile ill-suited to the conversation that had passed, a saucy playful smile, seeming to invite, in order to subdue me; at least, it appeared so to me. I resisted; it was the impulse of the moment to resist, and still walked on. I have since—sometimes—for a moment—regretted that I did not go back; but I know I was right. . ."

Edmund knows he was right; his principles, learned from Sir Thomas, tell him so, though till he turns to the conveniently available Fanny they are cold comfort. But Mary has fallen in love, and—unlike Sir Thomas or Maria—she hasn't misconceived the nature or extent of her feelings. She has had the bad luck to fall in love with an intelligent, straightforward young man whose principles and manners she finds rather stuffy (as Elizabeth found Darcy's), and whose intended vocation she regards as liable to submerge his qualities in the tedium of an illiberal routine:

"Oh! no doubt he is very sincere in preferring an income ready made, to the trouble of working for one; and has the best intentions of doing nothing all the rest of his days but eat, drink, and grow fat. It is indolence Mr. Bertram, indeed. Indolence and love of ease—a want of all laudable ambition, of taste for good company, or of inclination to take the trouble of being agreeable, which make men clergymen. A clergyman has nothing to do but to be slovenly and selfish—read the newspaper, watch the weather, and quarrel with his wife. His curate does all the work, and the business of his own life is to dine."

The point that the cast-iron plan intends to make here is that Christianity is the true faith, and Mary a flippant and disrespectful traducer: ordination is the subject according to plan, and Edmund's choice will determine not only his vocation but, very likely, quite eschatological matters. The point that the story itself makes is more terrestrial: that Mary is in love with Edmund alive—all of him, as Fanny could never bring herself to think about the range of her own feelings for Edmund—and that she does her best to protect him against any threat to all that he is. In a desperate stroke intended to prove her depravity and finish her off, the author has her react to the fear of losing him by offering him without a qualm what respectably or at least prematurely can't even be thought of—i.e. what against his principles he desires and what in her love for him she wishes to give and to have. But as with Emma Bovary, another spark in a bookful of duds, the immoderateness is bracing, it breaks the time barrier (Jane Austen's respectability, Flaubert's nihilism) and discloses possibilities of feeling and action otherwise unthinkable in such a setting. At any rate, whether or not Mary "deserves" Edmund, she's the only woman in the novel whose gaiety, conversation, intelligence, kindness, and beauty can elevate him to a level of responsiveness beyond Sir Thomas's killing principles. When Edmund turns to Fanny, the principles voluminously reclaim him.

As for Henry Crawford, he really is a smug and unpleasant woman-chaser till he falls in love with Fanny. Fanny may not be all he thinks she is; but for him at this moment she's the very woman who will enable him to deliver himself from his own triviality. Henry, like his sister, is struck by a prospect of fullness and delight; he has a vision of what might, behind Fanny's timorous manners, be sheer goodness, an unbroken unity of character. As a result, he becomes kind, generous, considerate, immensely patient and persevering, the very model of a gentlemanly wooer, who knows the value of the woman he courts: "'I could so wholly and absolutely confide in her,' said he; 'and *that* is what I want.'" Jane Austen is in fact so successful in dramatizing this transformation that, eventually, she has no alternative to pretending it never happened. Thus Henry, on the verge of winning his suit, explodes everything by running off, in a lunatic caprice, with a married woman he doesn't even like. The plan has no room for Henry's, or Mary's, kind of love.

Ultimately, Jane Austen sacrifices her novel to her plan. Henry and Mary must be cast out so that Edmund and Fanny may come together in a union of convention and sentiment, and Sir Thomas tardily vindicated. Elizabeth Bennet, that paragon of sense and vivacity, would have been nonplussed to catch her author setting up so crude a tableau of evangelical complacency; but then Elizabeth is one of the last bright spirits of the eighteenth century, and couldn't be expected to approve the thickening pieties of the nineteenth. Even the older Jane Austen, free of public obligations, could write to her sister three years after *Mansfield Park:*

> We do not much like Mr. Cooper's new Sermons;—they are fuller of Regeneration & Conversion than ever—with the addition of his zeal in the cause of the Bible Society.

Her ear for cant had been dulled just long enough to permit Edmund's subjection and Fanny's triumph.

Mansfield Park is a transitional novel, not only between early and late Jane Austen, but between two cultural epochs. Sir Thomas's eighteenth-century forms of convention begin to seem as unintelligent and stifling as Fanny's nineteenth-century forms of sentiment. Linking, temporarily, such opposing charges as Edmund and Mary or Henry and Fanny, Jane Austen glances at the possibility of overriding both convention and sentiment, of proposing a different range of experience: to invite and cherish the affections, to move out from the park into the great world. The power of this fractured novel is in the mutiny of feeling it must sooner or later, for the author's peace of mind, put down. Such internal stresses are hard to imagine if the reader strolls through her novels as through a museum, in which quaintly dressed figures utter, by means of concealed loudspeakers, miniature Johnsonian periods. But Jane Austen is a great novelist, and her museum is crowded with ghosts and troubled flesh.

Good and Proper (II)

"Propriety," wrote William Hazlitt, Jane Austen's contemporary, "is one great matter in the conduct of life; which, though like a graceful carriage of the body it is neither definable nor striking at first sight, is the result of finely balanced feelings and lends a secret strength and charm to the whole character." There's no evidence that Hazlitt ever read *Persuasion* (or, indeed, anything by its author, of whom only Sir Walter Scott among the literary figures of her time took serious notice); yet, describing this civilized virtue, he might have been beautifully describing its incarnation in the heroine of Jane Austen's last novel.

Propriety, in a more neutral sense than Hazlitt's, has of course always been Jane Austen's subject. In her novels, society—"three or four families in a country village"—is the unevadable basis, the decorum to which eventually one accommodates oneself. Character exercises and proves itself among the circumscribed social opportunities, most particularly in courtship and marriage. But her heroines have always been too high-spirited (Marianne Dashwood, Elizabeth Bennet), or too ingenuous (Catherine Morland), or too calculating (Elinor Dashwood, Emma Woodhouse), or too humble (Fanny Price), to make of propriety the virtue and fulfillment that Hazlitt celebrates. The guardians and exemplars of propriety in her earlier novels are likely to be fools, snobs, stuffed shirts: Mr. Collins, Mrs. Elton, Sir Thomas Bertram; as if the author deliberately separates herself by a margin of distaste from the society to which neither she nor her heroines have any prudent alternative. *Persuasion* is different: an epilogue of acceptance, a reconciliation. The proper parochial society that for a quarter of a century Jane Austen had been laughing at and amusing, despising and defending, at all events copiously memorializing, comes to its late flower in the unassuming grace, the finely balanced feelings, the secret strength and charm of character, of Anne Elliot.

Appearance nevertheless challenges and postpones reality. Though Anne is the heart, the vital breath, the crown of propriety, she merely is what numerous others, by the warrant of privilege and custom, plume themselves on being—nobody so much as her very silly father:

> Sir Walter Elliot, of Kellynch Hall, in Somersetshire, was a man who, for his own amusement, never took up any book but the Baronetage; there he found occupation for an idle hour, and consolation on a distressed one; there his faculties were roused into admiration and respect, by contemplating the limited remnant of the earliest patents; there any unwelcome sensations, arising from domestic affairs, changed naturally into pity and contempt. As

> he turned over the almost endless creations of the last century—and there, if every other leaf were powerless, he could read his own history with an interest which never failed—this was the page at which the favourite volume always opened. . . .

Sir Walter, besides, has been specially favored by nature in his role as the protagonist of this comedy of appearance:

> Vanity was the beginning and the end of Sir Walter Elliot's character; vanity of person and of situation. He had been remarkably handsome in his youth; and, at fifty-four, was still a very fine man. Few women could think more of their personal appearance than he did; nor could the valet of any new-made lord be more delighted with the place he held in society. He considered the blessing of beauty as inferior only to the blessing of a baronetcy; and the Sir Walter Elliot, who united these gifts, was the constant object of his warmest respect and devotion.

The comedy has a leading lady in his daughter Elizabeth (and even, back in the scullery, Anne as Cinderella):

> Sir Walter's continuing in singleness [after his wife's death] requires explanation.—Be it known, then, that Sir Walter, like a good father (having met with one or two private disappointments in very unreasonable applications), prided himself on remaining single for his dear daughter's sake. For one daughter, his eldest, he would really have given up anything, which he had not been very much tempted to do. Elizabeth had succeeded, at sixteen, to all that was possible, of her mother's rights and consequence; and being very handsome, and very like himself, her influence had always been great, and they had gone on together most happily. His two other children were of very inferior value. Mary had acquired a little artificial importance, by becoming Mrs. Charles Musgrove; but Anne, with an elegance of mind and sweetness of character, which must have placed her high with any people of real understanding, was nobody with either father or sister: her work had no weight; her convenience was always to give way—she was only Anne.

The comedy has, finally, a superb scheming toady, Mrs. Clay, who winds herself into the tangled narcissisms of Sir Walter and Miss Elliot by judiciously affirming their right to be stupid. Anne having ventured to speak well of the navy, Sir Walter states his objections to it:

> ". . . . First, as being the means of bringing persons of obscure birth into undue distinction, and raising men to honours which their fathers and grandfathers never dreamt of; and secondly, as it cuts up a man's youth and

vigour most horribly; a sailor grows old sooner than any other man. . . . they are all knocked about, and exposed to every climate, and every weather, till they are not fit to be seen. . . ."

Whereupon Mrs. Clay rushes in to make her corroborative qualifications:

"Nay, Sir Walter," cried Mrs. Clay, "this is being severe indeed. Have a little mercy on the poor men. We are not all born to be handsome. The sea is no beautifier, certainly; sailors do grow old betimes; I have often observed it; they soon lose the look of youth. But then, is it not the same with many other professions, perhaps most other? Soldiers, in active service, are not at all better off; and even in the quieter professions, there is a toil and a labour of the mind, if not of the body, which seldom leaves a man's looks to the natural effect of time. The lawyer plods, quite care-worn; the physician is up at all hours, and travelling in all weather . . ."

And so she eliminates, one by one, all the professions till she has proved by default that only the mild obligations of a country baronet are not hostile to "the blessings of health and a good appearance."

Propriety—modest public currency—can be easily counterfeited. Sir Walter and Elizabeth, imagining themselves models of propriety, have debased it into snobbery, name-worship, the sloth of self-love. Low-bred and penniless Mrs. Clay, who scrupulously cultivates the vices of others till she will be allowed to humor her own, takes the good name of propriety for her sycophancy and social-climbing. Mr. Elliot, as cunning as Mrs. Clay, uses his face, family, and manner to practice an opportunism that Anne is able to identify long before she has all the evidence of it:

who could answer for the true sentiments of a clever, cautious man, grown old enough to appreciate a fair character? . . .

Mr. Elliot was rational, discreet, polished—but he was not open. There was never any burst of feeling, any warmth of indignation or delight, at the evil or good of others. This, to Anne, was a decided imperfection. Her early impressions were incurable. She prized the frank, the open-hearted, the eager character beyond all others. Warmth and enthusiasm did captivate her still. She felt that she could so much more depend upon the sincerity of those who sometimes looked or said a careless or a hasty thing, than of those whose presence of mind never varied, whose tongue never slipped.

Mr. Elliot was too generally agreeable. Various as were the tempers in her father's house, he pleased them all.

False propriety may infect a nature neither vicious nor frivolous, even one as inclined to kindness and disinterested affection as Lady Russell's; for if Sir Walter's self-infatuation is the worst form of snobbery, Lady Russell's immoderate respect for name and family is snobbery enough to make her doubt and distrust merely personal virtues, and thus to effect Anne's disastrous refusal of Wentworth:

> Captain Wentworth had no fortune. He had been lucky in his profession, but spending freely what had come freely, had realized nothing. But, he was confident that he should soon be rich—full of life and ardour, he knew that he should soon have a ship, and soon be on a station that would lead to everything he wanted. He had always been lucky; he knew he should be so still.—Such confidence, powerful in its own warmth, and bewitching in the wit which often expressed it, must have been enough for Anne; but Lady Russell saw it very differently—His sanguine temper, and fearlessness of mind, operated very differently on her. She saw in it but an aggravation of the evil. It only added a dangerous character to himself. He was brilliant, he was headstrong.—Lady Russell had little taste for wit; and of anything approaching to imprudence a horror. She deprecated the connexion in every light.

Consistently with her social predispositions, Lady Russell is as blind to Sir Walter's silliness, Elizabeth's mean vanity, and Mr. Elliot's guile as she is to Wentworth's energy and Admiral Croft's shrewd benevolence. She is a good woman whose judgment is almost fatally incapacitated by the proper assumptions that she accepts without question from her class and time. Sure of being in the right, she is at the mercy of every façade.

Not that everyone is enlisted in this war of appearance versus reality: not the children, of whatever age, the amiable golden children (like Bingley and Jane Bennet in *Pride and Prejudice*) whose only motive is to be quickly pleased, and whom their author always treats with parental indulgence; the Musgrove girls, for example—

> like thousands of other young ladies, living to be fashionable, happy, and merry. Their dress had every advantage, their faces were rather pretty, their spirits extremely good, their manners unembarrassed and pleasant; they were of consequence at home, and favourites abroad. Anne always comtemplated them as some of the happiest creatures of her acquaintance; but still, saved as we all are by some comfortable feeling of superiority from wishing for the possibility of exchange, she would not have given up her own more elegant and cultivated mind for all their enjoyment. . . .

Or, as the observant Admiral Croft sums them up, "very nice young ladies they both are; I hardly know one from the other."

Captain Benwick, another innocent, by his extravagant responsiveness to Romantic poetry provokes Anne to a rare pitch of moral admonition:

> he repeated, with such tremulous feeling, the various lines which imaged a broken heart, or a mind destroyed by wretchedness, and looked so entirely as if he meant to be understood, that she ventured to hope he did not always read only poetry, and to say that she thought it was the misfortune of poetry

to be seldom safely enjoyed by those who enjoyed it completely; and that the strong feelings which alone could estimate it truly were the very feelings which ought to taste it but sparingly.

And when Benwick's heart, supposed to have been broken by his fiancée's recent death, recomposes itself and turns with butterfly lightness to one of the Musgrove girls, Anne accurately concludes: "He had an affectionate heart. He must love somebody."

Charles Musgrove, who must have been not quite so simple to begin with, has by this time declined into simplicity. Having first aspired to Anne and having had to make do with her querulous sister Mary, he sinks any prospects of maturity into the unthinking diversions that keep his marriage tolerable:

> he did nothing with much zeal, but sport; and his time was otherwise trifled away, without benefit from books, or anything else. He had very good spirits, which never seemed much affected by his wife's occasional lowness; bore with her unreasonableness sometimes to Anne's admiration; and upon the whole, though there was very often a little disagreement . . . they might pass for a happy couple.

If Charles isn't lucky enough to be as childlike and unfallen as the Musgrove girls and Captain Benwick, he's at least artless and good-natured, and only now and then childish.

As for Jane Austen's representatives of true propriety in *Persuasion,* it's no wonder that even for the well-intentioned Lady Russell they are—with the exception of Anne herself—so difficult to recognize and credit. Any conventional society is liable to mistake ceremoniousness for propriety; and Jane Austen's new exemplars (again, except for Anne) are about as vigorous and unceremonious as Lady Russell is slow and solemn. They are, after all, sailors. The personal hero of *Persuasion* is named Wentworth, and a very likable and dashing fellow he is; but the collective hero of *Persuasion* is the British Navy, at its zenith of power and reputation, just after the final defeat of Napoleon—Jane Austen's beloved navy, in which two of her brothers rose to the rank of admiral.

Her view of the navy may not have been altogether unprejudiced. It seems improbable that every British ship's captain was either a sentimental admirer of Scott and Byron like Benwick, or a pattern of conjugal felicity like Admiral Croft or Captain Harville, or, like Wentworth, the soul of unaffected manliness. Yet if Jane Austen had been critically seeking out a profession in which every sort of social duty and ambition was compatible with enthusiasm and physical grace, she could hardly have chosen better. The navy was, as Sir Walter remarks, "the means of bringing persons of obscure birth into undue distinction," i.e. of gratifying their honorable ambition for rank and money. Jane Austen lived in a pre-Marxian, almost a pre-industrial, society, still unencumbered by a sense of guilt about rank and money, in an epoch when war at sea was a patriotic and personal adventure, a double opportunity in which a ship's master could simultaneously serve his country and make his fortune by the straightforward means of capturing enemy ships. So Wentworth exclaims in fond remembrance:

> "Ah! those were pleasant days when I had the *Laconia!* How fast I made money in her.—A friend of mine, and I, had such a lovely cruise together off the Western Islands.—Poor Harville, sister! You know how much he wanted money—worse than myself. He had a wife.—Excellent fellow! I shall never forget his happiness. He felt it all, so much for her sake.—I wished for him again the next summer, when I had still the same luck in the Mediterranean."

And sensible Admiral Croft makes casually explicit the indispensable condition for another set of such blissful reminiscences: "'. . . if we have the good luck to live to another war. . . .'" No sensible person in Jane Austen's novels ever deludes himself against the authority and usefulness of money. A ship's captain has the advantage of being able to make his fortune rapidly, and the disadvantage that he can make it only in time of war. He must seize his chance, or renounce his hope of money and position, perhaps even his hope of a good marriage. Certainly, without money and the leisure it provides, Anne could not have become what she is; money is the foundation of true as of false propriety, and without it Wentworth doesn't deserve Anne. Her error was to let Lady Russell persuade her against Wentworth's destiny, against the temper and ambition that virtually guaranteed it. The sailor's life quite suits Jane Austen's purposes because his attitude toward money is the right one: direct, unpretending; as toward sails and keels, lifeboats and yardarms—whatever a sensible man would much rather not do without.

True propriety is, then, discretion still, for discretion and judgment have nothing to do with mere caution, conformity, moral sluggishness. One sort of propriety is the sailor's manliness, which is not rashness for its own sake, but passion and energy for the sake of the rewards that a man attains, if unassisted by birth, only by his own directed passion and energy. Jane Austen's attitude toward rank and money isn't that of, say, Dickens, an urban poor boy who grew up in the lengthening shadows of industrialism's Satanic mills, and for whom money is rubbish or magic. Jane Austen is neither enthralled nor repelled (of course she spent her life among the rural gentry, and some years before industrialism had decisively asserted itself); she isn't sentimental: Anne is Anne, the jewel of a particular setting, and Wentworth will deserve her if, socially as well as personally, he can bring what will maintain and enhance her very nature. Lady Russell thinks as well of Anne as every reader must; but Lady Russell confuses propriety with obliquity and ceremoniousness, with Anne's gentle reserve; she is unaccustomed to the manners of unevasive manliness, as when Admiral Croft comments on Miss Musgrove's fall:

> "Ay, a very bad business indeed.—A new sort of way this, for a young fellow to be making love, by breaking his mistress's head!—is not it, Miss Elliot?—This is breaking a head and giving a plaister truly!"

Admiral Croft's manners were not quite of the tone to suit Lady Russell, but they delighted Anne. His goodness of heart and simplicity of character were irresistible.

Moreover, as war is the unarguable condition for a sailor's advancement, so in *Persuasion* manliness is the condition for a happy marriage. Only in *Persuasion* does Jane Austen offer images of conjugal happiness; and, not content with one couple, she offers two: the Crofts and the Harvilles. Anne is always pleased to see the Crofts out for a stroll because they are so plainly and justifiably pleased with each other:

> She always watched them as long as she could; delighted to fancy she understood what they might be talking of, as they walked along in happy independence, or equally delighted to see the Admiral's hearty shake of the hand when he encountered an old friend, and observe their eagerness of conversation when occasionally forming into a little knot of the navy, Mrs. Croft looking as intelligent and keen as any of the officers around her.

And "the picture of repose and domestic happiness" at the Harvilles' is almost too much for Anne—feeling her own chance gone by—to contemplate without pain, even as it incites one of the Musgrove girls, in love with Wentworth, to rhapsodize on the sailor's monopoly of the manly virtues:

> Louisa . . . burst forth into raptures of admiration and delight on the character of the navy—their friendliness, their brotherliness, their openness, their uprightness; protesting that she was convinced of sailors having more worth and warmth than any other set of men in England; that they only knew how to live, and they only deserved to be respected and loved.

It isn't surprising that such qualities—though Louisa's partiality may overestimate their prevalence among sailors—seek out and attract admirable women, and make for better marriages than those of which Lady Russell would be likely to approve.

Anne, if she didn't have reasons for keeping her counsel, could speak even more rapturously than Louisa; but the decision she made seven years ago excludes her, so she must believe, from the hope that Louisa can entertain. Anne is a Cinderella who long ago, at the behest of her fairy godmother, rejected her prince. The coach has since been permanently retranslated into a pumpkin, the footmen into mice; the heartless sister triumphs at the ball; and the angry prince returns, irreconcilable, with eyes for any girl except the one who spurned him. If ever gentleness, sweetness of temper, kindness of heart, the charm of quiet spontaneous feeling, the unsounded depth of passion—if propriety, in a word, is ever to be tested, it will be by Anne; for Anne's ordeal is so private and un-confessable that it bereaves her of even the world's pity; it's so vivid and absolute that it leaves her no resource beyond the womanliness which her state of being defines.

Propriety, in *Persuasion,* is like the original bisexual humanity in Plato's parable. Once there was a "male-female sex . . . sharing both male and female." Humanity, having in this union of capacities "terrible strength and force," challenged the very gods, who thereupon sliced them "through the middle, as you slice your serviceberries through the middle for pickle, or as you slice hard-boiled eggs with a hair." Ever since, each half has sought and yearned for its complementary other. "So you see how ancient is the mutual love implanted in mankind, bringing together the parts of the original body, and trying to make one out of two, and to heal the natural structure of man."

The two halves of propriety are manliness and womanliness. They seek each other out, through the thickets of circumstance and misunderstanding; their natural and sufficient end is marriage. Anne's consummation is deferred, forever she believes; but her womanliness was the lodestar to Wentworth's manliness once. By seven years of regret and perfect fidelity she has proved his title as her fated complement, and her own claim to the last, undemanding privilege of womanliness. So she replies to Captain Harville's exclamation on the emotional trials of a sailor-husband:

> "Oh!" cried Anne eagerly, "I hope I do justice to all that is felt by you, and by those who resemble you. God forbid that I should undervalue the warm and faithful feelings of any of my fellow-creatures. I should deserve utter contempt if I dared to suppose that true attachment and constancy were known only by woman. No, I believe you capable of everything great and good in your married lives. I believe you equal to every important exertion, and to every domestic forbearance, so long as—if I may be allowed the expression, so long as you have an object. I mean, while the woman you love lives, and lives for you. All the privilege I claim for my own sex (it is not a very enviable one, you need not covet it), is that of loving longest, when existence or when hope is gone."

The plot of *Persuasion* could scarcely be more unitary. Its instigation is the return of Wentworth; its events are the stages of Anne's emotion, from despair to "joy, senseless joy": the inner agitation of a presence that never, in its bleakest moments, loses touch with the freshness of common reality—with Sir Walter's embarrassing fatuity, or Benwick's harmless sentimentality, or the Musgrove girls' vivacity, or Admiral Croft's unillusioned good nature. Anne, living her public life with open eyes and serviceable grace, is compelled to live her private life, painfully, at the center of a web of memory and speculation: what life was like when she and Wentworth were together; whether his feeling for her can now be—must it not be, in view of his attachment to Louisa?—entirely dead. The most trivial actions assume the proportions of hallucination and nightmare. At her sister's, one of Anne's nephews persists in clinging to her "as she knelt, in such a way that . . . she could not shake him off":

> In another moment . . . she found herself in the state of being released from him; some one was taking him from her, though he had bent down

her head so much that his little sturdy hands were unfastened from around her neck, and he was resolutely borne away before she knew that Captain Wentworth had done it.

Her sensations on the discovery made her perfectly speechless. She could not even thank him. She could only hang over little Charles, with most disordered feelings. His kindness in stepping forward to her relief—the manner—the silence in which it had passed—the little particulars of the circumstance—with the conviction soon forced on her, by the noise he was studiously making with the child, that he meant to avoid hearing her thanks, and rather sought to testify that her conversation was the last of his wants, produced such a confusion of varying, but very painful agitation, as she could not recover from, till enabled by the entrance of Mary and the Miss Musgroves to make over her little patient to their cares, and leave the room.

From the stunning fact of his mere proximity till the great scene of lovers' reconciliation at the White Hart Inn, Anne sustains the numberless shocks of her ordeal, the trial and vindication of her passionate fidelity. Only once before has Jane Austen considered such intensity of feeling—in Marianne Dashwood; and only to betray Marianne, at last, into an insipid match that is supposed to subdue sensibility to sense. If Marianne is Jane Austen's Juliet (without a true Romeo), Anne is her Penelope, the tender wife to a husband who will not yet acknowledge himself, the goal of the sailor's long journey, the radiance of conjugal love after years of battle and wandering. "Propriety is one great matter in the conduct of life"—Hazlitt's maxim is what Anne's life illustrates, and what she believes in even to extremity:

"I have been thinking over the past, and trying impartially to judge of the right and wrong, I mean with regard to myself; and I must believe that I was right, much as I suffered from it, that I was perfectly right in being guided by the friend whom you will love better than you do now. To me, she was in the place of a parent. Do not mistake me, however. I am not saying that she did not err in her advice. It was, perhaps, one of those cases in which advice is good or bad only as the event decides; and for myself, I certainly never should, in any circumstance of tolerable similarity, give such advice. But I mean that I was right in submitting to her, and that if I had done otherwise, I should have suffered more in continuing the engagement than I did even in giving it up, because I should have suffered in my conscience. I have now, as far as such a sentiment is allowable in human nature, nothing to reproach myself with; and if 1 mistake not, a strong sense of duty is no bad part of a woman's portion."

Wentworth is not yet quite so devout a believer as Anne:

He looked at her, looked at Lady Russell, and looking again at her, replied, as if in cool deliberation,

"Not yet. But there are hopes of her being forgiven in time. I trust to being in charity with her soon...."

Still, Wentworth is less grudging than he appears. Odysseus has never objected to a Penelope with loftier notions of fidelity and duty than his own.

Mrs. Harris and the Hend of All Things

JUDGED by the expectations of its already spectacularly successful author, *Martin Chuzzlewit* hadn't been a popular success. Dickens concluded that much of the fault was in its episodic construction; and, working on his next novel, he decided to curb his fancy and confine himself within a narrower and less hospitable plot. But the effort hurt. "You can hardly imagine," he wrote to a friend,

> what infinite pains I take, or what extraordinary difficulty I find in getting on FAST. Invention, thank God, seems the easiest thing in the world; and I seem to have such a preposterous sense of the ridiculous after this long rest as to be constantly required to restrain myself from launching into extravagances in the height of my enjoyment.

Such extravagances are the deepest passions of his blood; he does himself an injury when he denies them; and neither Dickens's own ambition to be a "serious" as well as a popular novelist, nor modern criticism's preoccupation with the all-too-unifying themes and symbols of his novels, can keep the dam from bursting and flooding out into the extravagances which identify the special Dickensian ridiculous; which compound and concentrate it, touch it with the sinister, disclose the lesions of its apparent solidity, accelerate it to the edge of psychosis, round it back into the merely human. Nor is it a quality easily fixed and described, even by so careful a critic as Santayana. Dickens, according to Santayana,

> was the perfect comedian. When people say Dickens exaggerates, it seems to me that they can have no eyes and no ears. They probably have only *notions* of what things and people are; they accept them conventionally, at their diplomatic value. Their minds run on in the region of discourse, where there are masks only and no faces, ideas and no facts; they have little sense for those living grimaces that play from moment to moment upon the countenance of the world. . . . Pure comedy . . . brutally says to the notions of mankind, as if it slapped them in the face, There, take that! That's what you really are! At this the polite world pretends to laugh, not tolerantly as it does at humour, but a little angrily. It does not like to see itself by chance in the glass, without having had time to compose its features for demure self-contemplation. "What a bad mirror," it exclaims; "it must be concave or convex; for surely I never looked like that. Mere caricature, farce, and horse play. Dickens exaggerates; *I* never was so sentimental as that: *I* never

say anything so dreadful; *I* don't believe there were ever any people like Quilp, or Squeers, or Serjeant Buzfuz." But the polite world is lying; there *are* such people; we are such people ourselves. . . .

This formulation covers the honest staple of Dickensian comedy—Mrs. Todgers or Mr. Mould—and it suggests that, however massively simple they may seem, Dickens's comic successes aren't humors but as coarse and close as life. Mrs. Gamp, for example, begins as a garrulous, gross old toper of a nurse, assistant at births and deaths, who "went to a lying-in or a laying-out with equal zest and relish"; enough, it seems, for us to laugh at and keep our distance from; "mere caricature, farce, and horse play"; nothing but art. Yet even at the beginning her talkativeness isn't blind and redundant; it aspires if not to consciousness at least to cunning; it beats suddenly away from its bare prepossessions, darts out here to set up a compromise between charity and practicality, there to fabricate and cross-examine the alter ego who shelters her from the world by acting as its benevolent proxy:

". . . If it wasn't for the nerve a little sip of liquor gives me (I never was able to do more than taste it), I never could go through with what I sometimes has to do. 'Mrs. Harris,' I says, at the very last case as ever I acted in, which it was but a young person, 'Mrs. Harris,' I says, 'leave the bottle on the chimley-piece and don't ask me to take none, but let me put my lips to it when I am so dispoged and then I will do what I'm engaged to do, according to the best of my ability.' 'Mrs. Gamp,' she says, in answer, 'if ever there was a sober creetur to be got at eighteen pence a day for working people, and three and six for gentlefolks—night watching,'" said Mrs. Gamp, with emphasis, "'being a extra charge—you are that inwallable person.' 'Mrs. Harris,' I says to her, 'don't name the charge, for if I could afford to lay all my feller-creeturs out for nothink, I would gladly do it, sich is the love I bears 'em. . . .'"

Mrs. Gamp is no fool; she is proficient at her vocation and so pricked by the multiplicity of her professional skills that she gazes at an unconscious and delirious patient

as a connoisseur might gaze upon a doubtful work of art. By degrees, a horrible remembrance of her calling took possession of the woman, and stooping down, she pinned his wandering arms against his sides to see how he would look if laid out as a dead man.

Not only art, but sentiment, moves her: as a midwife, her sentiment for infants, even unborn ones—

Which . . . is well beknown to Mrs. Harris as has one sweet infant (though she do not wish it known) in her own family by the mother's side, kep' in spirits in a bottle, and that sweet babe she see at Greenwich Fair, a-travelling in company with the pink-eyed lady, Prooshan dwarf, and livin' skelinton, which judge her feelins when the barrel organ played, and she was showed her own dear sister's child, the same not bein' expected from the outside picter, where it was painted quite contriary in a livin' state, a many sizes larger, and performing beautiful upon the Arp, which never did the dear child know or do, since breathe it never did, to speak on, in this wale! . . ."

Mrs. Harris is the honey and consolation, the bribed judge and stacked jury of Mrs. Gamp's private trials ("'Sairey,' says Mrs. Harris, 'sech is life. Vich likeways is the hend of all things'"); and one of the crises of the novel occurs when Betsey Prig, turncoat, pronounces the grand denial:

"Mrs. Harris, Betsey—"
"Bother Mrs. Harris!" said Betsey Prig.
Mrs. Gamp looked at her with amazement, incredulity, and indignation, when Mrs. Prig, shutting her eye still closer and folding her arms still tighter, uttered these memorable and tremendous words: "I don't believe there's no sich a person!"
After the utterance of which expressions, she leaned forward and snapped her fingers once, twice, thrice—each time nearer to the face of Mrs. Gamp—and then rose to put on her bonnet, as one who felt that there was now a gulf between them which nothing could ever bridge across.
The shock of this blow was so violent and sudden that Mrs. Gamp sat staring at nothing with uplifted eyes and her mouth open as if she were gasping for breath, until Betsey Prig had put on her bonnet and her shawl and was gathering the latter about her throat. Then Mrs. Gamp rose—mentally and physically rose—and denounced her.
"What!" said Mrs. Gamp, "you bage creetur, have I know'd Mrs. Harris five and thirty year to be told at last that there ain't sech a person livin'! Have I stood her friend in all her troubles, great and small, for it to come at last to sech a end as this, with her own sweet picter hanging up afore you all the time, to shame your Bragian words! . . ."

The comic grimace that Santayana speaks of is here almost in ruins—we are more nearly alarmed than amused—and one would suppose that after such a climax, Dickens has exhausted both Mrs. Gamp and Mrs. Harris. But something much more astonishing is to come. Jonas Chuzzlewit, murder on his conscience already, fearing that Chuffey can inform against him, has hired Mrs. Gamp to watch the dotty old man:

"Where is the other woman?"
"The other person's with him now," she answered.
"That's right," said Jonas. "He's not fit to be left to himself.
. . . You told me the other woman's name. I forget it."

> "I mentioned Betsey Prig," said Mrs. Gamp.
> "She is to be trusted, is she?"
> "That she ain't!" said Mrs. Gamp; "nor have I brought her, Mr. Chuzzlewit. I've brought another, which engages to give every satigefaction."
> "What is her name?" asked Jonas.
> Mrs. Gamp looked at him in an odd way without returning any answer, but appeared to understand the question too.
> "What is her name?" repeated Jonas.
> "Her name," said Mrs. Gamp, "is Harris."
> It was extraordinary how much effort it cost Mrs. Gamp to pronounce the name she was commonly so ready with. She made some three or four gasps before she could get it out, and when she had uttered it, pressed her hand upon her side and turned up her eyes, as if she were going to faint away. . . .

It's the ultimate nightmare of alienation, as the ego begins to crack like an ice floe. Mrs. Gamp, for the sake of the plot's last surprise, has ventured to the farthest outstation of consciousness, where at last there is only self and no other. Santayana didn't perceive that behind the mask of decorum—in Dickens's finest moments at any rate—the comic grimace is itself a mask. Comedy itself runs the risk of exposure.

Surely Dickens has done, then, as much as can be done with so extreme a development in a comic novel, for a comic figure; surely he wouldn't dare something comparable in the same novel. But he does. Pecksniff is the other comic prodigy of the novel—not only a hypocrite, but a doting anxious father, a bully, a devourer of praise and admiration, a gull for scoundrels cleverer than himself, sometimes a brutal sensualist, sometimes a mawkish drunken sensualist:

> "She was beautiful, Mrs. Todgers," he said, turning his glazed eye again upon her, without the least preliminary notice. "She had a small property."
> "So I have heard," cried Mrs. Todgers with great sympathy.
> "Those are her daughters," said Mr. Pecksniff, pointing out the young ladies, with increased emotion.
> Mrs. Todgers had no doubt of it. . . .
> ". . . .You are like her, Mrs. Todgers."
> "Don't squeeze me so tight, pray, Mr. Pecksniff. If any of the gentlemen should notice us."
> "For her sake," said Mr. Pecksniff. "Permit me. In honour of her memory. For the sake of a voice from the tomb. You are *very* like her, Mrs. Todgers. What a world this is!"

Pecksniff's most enthusiastic devotee is the naive and humble Tom Pinch. Yet Tom serves Pecksniff as Mrs. Harris serves Mrs. Gamp: X worships me, therefore I exist; I bless, therefore I am. Comes the day when Tom accepts the truth about

Pecksniff, while the great hypocrite eavesdrops, fascinated, behind a pew in church. Alone again, he is neither angry nor amused, nor even puzzled; he is *restless*:

> He was in a curious frame of mind, Mr. Pecksniff—being in no hurry to go, but rather inclining to a dilatory trifling with the time, which prompted him to open the vestry cupboard and look at himself in the parson's little glass that hung within the door. Seeing that his hair was rumpled, he took the liberty of borrowing the canonical brush and arranging it. He also took the liberty of opening another cupboard; but he shut it up again quickly, being rather startled by the sight of a black and a white surplice dangling against the wall, which had very much the appearance of two curates who had committed suicide by hanging themselves. Remembering that he had seen in the first cupboard a port-wine bottle and some biscuits, he peeped into it again and helped himself with much deliberation, cogitating all the time, though, in a very deep and weighty manner, as if his thoughts were otherwise employed.
>
> He soon made up his mind—if it had ever been in doubt—and putting back the bottle and biscuits, opened the casement. He got out into the churchyard without any difficulty, shut the window after him, and walked straight home.
>
> "Is Mr. Pinch indoors?" asked Mr. Pecksniff of his serving-maid.
>
> "Just come in, sir."
>
> "Just come in, eh?" repeated Mr. Pecksniff, cheerfully. "And gone upstairs, I suppose?"
>
> "Yes, sir. Gone upstairs. Shall I call him, sir?"
>
> "No," said Mr. Pecksniff, "no. You needn't call him, Jane. Thank you, Jane. How are your relations, Jane?"
>
> "Pretty well, I thank you, sir."
>
> "I am glad to hear it. Let them know I asked about them, Jane. Is Mr. Chuzzlewit in the way, Jane?"
>
> "Yes, sir. He's in the parlour, reading."
>
> "He's in the parlour, reading, is he, Jane?" said Mr. Pecksniff. "Very well. Then I think I'll go and see him, Jane."

Pecksniff, more adaptable than Mrs. Gamp, is reëstablishing after the blow, by a sort of incantatory nominalism ("Jane, Jane": others have names, therefore they exist), his shaken conviction of his own existence; but the blow brought him to the same confrontation of the void: oblivion is in those dangling surplices. "We are such people ourselves," said Santayana, as we see ourselves at last, for a moment, in the parson's undistorting mirror; and what we see is neither the social smile nor the comic grimace, but an inanition antecedent to both.

Pecksniff and Mrs. Gamp are, as the world knows them, nothing but their personalities, their visible and audible idiosyncrasies; to the world they are stable suspensions of oddities, they are reliable, they run on like clocks. In fact, however, the personality of each is precariously epiphenomenal: it derives from, feeds on, and masks a secret self, an identity so distinct from the mask, and so helpless in its unevolved primordial blankness, as to be threatened with extinction when the mask is off even for a moment. With Pecksniff and Mrs. Gamp we are out of sight of the comic prototypes of Dickens's eighteenth-century masters, Smollett and Fielding, not to mention the scapegoat of comic drama from Aristophanes to Jonson. Both Pecksniff and Mrs. Gamp resemble their literary predecessors in being instantaneously recognizable by tics, mannerisms, prepossessions, obsessions, peculiarities of diction and gesture—amusing, that is, for all the outlandish ways which we enjoy in others, and which distinguish them from our ideal conception of ourselves. So these two customarily appear. But unlike, say, a Squire Western, they are susceptible to traumas that drive them back beyond comedy, beyond the conditions of daily life, into intimations of unacknowledgeable identity. The effect is similar (and, because less foreseeable, superior) to the shattering of Jonas Chuzzlewit's mere wickedness or personality, when, having committed murder, he returns to his secret room, expecting to encounter there if not himself, then the murdered man, who drives him back into an anterior identity that occupies his very space and that he will be unable to sink again except by suicide:

> The passage-way was empty when his murderer's face looked into it. He stole on to the door on tiptoe, as if he dreaded to disturb his own imaginary rest.
> He listened. Not a sound. As he turned the key with a trembling hand and pushed the door softly open with his knee, a monstrous fear beset his mind.
> What if the murdered man were there before him!

Jonas and Mrs. Gamp are equally schizophrenic: it's a state of mind that Dickens (like his disciple Dostoevsky) seems to have found almost congenial; related to his infatuation with the theater and acting; the common focus of his comedy and his melodrama. Dickens was much interested in hypnotism and became an expert practitioner; one of Mrs. Dickens's ordeals was to sit at home while her husband was off "curing" a Mrs. De la Rue of delusions by hypnotizing her, "urging her to have no reticences with him, insisting that it was dangerous and might invalidate the cure if she kept any secret from him."[1] While writing dialogue, Dickens would often jump up to stand before a mirror and, speaking in the voice of the character he was inventing, match his expressions to his words with a total unawareness of anybody else in the same room. When he undertook, toward the end of his life, the public readings that wasted him like a mortal illness, his aim was to produce not acclamation but a trance of sympathy or terror in the audience. He didn't in fact do a reading; rather he acted out all the roles in their proper voices, with gestures and grimaces and stage effects, as in the sensational murder scene from *Oliver Twist:*

---

[1] Una Pope-Hennessy, *Charles Dickens* (Howell, Soskin, 1946). p. 217.

On the night of the reading the ladies' doctor, Priestley, buttonholed Dickens and said, "You may rely upon it that if only one woman cries out when you murder the girl, there will be a contagion of hysteria all over the place." . . . When the reading was over, the bright gas reflectors were turned by Dickens's order away from himself on to the guests. Though the ladies in their coloured dresses looked like "a great bed of flowers and diamonds," their faces were pale and horror-stricken. No one could question the success of the experiment in mass-hypnotism.[2]

Dickens liked to strike at the ostensible unity of personality, in life as well as in art; and in *Martin Chuzzlewit* he conducts his experiment on a grand scale. Not only Pecksniff, Mrs. Gamp, and Jonas: from this standpoint, the novel has at least as many failures as successes. The mean, fawning vagabond and cadger of small loans, Montague Tigg, hanger-on and encomiast of Chevy Slyme, is abruptly converted into Tigg Montague, with more than his name reversed—now a plausible and articulate highbrow of a swindler, elevated enough to compete with governments for the people's funds. Slyme himself, who in his first appearances is an emblem of sloth and absurdly self-important discontent, turns up at the end as—because the book needs one—an efficient and rather compassionate policeman. Mercy Pecksniff is at first Pecksniff's true daughter, a bundle of self-serving charm, "all girlishness, and playfulness, and wildness, and kittenish buoyancy . . . the most arch and at the same time the most artless creature"; but, having married Jonas, she reappears at once as an oleograph of abused and forgiving Victorian womanhood:

". . . Tell him that I don't blame him, but am grateful for the effort that he made; but ask him for the love of God, and youth, and in merciful consideration for the struggle which an ill-advised and unawakened nature makes to hide the strength it thinks its weakness—ask him never, never, to forget this, when he deals with one again!"

Even so marginal and entertaining a personage as Mrs. Todgers, "affection beaming in one eye and calculation shining out of the other," becomes poor Mercy's noble-hearted confidante, presumably because Mercy deserves one. As for Young Bailey, his leaps from role to role are justified only by the memorable *sic transit* exchange that the report of his death evokes between Sweedlepipe and Mrs. Gamp:

". . . And what a life Young Bailey's was!"
"He was born into a wale," said Mrs. Gamp, with philosophical coolness; "and he lived in a wale; and he must take the consequences of sech a sitiwation. . . ."

As a matter of fact, it's hard to determine when these plural characters with the same (or reversed) names are modified according to the exigencies of the plot, and

---

[2] Ibid., pp. 458-59.

when Dickens's intention—whether or not fulfilled—is to demonstrate that everybody is AB: that in ordinary circumstances he has the face of A and in crises he splits off into B. Nor, in these cases, is A or B necessarily more interesting or basic than its alternative. Slyme is dull in both; Mercy Pecksniff is an appropriate pendant to her father in A, and pasteboard in B; Montague Tigg is a low-life palaverer in an ebb of his creator's fancy, Tigg Montague a smooth and convincing villain worthy of Jonas's special attention. All we can be sure of is Dickens's own fascination with the process, as he illustrates it not only in his work but by the events of his life. The Dickens who hypnotized Mrs. De la Rue in private and his exclusive audience in public is something of a charlatan, a sideshow magician, an English Poe enchanted by chiaroscuro, inexplicable discontinuities, the thunder and lightning of melodrama: Old Martin playing his deep (and tedious) game; young Martin learning about selfishness; Mercy learning about life. And the other Dickens, oracle and seer, makes a few passes and conjures up such vital mysteries as Pecksniff, Jonas, Mrs. Gamp. Dickens himself had a touch of Pecksniff. He shocks us by his unprincipled doubleness, this Victorian genius of domesticity—patron of the hearth; celebrant of so many sweet and mutually indistinguishable heroines, among them Ruth Pinch and Mary Graham—who abandoned his wife, behaved "like a madman" toward his children, and spent his last years in a liaison with a young actress.

Of course there's also Dickens the intelligent and sardonic reporter, who rehearses out of his disillusioning American tour what foreign reporters always discover, the America that confuses violence with courage, intimidation with justice, chauvinism with pride, conformity with freedom. Then Dickens the heir of Fielding, sponsor of Mark Tapley, Mrs. Lupin, and other generous and lively ornaments of the English countryside—hearts of gold that seldom ring hollow and that gather with the principal characters at climactic feasts of reconciliation and love. And Dickens the journeyman novelist, explaining that his diffuse novel will be united by the theme of selfishness, and occasionally remembering to enforce the lesson by having someone or other exclaim, "Self, self, self!"

In *Martin Chuzzlewit,* however, the Dickens who holds our attention is occupied with other matters—not a parable, but labyrinths whose jogs and nooks and dead ends we laugh at as we laugh at a problem in order to postpone acknowledging its insolubility; but Mrs. Gamp is even less of a joke than Jonas Chuzzlewit. In the general distribution of roast-beef-of-England justice at the end, Old Martin makes an effort to admonish and reform her. But Mrs. Gamp is out of reach in another world altogether—a world of homeless and unreformable anxieties—whereas Old Martin is as dead as Queen Victoria.

The Return of Marvin Mudrick

During my first semester at the College of Creative Studies (CCS), I wrote about Marvin Mudrick in a university magazine. Twenty years later, the magazine asked me to write another article about him. My posting of that second article on my blog started the correspondence that led to the creation of this book series. One of Marvin's daughters, Ellen Mudrick, came across the blog post and wrote to me. She then introduced me to her sister and mother, and soon I had been connected, or reconnected, with a group of former students who were digitizing some of his books.

In this collection, you'll hear from some of them, as well as from two other people who knew Marvin well. The introductions they have written are personal. As James Raimes, the editor who worked with Mudrick on *Books Are Not Life, But Then What Is?* (Oxford University Press, 1979) and *Nobody Here But Us Chickens* (Ticknor and Fields, 1981), put it in an email, "We all want to connect again with the man and his mind." Over the years, Raimes found himself rereading Mudrick. After his retirement, he wrote a memoir, and browsing the web, found me. "Marvin Mudrick is the hero of my memoir," he emailed. In his introductions to *Mudrick Transcribed* and *Nobody Here But Us Chickens*, Raimes relates his admiration of Mudrick and his difficulties as champion of the idiosyncratic author.

One of my fellow students at CCS was Jervey Tervalon, who wrote stories about growing up in an African American neighborhood in Los Angeles. Encouraged by Mudrick, he published his first novel a few years later. Now an award-winning novelist, poet, and dramatist who teaches at CCS, Tervalon exemplifies the effect that Mudrick had on his students. It feels exactly right to have him introduce, in his vivid and very personal way, *Books Are Not Life But Then What Is?*

Kia Penso, another former student, wrote the introduction to *On Culture and Literature*. She explains that it's the book where he drew the line between himself and the litcrit profession, and where he discussed ideas about the nature of literary experience that were a turning point for him, making it a launch pad for the later books. It also includes essays that critics nowadays are most likely to cite, including those on Norman Podhoretz and on Diana Trilling.

William Pritchard, author, poetry critic, and Henry Clay Folger Professor of English at Amherst College, who wrote the introduction to *The Man in the Machine*, knew Marvin Mudrick through the *Hudson Review*, where they both published for many years. When I contacted him, he turned out to have an office at the college adjacent to that of Allen Guttmann, with whom I worked on many projects, so we may literally have crossed paths unwittingly. Similarly, a great admirer and friend of Mudrick, Pauline Kael, the *New Yorker* film critic, turned out to have lived up the street from the Berkshire Publishing's office in Great Barrington, Massachusetts; and another former student lives just around the corner. Marvin Mudrick has never really been so far away.

I wrote the introduction to *Jane Austen: Irony as Defense and Discovery*, Mudrick's first book, because no one else in our working group seemed to know much about it. For me, it was life changing, and I was delighted to find that it remains enjoyable and enlightening, and subversive.

The final book in this collection, *Mudrick Transcribed: Classes and Talks*, exists only because of the diligence and ingenuity of another student, Lance Kaplan. Kaplan first started to record Mudrick's Writing Narrative Prose class to send to his brother, a former student. After Mudrick's untimely death in October of 1986, Kaplan began to transcribe and edit his recordings as well as recordings made by other students over the years. *Transcribe* and *edit* are accurate but inadequate words to describe the creation of this extraordinary book. A professional court reporter and editor couldn't have done it. It required someone who knew Mudrick's voice and temperament through and through—to paraphrase Boswell, someone permeated by the Mudrickian ether. The book is a kind of miracle of attention. It's also entertaining, freakishly smart and full of love—of life, books, music, and people. Previously published only in a limited, private edition, it may well be the gem of the collection.

Other people have been essential to this project. Marvin Mudrick's daughter Janie Mudrick has taken the lead in coordinating details with Berkshire Publishing and I've been able to get to know her through phone calls and Facebook. Marvin's wife, Jeanne Little Mudrick, put a great deal of time into preparing and proofreading typescripts of several of the books. It's a great pleasure to put the new editions into her hands. We also thank Lee Mudrick, Ann Mudrick White, and Ellen Mudrick for their support and advice.

We also thank Kate Johnston, Bob Blaisdell, author of the memoir *Mr. Mudrick Said*, Sheila Oviatt Ham, who originally put Mudrick's essays into my hands, Derek Attridge of the University of York, and Kia Penso, who wrote the introduction to *On Culture and Literature*, for their review of the introductory material, and Robert Dugan, dean of libraries at the University of West Florida, for so kindly digitizing several of the books.

One thing that is clear in all six books, as it was clear in every encounter with Marvin, is that he rejoiced in writing and writers, and that he counted on us students to read with the same intense interest and enthusiasm as he did. He assigned more books each week than any human being could possibly manage, but because of that we read an immense amount. And reading a book was always more fun when there was the prospect of hearing what he would have to say about it.

While Mudrick excelled at criticism and at pricking holes in literary pretension, he didn't do it casually. Roger Sale, in a review of *On Culture and Literature*, explains:

> When Mudrick is not writing he must be reading; there simply are not enough hours in the day for anything else. Not long ago the man whose office is next to mine, David Wagoner, had his fifth novel reviewed by Mudrick

in *The Hudson Review*. Mudrick had not liked the novel very much, but, not content with that, he had gone back and read Wagoner's first four before describing his opinion of the fifth. Wagoner was understandably not very happy at Mudrick's dislike of his novels, but more than that he was dumbfounded by Mudrick's procedures. I could only tell him that this was just like Mudrick, and also that I too knew no one else who would read five novels by a man in order to be able to level against one in just the terms he wanted. (*On Not Being Good Enough,* 1979)

In republishing Mudrick's books, our aim is to invite modern readers to the classroom we remember, to his English department office where we would hang out in the afternoon, and to the conversations that he would have with the colleagues he most admired and trusted. You will hear his voice, and not only in the volume *Mudrick Transcribed,* which consists of extraordinarily entertaining transcripts from his classes. As his colleagues at CCS, John Ridland, Alan Stephens, and Logan Speirs, wrote: "The voice in all of his writing reproduces his own living voice in an almost uncanny way. That voice is cantankerous, loving, aggressive, spiteful, charming; it abounds with energy and fierce humor."

I can still hear that voice, and see him at a table at the front of a classroom, his socked and sandaled feet flexing up and down as he sifts through the pile of papers dropped there by students as we walked into the room.

Besides that, he was in his office and ready to talk to us every single afternoon, and we felt that we could talk to him about anything. It was impossible not to feel awed by his brilliance, and he was as tolerant of adoration as he was of our various waywardness. We came to him even when we had no assignment to discuss. We would take a seat and join in a conversation, or just listen, perhaps waiting for the others to leave so we could ask a confidential question. He was, in his own unassuming way, entirely welcoming.

We are publishing Marvin Mudrick's six books to coincide with the fiftieth anniversary of the College of Creative Studies, which he created and led. The collection is a celebration of the man we knew and loved and admired as well as a fresh contribution to literary criticism and literary conversation. We hope that his essays will draw you to wonderful writing from all over the world and from different centuries (oh, how he loved Chaucer!), and that you'll be coming to new appreciation of writers you might otherwise have missed. Happy reading.

Karen CHRISTENSEN
College of Creative Studies '81
CEO, Berkshire Publishing Group

BERKSHIRE CLASSICS
The Marvin Mudrick Collection

Jane Austen: Irony as Defense and Discovery (1952) by Marvin Mudrick,
with a new introduction by Karen Christensen

On Culture and Literature (1970) by Marvin Mudrick,
with a new introduction by Kia Penso

The Man in the Machine (1977) by Marvin Mudrick,
with a new introduction by William Pritchard

Books Are Not Life, But Then What Is? (1979) by Marvin Mudrick,
with a new introduction by Jervey Tervalon

Nobody Here But Us Chickens (1981) by Marvin Mudrick,
with a new introduction by James Raimes

Mudrick Transcribed: Classes and Talks (1986), edited by Lance Kaplan,
with a new introduction by James Raimes

Find out more about this series and Berkshire Publishing Group's revival of selected authors at http://www.berkshirepublishing.com/classics/

About Marvin Mudrick

Marvin Mudrick (1921–1986) was a literary critic, English professor, and founder of the College of Creative Studies at the University of California, Santa Barbara (UCSB), which is known as a "graduate school for undergraduates" with programs in math, biology, physics, and computer science as well as the arts. Mudrick wrote extensively for the *Hudson Review* and published five collections of essays. He also wrote for the *New York Review of Books* and *Harper's Magazine*. Known for his distinctive critical voice and his willingness to tackle histories as well as fiction, he had many admirers, and more than a few detractors. In addition to literature, he loved and occasionally wrote about classical music and ballet.

Marvin Mudrick was born on 17 July 1921 in Philadelphia. He received his AB degree from Temple University in 1942 and joined the army. At the end of the War, en route to California from the Philippines, he discovered Jane Austen. He would go on to write his first book about her novels. After receiving a PhD in English from UC Berkeley, he joined the English faculty at the newly established UCSB in 1949 and remained there until his death in October 1986. In 1967, he founded the College of Creative Studies (CCS) and became its first provost.

Although he was deeply suspicious of the word "teacher," he was a brilliant one, in the classroom and also through the stream of books and essays he produced while continuing the almost superhuman task of running the College, teaching several courses, and maintaining close contact with its students past and present. From the first, he conceived of the College as a necessary addition to campus life, fulfilling the special needs of a portion of its students, never as a body which competed with the university or opposed its fundamental purposes.

Mudrick was the author of five books: *Jane Austen: Irony as Defense and Discovery*; *On Culture and Literature*; *The Man in the Machine*; *Books Are Not Life But Then What Is?*; and *Nobody Here But Us Chickens*, as well as the posthumously published collection of classroom recordings, *Mudrick Transcribed*.

His later books are collections of critical essays of a particular kind that he developed during his long association with the *Hudson Review*. The first of them appeared in the spring of 1953.

Thereafter, they were produced in astonishing quantities and on an astonishing variety of subjects. The 103rd appeared posthumously in the winter issue of 1987.

As a writer, Mudrick never confined himself to the works he was ostensibly reviewing, but saw these as opportunities to learn more about the authors' achievements and the way they lived their lives. It was life that engrossed him. He saw art as the medium through which we stand most completely revealed as ourselves. He was on the alert to intercept evidence of an artist's nature from any clue that the work provided.

The essays he wrote, now published again as Berkshire Classics, use layer upon layer of quotations, which he selected in a particular way. His quotations are always unexpected, yet always come to be recognized as important moments of truth, like telltale changes of expression on a face that is being watched with relentless attention. Character portraits of a special kind are Marvin Mudrick's medium and embody his critical method. Through them he reminds his readers that no artistic statement can be separated from the human being who has made it. Often he pursues what he perceives as personality defects with a cruel and relentless wit, hunting down particular words and actions, and using these against the subject with devastating effect. At other times, he joyfully pursues evidence of personal heroism, of a mind which has dared to be true to itself.

Mudrick's writing voice reproduced his own living voice in an almost uncanny way. Cantankerous, loving, aggressive, spiteful, charming: his voice abounds with energy and fierce humor. His very funny wordplay remains, along with his gift for parody as well as his enormous love and need for the arts, as though his own life depended on them.

In the preface to one of his books, Marvin Mudrick described the theoretical choices that guided him in life and literature:

> High spirits over low, energy over apathy, wit over dullness, jokes over homilies, good humor over jokes, good nature over bad, feeling over sentiment, truth over poetry, consciousness over explanations, tragedy over pathos, comedy over tragedy, entertainment over art, private over public, generosity over meanness, charity over murder, love over charity, irreplaceable over interchangeable, divergence over concurrence, principle over interest, people over principle.

Remembering Mudrick, and his continuing presence within his work, it is tempting to quote from Hamlet, the dramatic hero who aggravated him most: "He was a man, take him for all in all / I shall not look upon his like again."

This essay by John Ridland, Alan Stephens, and Logan Speirs, who were professors at the University of California, Santa Barbara and taught in the College of Creative Studies, has been lightly edited and updated.

About Jervey Tervalon

Jervey Tervalon is the author of *Understand This*, for which he won the Quality Paper Book Club's New Voices Award, and *Dead Above Ground*, a *Los Angeles Times* bestseller. His latest novel, *Monster's Chef*, was published June 2014. He graduated from the College of Creative Studies at UC Santa Barbara in 1980, and received his MFA in Creative Writing at UC Irvine, where he worked with Thomas Keneally. He is the executive director of *Literature for Life*, a literary magazine and educational advocacy organization, and literary director of the Pasadena LitFest. Tervalon teaches at the College of Creative Studies and divides his time between Los Angeles and Shanghai with his wife, Jinghuan Liu Tervalon, and their kids.

www.ingramcontent.com/pod-product-compliance
Lightning Source LLC
Chambersburg PA
CBHW061439300426
44114CB00014B/1759